THE CYRENIAN:
CROSSROADS AND A CROSS

"There is no greater love than this: that a person would lay down his life for the sake of his friends."

—John 15:13 (Aramaic Bible in Plain English translation)

by Donovan Peterkin

The Cyrenian: Crossroads and a Cross

Trilogy Christian Publishers A Wholly Owned Subsidiary of Trinity Broadcasting Network

2442 Michelle Drive Tustin, CA 92780

Copyright © 2023 by Donovan Peterkin

No part of this book may be reproduced, stored in a retrieval system, or transmitted by any means without written permission from the author. All rights reserved. Printed in the USA.

Rights Department, 2442 Michelle Drive, Tustin, CA 92780.

Trilogy Christian Publishing/TBN and colophon are trademarks of Trinity Broadcasting Network.

Cover design by: Sierra Deyoe with assets from DaFont and Adobe Stock

For information about special discounts for bulk purchases, please contact Trilogy Christian Publishing.

Trilogy Disclaimer: The views and content expressed in this book are those of the author and may not necessarily reflect the views and doctrine of Trilogy Christian Publishing or the Trinity Broadcasting Network.

10 9 8 7 6 5 4 3 2 1

Library of Congress Cataloging-in-Publication Data is available.

ISBN: 979-8-88738-936-3

E-ISBN: 979-8-88738-937-0

This book is dedicated to those who:

Have never heard the story of Salvation.
Have struggled with the story of Salvation.
Have fought the story of Salvation.
Have embraced the story of Salvation.
Have read the Bible.
Have never read The Bible.
Have never missed Church.
Have never been to Church.
Have stopped going to Church
Have fallen asleep in Church.
And everyone else.
God loves you, and so do I!

ACKNOWLEDGEMENTS

I wish to first thank my God, my Jesus and the Holy Spirit for the gifts and inspiration to write this book. You've given me a great story to tell. I am forever thankful, and forever in Your service.

I also wish to thank my dear wife Diane, who has been my support and my anchor, especially during the roughest of times. I love you. Thank you for every sacrifice.

I wish to thank my Peterkin family and extended Goetze family for the love and support that I can always count on.

Thank you, Mom, and Dad in Heaven. On top of all that I could say here, you bought me books that you couldn't afford, (especially our World Book Encyclopedias) and made reading a joy for me. I miss you. Your spirits live on in this project. I love you from here to eternity.

I thank the late Professor Samuel Draper, my Honors English professor at Rockland Community College, Suffern, New York, and my "Yoda". You opened the entire world of Writing for me. You always said that I'd be the author of a book someday. We did it!

I also want to say a special and deeply heartfelt "Thank you!" to my sister Maureen Peterkin-Byrd, and my "Brother from Another Mother and Sisters from Another Mister", Matthew, Suzanne, and Kathy Ruley for all your support. I love you more than words can say.

To my dear friends too numerous to name here, THANK YOU for your love, support, and your belief in me.

My thanks also to the Trilogy Publishing Team, especially my wonderful Publishing Executive, Ashley, and my Project Manager, Cammy, who were awesome all through the process.

Last but certainly not least, to Reverend Dana "Action" Jackson, it was your belief and energies that opened the door to my publisher. By His grace, you set the wheels in motion. May you be blessed one hundred-fold! Thank you for your prayers and all your help. I look forward to working together in the days to come.

I wish to thank most of all, everyone who indulges in these pages. I pray that this project will touch you as you read as it touched me as I wrote. Thank you, and I wish Peace to all who enter here.

Blessings,
Donovan F. Peterkin

TABLE OF CONTENTS

CHAPTER 1. THE DREAM 9

CHAPTER 2. THE CITY. 11

CHAPTER 3. "STRONG LITTLE PRINCE" 15

CHAPTER 4. CHANA 21

CHAPTER 5. JUDEA: THE VORTEX 27

CHAPTER 6. FORTUNES. 33

CHAPTER 7. A NEW TIME MARCHES ON. 41

CHAPTER 8. BY THE SEA. 47

CHAPTER 9. WHEN NOT IN ROME... 53

CHAPTER 10. PACTS AND PROMISES 61

CHAPTER 11. WINDS OF CHANGE. 71

CHAPTER 12. THE BROKEN ROAD 79

CHAPTER 13. RED DAWN 87

CHAPTER 14. MISSING IN ACTION 95

CHAPTER 15. SANDS IN THE HOURGLASS. 107

CHAPTER 16. SUMMITS AND SUMMITS 119

CHAPTER 17. THE EYE OF THE STORM 127

CHAPTER 18. CAESAREA MARITIMA .133

CHAPTER 19. MILE MARKERS 141

CHAPTER 20. NEW ARRIVALS. 147

CHAPTER 21. REVERSAL OF FORTUNE. 155

CHAPTER 22. THE HOME STRETCH .163

CHAPTER 23. SIGNS AND WONDERS 171

CHAPTER 24. ONE AGAIN. 183

CHAPTER 25. PIVOT POINT 187

CHAPTER 26. TRUTHS BE TOLD. 195

CHAPTER 27. "…AND AGAINST SPIRITUAL WICKEDNESS IN HIGH PLACES" (Ephesians 6:12, NKJV). 213

CHAPTER 28. OUT OF MOURNING COMES MORNING. 225

CHAPTER 29. MAYBE FATE WILL LEND A HAND 233

CHAPTER 30. POINTS OF NO RETURN 245

CHAPTER 31. THE BEGINNING OF THE END BEFORE THE BEGINNING 253

CHAPTER 32. THE FINISH LINE CROSSED 267

CHAPTER 33. NO REST FOR THE WICKED. 279

CHAPTER 34. VICTORY COMPLETE .283

CHAPTER 35. THE POWER AND THE GLORY 289

CHAPTER 36. COMMISSIONED 295

CHAPTER 1. THE DREAM

The noise of the crowd continues to rise, growing rapidly from the shouting of individual voices to the din and cacophony of a maddened crowd. Yet, with all this noise, the words themselves are unintelligible. In addition, there is an ever-present feeling of spinning and falling while, at the same time, the feeling of being physically gripped by an unknown and unseen force. Then—the eyes. No face, just eyes. Piercing, glaring, and fiery eyes that speak as loudly as the actual voice that follows. A booming, echoing voice uttering only one word—"YOU!!!"

The scene ends as quickly as it begins. Reality returns in the same manner as always, replete with sweating, gasping, shudders, and wide-eyed terror. The sound of the crowd is instantly replaced by the pounding sound of the blood coursing through the ears being pumped by a hyperactive heart. The cold but familiar darkness of the room once again reassures Simon that while he was shaken, he is safe. Safe but, at the same time, troubled.

Fortunately for him, his greatest reassurance also comes at that very moment, in a much more desirable and welcome form. A soft voice and a warm touch let him know that his loving wife, Chana, is awake now as well.

"Are you alright, my husband?" she whispers.

"I am—don't worry," he says, squeezing her hand as he gets out of bed. "Just that dream again."

She sighs, "The same one?"

"Yes, exactly the same one," he answers.

There is no mistaking his frustration—or his deep concern. He is convinced that there is no doubt a message here, but what is it and from whom? Once again, however, he must put all his thoughts and questions on hold.

It's another new day in Cyrene. Another day, and it is time to get ready for whatever this day will bring. Though the outcome of this day is yet to be seen, one thing is for sure—there will be nothing routine about it. Cyrene is a lady of many faces. She has her wonders… her beauties… her mysteries…and her challenges. To live here is to know that, sooner or later, for better or for worse, one will come to know her. All of her.

CHAPTER 2. THE CITY

Simon quickly washes up and gets dressed. He tries his very best not to awaken his two sleeping sons, Alexander and Rufus, as he rushes about their fine home. They will be awakened by his wife soon enough so that they can go to work in the family-owned fields of Silphium, a highly prized medicinal herb, as well as Cyrene's chief export.

Simon has done very well for himself after taking over his late father's farm and becoming a key merchant in the Silphium trade. He travels often to establish and maintain his circle of buyers. It is a necessary duty that takes him away from the family, sometimes for weeks or even months at a time, but the duty has its rewards. He has built a solid name for himself, and he is considered one of the city's most wealthy and prominent residents. His status affords him substantial financial and political clout. Simon is both admired and envied by many members of the Cyrenian high society, a position that will prove to be both a blessing and a curse. The hardest part of it all is telling the two groups apart. This task alone is a full-time occupation.

Simon has received many an accolade for his accomplishments and for his benevolence. He is a person who believes in "paying it forward" and, as a matter of practice, contributes both his time and money to meeting the needs of the poor and orphaned. The latter is a cause that is near and dear to Simon's heart, as he became an orphan himself at a young age. He also provides work to the

The Cyrenian

willing in his fields and encourages the youth to become self-sufficient. These are the values instilled in him by his late Hellenistic Jewish father, passed down to him through the generations going back to his roots in Greece, and his strong and beautiful Ethiopian mother. At the same time, he naturally draws the masked ire of those who are jealous of his position in life. Simon is known to be a fair and brilliantly shrewd businessman. While he is generally a pleasant individual, he can be most fierce when defending both his family and territory. He has no problem calling out those who have sought to undermine him or extend to him anything less than the level of respect that he feels he has earned and rightfully deserves. This is an even bigger issue for him since Cyrene is now under the rule of the Roman Empire.

The Jews no longer have the equal rights that they have enjoyed under previous regimes. Therefore, there is now the constant watchful eye and iron-fisted control of Rome in every aspect of Cyrenian life to contend with. In addition, the Greeks, over time, have become a much larger and more autonomous population in Cyrene. Both factions represent constant oppression and suppression of the Jewish people in every sense of the word. One who is Jewish must vigilantly watch out for any hint of treachery, for it takes nothing to be accused and/or be suspected of insurrection and thus be branded an "enemy of the state." This is the most feared label, one that can and often does cost one everything—up to and including one's very life and those of friends and family. Even on a good day, one can be easily facing a life sentence of slavery if one falls on the wrong side of Rome's favor. These thoughts and concerns are always on Simon's mind. He does, however, have the advantage of being a good tax-revenue source for the Empire. This fact affords him a certain level of privilege and much coveted Roman favor.

Despite the complications, there is still much to be thankful for. Cyrene is one of the most beautiful and cultured places to live in the known world, an oasis located directly on the Mediterranean, surrounded by the sands of Libya at the top of North Africa. In addition, Simon has a loving and attractive wife, obedient and respectful children, and a success that provides the financial resources to weather virtually any storm. He sees reminders daily that he could be much, much worse off.

Simon steps out into the fast-rising sun and can't help but look to the heavens, close his eyes, and let the warmth caress his face. He breathes in deeply, taking in the salted perfume of the sea breeze. "It is a good day to be alive," he says aloud to himself. He stretches and begins down the path that leads to his fields. There is much to do as he is expecting some new buyers from Caesarea Maritima to arrive later in the evening, seeking to form a new trade alliance with him. Simon is very excited at the prospect, as he knows that he is well on the way to a bumper crop this season. Most of his competition is struggling due to their inferior farming skills and understaffing. This possible new partnership has the potential of making Simon the premier exporter of Silphium to Rome proper. Not to mention the potential to make him far richer than he can possibly imagine. He has labored long and hard in doing his homework and making all of the right connections. His well-earned reputation also helps a great deal. Nonetheless, he is leaving nothing to chance. Besides, Simon has a secret weapon up his sleeve. He knows that on top of everything, he can count on Chana to completely win them over with her charm and her unmatched prowess as a hostess. "Nobody in Cyrene does it better!" he cheerfully says to himself. Between her cooking, her smile, and her natural ability to make one feel at home, Simon is confident that the new agreement is as good as his. Without having a conscious thought to do so, Simon quickens his pace, his steps having found extra spring.

CHAPTER 3. "STRONG LITTLE PRINCE"

It could be argued that there is no place in all of Rome that cannot *not* hear the steady beating of swords against shields and the rhythmic shouts of enthusiastic soldiers in unison emanating from the Roman garrison today. This is the sound of warriors, but not the sound of warfare. No, this is, in fact, a celebration. The sun glints off their razor-sharp and polished weapons, as well as the pure silver *phalerae* or war medallions displayed on their garments. They are the medals worn by those soldiers who are so honored for their acts of bravery. The very sight of the perfectly straight and even columns of fighting men moving in perfect time inspires both awe and primal fear in those who aren't members of this elite war machine. The awesome display is only outdone by the appearance of a most imposing figure, who authoritatively takes his place at the head of this block of armored humanity. His bodily decorations declare loudly that he is a man of great power and position. His larger-than-life presence and grey locks also declare that he is a man of tried-and-true military experience, one who has survived to live out its rewards. His name, Legate Marcus Maximus, means "God of War," and those who know him or his reputation as a General of the Roman Army will be the first to testify to the absolute, perfect prosody of the name to the man.

In what is but a minuscule display of his authority, he merely raises his hand, and there is immediate silence from the throng. In a voice equal to his stature, he begins his proclamation.

"Men of Honor! Today, we celebrate the promotion of one of your own to the honored rank of Centurion. It is a special man indeed who can work hard enough, fight gallantly enough, lead fearlessly enough, and most importantly, live long enough to reach this coveted place. He will be charged not only with unconditionally carrying out the wishes of Caesar but also with the very lives of the men under his command. You will either live or die according to his leadership, and you will either live or die by your unquestioning obedience in following him. Your lives will be forever joined if you serve under this banner. That is why only the finest example of a soldier can be a Centurion. I have had the honor and privilege of hand-picking this very man myself. I have known him since he was a young boy. His father and I fought side by side in many a campaign until he died with honor on the battlefield. His grandfather served with my father. His blood carries the legacy of a grand tradition of fighting men. I know for a fact that, in this case, the fruit has truly fallen very close to the tree. Therefore, it is with great pride that I call forward Drusus Regulus, the 'Strong Little Prince' and now a Centurion of the Roman Legion."

Once again, the soldiers reprise the previous symphony of swords and shields until Drusus stands at attention before them. He is a tall, young, handsome, and athletically built specimen of a man. He has a youthful fire in his eyes that is most definitely reflective of the fire in his soul. The General removes the helmet of a soldier from Drusus' head and replaces it with the symbolic headdress of his new office. As cheers rise from the men, Marcus Maximus reaches for the *vitas*, or "vine stick," another symbol of the rank that was being held out by his assistant. The vitas, a thick baton of vine that is used to meter out punishment and to keep crowd control, is an effective tool.

At this very moment, a senior Centurion and longtime friend of Drusus named Gallus (nicknamed "The Rooster") steps forward and salutes the General. He then says, "Sir, begging your pardon, as a tribute and a welcome, the senior Centurions would like to present the vitas to Drusus in a special way if you have no objection."

The half-smile on his face is a tell-tale sign that something is afoot.

The General winks and answers, "You may proceed."

With that, about a dozen seniors line up single file and spread their legs. They then instruct the soldier holding the vitas to move to the head of the line.

Gallus continues, "Now, Drusus, your first lesson as a new Centurion is that if you are going to meter out punishment, you must also be able to take it. Therefore, you must crawl through the legs of each of us until you reach your symbol of rank."

Laughter breaks out as it becomes apparent what is about to happen. Drusus does his best to maintain his dignified and cool demeanor, while inside, all he can do is tell himself that the hazing will pass quickly and that he can handle anything they dish out. He must.

"Well?!" Gallus goads. "We're waiting!"

Reluctantly and stiffly, Drusus gets on his hands and knees, beginning his migration through the tunnel of legs. Immediately, the Seniors each brandish their own vitas' and waste no time in attacking Drusus's tender posterior flesh. Unfortunately, his athletic frame means that his progress is slow, thus giving his assailants multiple opportunities at targeting perfection. Some strikes land with resounding slaps, while others miss the mark and find exposed rear thigh skin instead. Regardless, each blow is followed by peals of laughter as they watch and hear their new fellow commander wince and yell curse words while moving along red-faced in this most compromising position. Finally, Drusus decides that enough is enough, and he puts on a burst of speed while on his belly, something akin to a fleeing giant lizard. Reaching the front of the line, he springs up, partially laughing but mostly speaking in now amplified profanities. But before he can fully give them what for, he is mobbed by his fellows and lifted upon their shoulders. This will prove to be a moment of both great affection and discomfort beyond description. After parading Drusus around for a few minutes, they let him down to begin the celebratory toasts. By now, even the mighty General is laughing uncontrollably when he calls out to the servants, "Wine for the new Centurion!" while at the same time looking to hand him his hard-fought-for trophy. But in all of the confusion, the new Centurion has disappeared from sight. He has found a full water trough for watering the horses in the stable and has immediately taken a seat in the cooling water, seeking relief for his stinging and welted buttocks. While doing so, he resigns himself to the fact that the ride on horseback to the port in the coming days may very well end up being more of a foot march for him. For Drusus, that would be preferable under the circumstances at the moment. Besides, it is what foot soldiers do. However, due to his family's political standing and connections in high places, he is given the rare privilege of admission to the Equestrian military class and a horse. Normally, he would not be mounted at his rank, but as they say, it's all in who you know. Riding, therefore, is a must, regardless of his current discomfort—at least initially.

Today has been one of those rare and brief moments of levity in the lives of these fighters. The reality is that for a Roman Legionnaire, life is hard, dangerous, and oft-times, short. Comfort is not a consideration. Keeping order in Caesar's world requires a level of discipline and of sacrifice uncommon to the average man. Orders are carried out swiftly and without question or hesitation, regardless of their logic or fairness. In fact, cruelty is the preferred weapon of the day and is used frequently on both insubordinate subjects and soldiers alike. For a Roman soldier, failure in any form is not an option. To question or fail at your task is to risk death on the cross or under the scourge. The incentive to succeed cannot be higher. The subsequent results are also undeniable. One needs only to look at the current map of the Empire to understand fully the effectiveness of the forces of Rome. Therefore, only the most select men can reach the coveted position of command.

Drusus is one of these men, and every soldier there knows it. He is a fierce and skilled fighter with many a kill to his credit. His men revere him and will indeed willingly follow him, regardless of their obligation to do so. He is one of their own, who has come up through the ranks, equally sharing in every aspect of the life of a soldier. This makes respecting and committing to him as their new leader easy. They will now write a new chapter in the story of conquest together in lockstep as they prepare to embark on their journey as a part of the new police force assigned to Cyrene.

CHAPTER 4. CHANA

By now, Alexander and Rufus have completed their morning routines and are about to head off to the fields to get to work, readying the crops for sale and export. They are good boys and hard workers. They are also considered good role models for the youth in the city. Today, they are doing their favorite chore. They are taking a shipment of Silphium to a merchant ship docked in the harbor at Apollonia, which is about ten miles from home. They love the freedom and the scenery of the trip, as well as the chance to do some swimming later after the goods are loaded. Best of all, they will have some of their mother's delicious special bread and roasted lamb with them to enjoy for lunch. The weather is perfect, as it is almost all of the year. In fact, it is not unusual for the farms to yield multiple harvests during the year due to the perfect perpetual planting conditions of the lush valley. This fact only adds to the success of the family business, as Silphium is always in very high demand.

Chana stands at the door so she can kiss her sons goodbye and give them their basket containing the savory lunch items. She is proud of the men that they are becoming, while at the same time, she is sad that they are growing up so quickly. She finds herself mentally going back in time. With Simon traveling so often, loneliness was a constant companion. She was a young girl when she became his wife, as was the common custom. While her husband traveled, she spent time with the other girls and women in the city, learning and perfecting her homemaking skills. She could sew, bake, and cook very well. She proved to be a natural at running an efficient household. What's more, her reputation as a hostess was widespread and well-deserved. Unlike many women of the time, Chana also has the added ability of running a successful business. Simon wisely trained her to handle most everything for him in his absence. Her skillsets include accounting, banking, inventory control, and management of the labor force. She can wheel and deal quite well with the buyers and is not someone that you would want to try to take advantage of. These traits have given her a unique and distinct advantage in their society. Women, in general, are relegated to the typical domestic duties and the raising of children. Most aren't even literate. Simon, in his wisdom, knew early on that he would need someone as a partner that he could also trust to be an ally. He knows without question that he can trust Chana unconditionally. She is loyal and honest, almost to a fault. She is a woman of rare virtue and, as her name reflects, a woman of grace.

None of her achievements came without sacrifices, however. Chana's early married life was one of mundane solitude, often to the point of sadness. However, that all changed when Alexander was born. Suddenly, there was a new-found joy in the house. The sound of his cooing was like music in her heart. Soon, he was a toddler with the uncanny ability to disappear without a moment's notice. She remembered how he would love to hide in the house until his giggling would give away his position. Giggling would give way to full-blown laughter once Mom or Dad captured and tickled him profusely as a reward for his mischief. Their joy was doubled soon thereafter when Rufus was born. These precious pictures from her memory pass through her mind's eye like a parade of murals in just milliseconds, right up to the present moment when her grown boys throw their arms around her and kiss her cheeks.

"We'll see you tonight, Mother!" Alexander says in an enthusiastic tone.

"Be careful and be home before dark!" she answers in a typical motherly fashion.

"We will, Mother!" Rufus chimes in as he bolts out the door to join his big brother.

Chana waves to them and shakes off the familiar feelings that come from parting with loved ones, if only even for a short while. In the meantime, it is good that she has things to do. Her guests are due later tonight, and she is determined to make everything perfect. She readies herself for the short trip to the market, for it will soon be time for her to cast her spell in her role as "The Hostess," as she is affectionately known.

Chana arrives at the market, which is alive with activity and the sounds of both the sellers hawking their wares and the buyers haggling over prices. This is also no place for beginners. One can either come home well supplied or with meager quantities after spending their budget, all depending on their level of experience as a shopper. Chana begins her rounds, starting with her friendly merchant regulars and saving the more troublesome ones for last. As usual, she runs into many of her neighbors and friends, so shopping time is also a welcome social time.

Chana reaches out to inspect some tomatoes when suddenly, she feels someone clench her wrist. Startled, she turns to find herself face to face with a young man in a hooded cloak who she does not recognize.

"Who are you?! What do you want with me?!" she barks.

The man lets go of her and puts his finger over his lips, indicating that he wants her to hush. "You don't know me, but I know of both you and your husband. You have helped members of my family with your kindness in the past. Now I wish to help you," he says in a voice barely reaching above a whisper.

"Help me? Help me *how*?" she asks, her voice shaking partially from shock and partially from anger.

He looks around cautiously and says, "There are people watching you both. Powerful people. They are not to be trusted. Beware of strangers and trust no one—you hear, NO ONE! I cannot say anymore. I must go now."

He spins around and disappears into the crowd before she can say anything or inquire anymore about his cryptic message. For a moment, Chana feels like the world is standing still. The silence is only broken by the voice of a man asking, "Are you going to buy the tomatoes or just squeeze them to death?!" She refocuses quickly and answers, "Yes—I'll take these." She finds herself looking off into the distance, hoping to catch a glimpse of the strange messenger, but to no avail. Still somewhat dazed, she gathers her packages and heads for home at a pace that is only nearly as fast as her breathing.

Chana bursts through the door in tears to find that Simon is thankfully already home. She tries to find the right opening words but instead finds it easier just to rush into his arms and hold him like the frightened wife that she is. He can easily feel that she is shaking and is immediately and deeply concerned.

"What is wrong, Chana?" he asks with great concern in his voice.

Her words keep failing her as she tries to describe the encounter and the anxiety that she is feeling—especially because they will soon have unfamiliar guests arriving. After she manages to get through the story, her anxiety turns into a rage after he responds.

"My love, you're overreacting," he starts while stroking her forehead. "This new deal is not a secret, as much as I wish it was. There are many would-be competitors who know that this potential new alliance can virtually lock them out of the Silphium game for good. They can't afford to meet our price based on the sheer volume that we can supply. This is probably just a tactic on their part to intimidate us and throw us off our game." His attitude only infuriates her even more.

"NO!" she yells, her dander at full strength. "You're wrong! This is different. Something is going on, and you are being too stubborn and dismissive to take me seriously. Something is happening unbeknownst to us—I can feel it!"

Simon realizes at that moment that a full-frontal response might not be the wisest move. He instantly drops his tone to the point of perfect softness and says, "My dear Chana, think about it. We have a stranger telling us to beware of strangers. Do you see what I mean? How many games have we seen played in our years together? This is the biggest business deal of our lives. Is it not natural to expect the biggest opposition of our lives as well?"

He puts on his best little boy smile and pushes out his bottom lip—a move that almost always gets her to smile and relax. Once again, his gamble pays off.

"Maybe," she says softly.

"That's my girl. Now, let's unleash your magic. Time is short!" he says as he hugs her reassuringly. She capitulates but is in no way fully convinced.

Chana will be watching all parties tonight with great scrutiny and skepticism. As far as she is concerned, everyone but Simon is suspect, period. Only time will tell which one of the two of them is right.

CHAPTER 5. JUDEA: THE VORTEX

Israel these days is a very complicated place, especially the state known as Judea. Judea is indeed the seat of both Roman power and Roman frustration in the region. Taming the winds of defiance and revolution is proving to be a task of Herculean proportions. The constant display of Caesar's might is a necessary element if order is to be kept. Civil unrest is both rampant and unacceptable in the eyes of Rome and must be stamped out at all costs—and quickly. Overall, the main problem is that there are many opposing forces at work here, with many factions and philosophies, each vying for dominance. The constantly growing cast of individual players all have their agendas as well.

First, there is the religious side of things. The Jews view this land to be the Promised Land ceded to Abraham, Isaac, and Jacob (now "Israel") by God. Therefore, there is a venomous resentment aimed toward the Roman occupation. Some of the Jews, known as the *Zealots*, consider themselves to be patriots and the designated holy guardians of Israel, whose duty it is to remove all oppressors and intruders by any means necessary. Any means, that is, right up to and including assassination. Their belief is that they are commissioned by Jehovah to do so in His name to save and protect His people. They live in the shadows, planning and waiting for any and every opportunity to further their cause. There is arguably not a more dedicated and motivated band of men who are wholly pledged to achieving their objective. Death while trying or after trial is a price that they are willing to pay, fully believing that they will be rewarded by God in the end for furthering His kingdom.

Even more fanatical are the *Sicarii* or *Dagger Men*. This is a much more violent and deadly branch of the Zealot sect, who will kill anyone who stands against them in their inciting war against Rome, even other Jews. They do not discriminate either. Their list of targets may include even the individual priests of the Jewish Temple whom they may disagree with—and their families are not off limits either. Originally, the Sicarii were based in Galilee, but they have moved their base of secret operations and hiding to Cyrene. Finding and eliminating them will be the core of Centurion Drusus' "Search and Destroy" mission for Rome. Such is the military side of the equation.

In addition, there is the complex political side. The Jewish Temple is allowed to exist by the Romans mainly as a matter of convenience. The social control of the Jews is left to the *Sanhedrin*, a tribunal assembly of rabbis and the governing body of the Temple. That is, so long as they stay within the rules and regulations of the Roman fiats. The constant and ever-present Roman threat of destroying the Temple at any time for any reason also keeps the Jewish leaders in check. Make no mistake, though. The Sanhedrin is quite powerful, and its leaders quite savvy in the ways of political manipulation and control. They are not only powerful, but they are ruthless. They will use any means available, including coercion, extortion, intimidation, fear-mongering, false accusation, propaganda, misinformation, and all-out framing, to achieve their agendas and maintain or otherwise increase their power and control over the people.

The current Jewish king, Herod Antipas, is also allowed by Rome to ceremonially retain his throne as a symbolic gesture to give the illusion of Roman benevolence. Essentially, he is a "king" without the official title or the independent power of the office. He is limited in power and controlled by the Romans, who can remove him at their own discretion at any time. He was made the symbolic king or *Tetrarch* after the Roman removal of his brother Archelaus, who was so tyrannical and cruel that even the Romans found it best to unseat him and replace him with someone of their own choosing. Antipas is not much better than Archelaus, but he is more controllable in the eyes of Rome. Both are the sons of the late Herod the Great, who was a powerful, paranoid, and murderous tyrant. On the other hand, some at the same time regarded him to be a genius of sorts. He was a gifted architect and prolific builder who created many major infrastructure projects. Some of his most notable accomplishments include building three distinctly ornate palaces as well as the massive and beautiful Temple of Herod in Jerusalem. There are no other constructions such as these anywhere in the known world, and they were all built by his unmatched army of slaves. He also provided Rome with a strong tax revenue base, which was a main contributing factor to him currying Rome's current favor. Herod and his lineage are Jewish by religion and tradition only. They are Edomites, partial Jews who are hated by the traditional Jewish people, even above the Romans, for their tyranny and cruelty. Adding to the list of religious complications among the Jews are the many deep divides in core religious beliefs among sects.

Last, but certainly far from least, comes the Roman position. It can be said that the current Roman occupation is the lesser of two evils in the eyes of its subjects. The real fact is that the new Roman *Prefect* (or Governor), Pontius Pilate, is only interested in finding effective ways to rule Judea with a minimal amount of interaction with these people. His main concern is to keep nothing but either good news or no news in the ears of Caesar. His next highest priority is to keep the tax revenues from the Jews flowing, to fuel the Roman conquests. Though they are under heavy Roman control, Pilate allows the Jews to indulge in their customs and celebrations

The Cyrenian

more to hopefully keep their subjects occupied and quiet than anything else. Not to say that Pilate is in any way an easy mark. Any deviation from his decrees is met with swift and public retribution. Rome is always present, observing every move. There are spies everywhere who are especially suited for that purpose. Some are even paid Jewish informants. Anything but complete order and control will not be tolerated, especially from these stiff-necked and vocal people.

In any case, for a Judean Jew, the wisest way to ensure one's survival under the circumstances is to "toe the line," especially wherever one can be observed or heard. Outside of that, one can only silently pray that those with the courage to become Zealots will succeed in their efforts—and soon. Their failure, however, would mean increased suffering for the Jewish people.

Conversely, though, there is also a new wave of hope sweeping Judea. There is a message of hope spreading far and wide that promises a new life of freedom, prosperity, and peace in an everlasting kingdom of the same. What is most amazing is that this new life and subsequent new kingdom would not be the product of armies, wars, or Zealots. On the contrary, it will come via a man—a *Messiah* ("Deliverer"), who, it is said in Jewish scriptural prophecy, will be sent by God to liberate the Jews from oppression and crush their enemies forever. That said, there is news traveling like wildfire throughout the land about a young rabbi who is supposedly endowed with supernatural gifts from God. There are stories of him healing people of every imaginable malady by the mere touch of his hand. There are reports of the dead coming back to life at his command and evil spirits being cast out of their victims by his spoken word. Many are claiming to be eyewitnesses to these miraculous manifestations. Some even claim to be recipients of the same.

On the other hand, there are others that are convinced that this Deliverer is of the devil and his works are black arts or magic tricks. This view is most popular with the Temple leaders and many religious scholars for many reasons. Still, others are writing off the tales to some form of mass hysteria or perhaps propaganda. Whatever the excuse, it is imperative to those of the current governing religious establishment that the status quo be maintained at any cost. Their positions, agendas, and very futures depend on it. Besides, it wouldn't be the first time or the last time that desperation has given birth to hope in the form of myths and legends. But there is something that sets this story apart from the others...a *promise*.

The Jewish scriptures have prophesied that this Deliverer, this Messiah, will usher in all of these very things that are being espoused. There isn't a mature Jew who hasn't prayed for this Messiah to arrive in their lifetime. This same prayer was shared by others for generations, but what if this time it really is the promise come true? What a wonderful and, at the same time, potentially dangerous possibility to share! Is it rumor or reality, though? Only time will tell, but one thing is certain. Convergence is coming.

CHAPTER 6. FORTUNES

The torch lights from the house on the hill announce that something special is going on in the House of Simon tonight. There is the sound of the musicians who are serenading the attendees with their melodious tapestries. If one is close enough (and lucky enough) to be near the fire pit, they will be enraptured by the aroma of perfectly seasoned lamb being slow-roasted to savory perfection. Laughter and new wine are both flowing without restriction. The festive night is indeed going nicely for all but Alexander and Rufus. Exhausted from their day on the road and a frolicking swim session, they eat in their room and go to sleep early. In a rare display, they don't mind taking a pass on the adult activities tonight.

Simon raises his cup in a toast, "To our honored guests, Saccius and Aemilius. Welcome to our house!" His gesture is met with a hearty echo of cheers from the servants and hosts alike.

Saccius speaks, "Never before in my travels have I ever been treated or fed so well. In fact, I may never leave!"

Joining in the spirit of the moment, Aemilius chimes in, "Nor I! We cannot thank you enough for this wonderful night."

Simon turns to his smiling, though now tired wife, who is helping to clear the table. "Now," Simon continued, "I wish to toast the true marvel of the evening. Here's to…"

"No, allow me!" Saccius jumps in, anticipating Simon's goal. "Our thanks to our lovely and most gracious hostess, Chana. You have made us feel almost as rich and as blessed as your husband."

The Cyrenian

"That I am!" says Simon gleefully as he finds Chana's cheek with his lips.

Aemilius adds, "The best part is, you are possibly about to become even richer!"

Chana recognizes that this is the opportune time to vacate the space and allow the men to begin their negotiations, "Gentlemen, the pleasure is mine. I am delighted to have such fine guests. Thank you for your kind sentiments. I must leave you now and prepare your quarters for the night. I'll see you when you are ready to turn in."

She bows her head and leaves the room in a picture-perfect exit. Simon knows that even though she is physically separated from them, Chana's legendary hearing will not be. In fact, he is counting on it.

"Simon, my friend, all men should do as well as you have. Our sentiments are not empty ones," says Porcius, his tone becoming more business-like. "It is our aim tonight to increase and enhance your position—rather OUR positions if possible."

"What better deal can there be than the kind where all parties are enhanced?" Simon responds.

"Agreed. Aemilius, my partner, would you like to begin?"

"Thank you, Saccius," says his partner. Everyone sits up in full focus. "I needn't lecture you on the market," he begins, "as I am sure that you know probably better than I what is going on. But nonetheless, here are a few key points for the record. Silphium has become exponentially more valuable of late for several reasons. First, outside of its traditional use as a most effective contraceptive, new medical benefits have arisen. It is now being prescribed for everything from coughs, sore throats, and fevers to indigestion, pain, and even warts. But that is only part of the story. In Rome, it is considered an aphrodisiac of such potency that it is being immortalized in songs and poetry. It's now even a coveted cooking spice. Moreover, it is said that the animals that graze upon it possess the most flavorful and tender meat. I'll need only to taste Chana's lamb to attest to that fact!"

There is a burst of believing laughter at the comment.

"On another note, though, there are other factors working in your favor. Silphium only grows in this region of Cyrenaica and is being harvested almost to extinction by those who cannot cultivate it since many of the farms were forcefully taken over from the Greek owners by Roman nobles, who are the biggest culprits and the least qualified to grow it. Fortunately for you, that hasn't happened here—yet. Silphium doesn't seem to replenish itself like most other crops, and many farms are now either out of business or searching for a substitute plant to grow. You, on the other hand, have a thriving farm that is, up to now, not showing any sign of slowing down. In the meantime, your competition is getting smaller almost daily. You have succeeded where others have failed. Best of all, Rome is aggressively looking for new suppliers." Porcius now enters the sales pitch. "That's where we come in. We have been given the exclusive license from Caesar himself to import Silphium to Rome from here in Cyrene."

At that moment, he produces a very official-looking parchment for Simon to inspect.

"Since we will be operating under his Seal, your farm will be protected and safe from the annex, at least for the foreseeable future. In addition, by partnering with us, you will be the sole supplier to Rome. You—I mean, WE can't lose!" he says most enthusiastically. "Say the word, and all is done!"

Simon sits still, rubbing his chin and silent for the moment. His two guests look at each other, visibly surprised that Simon is not more excited.

"Does this news not please you, Simon?" they ask.

He straightens up. "I apologize, but I have some concerns. For instance, how much will this partnership cost me?" he queries.

The Cyrenian

Saccius responds, "We were thinking that since we have the Seal and market and you have the product, we could be equal partners."

"I see. So, I can assume that we will share all the expenses and the taxes evenly as well?" says Simon, carefully watching their every move.

"Well, we figure we will handle things like transportation from here to market and final distribution. And, of course, we can discuss taxes and such. The important thing is that we can offer you an exclusive market and the protection of Rome. Nobody else can say that."

Simon counters, "I must admit that I do see some advantages in your offer, but while Rome is a much bigger market and offers higher possible returns long-term, I also must consider my own risks. Roman rulers and governors change often, and who knows what terms may change and when. Besides, I have the labor costs, the production costs, and I also must consider the fact that many of my long-established customer relationships would have to be severed. I've done well with them thus far, and they have been the reason that I am in my current position. That would be a tough decision to make. Furthermore, I would not even consider this deal for less than an 80 percent share if I did it at all."

Aemilius now speaks up, politely but emphatically, "The times are changing, Simon. I strongly urge you to reconsider. You are right—the terms can change for all of us and at any time. But for right now, the winds are blowing in our favor. We may not get this chance again."

Saccius quickly spouts, "Sixty-forty?" testing the water.

Simon stands up, stretching after what has been a long night of sitting. "Gentlemen, you have given me much to ponder. Truthfully, though, I cannot decide at this moment. Wine, a full belly, and the need for sleep also seek to cloud my judgment," he says, grinning. "Let us rest now and explore things in the morning."

Sensing the obvious halt to the night's negotiations, his two guests take the soft approach.

"You are right, Simon. Perhaps a break for the night is in order. We thank you again for a delightful evening and will look forward to a fresh start tomorrow. Now, where is your charming wife that we might say goodnight to her also?"

As if on cue, Chana and her smile enter the room. "Begging your pardons, gentlemen, I was just coming to tell you that your room is ready. What timing!" she says cheerfully. "Our steward will show you the way."

"In that case, we shall retire. Sleep well, our wonderful hosts," smiles Saccius.

"Until morning then," smiles Simon.

When they are gone, Simon turns to his wife and asks, "So, how much did you hear?"

Winking, she replies, "Enough."

Once in bed, Simon and Chana begin their much-anticipated pillow talk while also being ever-mindful to keep their voices low. Chana does not hesitate to make her feelings known.

"I don't like it. I don't trust them. In fact, I don't believe that you even need them. You've done well on your own all these years, and your base of clients is well-established. Your reputation is impeccable and has traveled far and wide, obviously even to Rome. As far as I'm concerned, they need you—not the other way around."

Her face and her tone are most serious. This won't be an easy sell for Simon, especially since her points are iron-clad in their validity.

"I agree with you fully, my dear. I don't blame you at all for your feelings. Our first thoughts are the same."

She feels Simon's next line coming and prefaces it, "But."

Simon continues the thought, "But there is a major fact that we must consider. Aemilius is right. Rome has pretty much taken away the farms of many of our friends, generally without a moment's notice. They went from being owners to being servants or, worse, homeless. There was no negotiation involved whatsoever. I also know that we are on borrowed time, as much as I hate to admit it. I hear the rumors out there. We can't hide our success, and now that the supply of Silphium is getting scarcer, we are a prime prospect for takeover. We would be foolish to think that what has happened to others can't happen to us. We've been lucky to have enjoyed peace under a good Roman Prefect, but things are changing rapidly under the new Emperor, Caesar Augustus. No one is sure what will happen now under the new Prefect, Pontius Pilate, either. It was tough enough to be a Jew in a Greek world, but now we are Jews in a Roman world. It might be wise for us to take this deal and at least have some guarantee of our existence, albeit possibly subject to future changes, good or bad. In any case, it would buy us some time to come up with a long-term plan. We both know that nothing lasts forever, especially in these times that we are living in. Change is the only thing we can be sure of. I've even thought of selling the farm after this harvest and retiring to a quiet life on the coast. Then, on the other hand, the deal might work out in our favor. We're talking about having exclusive rights to a much larger marketplace than we've ever had. Who knows? All in all, I'm thinking that it might be wiser for us to operate as a partner of Rome than as a target of Rome. It's the lesser of two evils in my mind."

These are sobering words indeed. Chana ponders the words of her husband and weighs them against the intuitions that she is feeling. She knows that Simon is a smart and prudent man and that his thoughts are almost always well-crafted and well-rooted in truth. However, there is still one factor that she can't shake off.

"I still don't trust these two men, don't ask me why. Can't you go to Rome and cut the deal yourself?" she asks.

Simon answers without hesitation, "As a Jew and an outsider, I wouldn't stand a chance. I doubt that I could even get an audience. In fact, getting one might accelerate their annexing us after I state my case. Rejecting this offer might also have the same effect once word got back to Rome. Unfortunately for us, Rome's position would be that I need them, but they don't need me. No, my dearest, we may have to choose to deal this time. The more I think about it, the clearer the answer seems to be. This is a major paradox, and there is much more at stake now than money."

Both lay there silent for a time until Chana whispers, "What about the warning I got about trusting strangers?"

"Now, Chana, we've already been over that. I'm not worried about some strange madman's rant. While it's true that they are strangers, right now, they represent our best possible option for survival, regardless of our feelings. Look, my love, I hate being in this position as much as you do, but we must face reality. Time is not on our side. Speaking long-term, we don't really have a choice this time but to trust them, however cautiously. We could take our chances, but we would risk losing everything. I don't see a better way. But believe me, I'll be watching their every move, I promise."

He kisses her forehead. There is no mistaking the angst in her eyes. She knows he is twisting inside as well, though. She stares into his eyes and touches his hand in support, saying, "I don't like the whole thing, but I do understand. Of course, I will trust your judgment. It has served us well all these years. It will bear out again. I believe in you, my husband."

They trim out the lamp and roll over to attempt to sleep, knowing now that the decision has been made.

The wonderful smell of smoke and roasted lamb still permeates the house. The conversations of the evening will soon serve to forever permeate their lives.

CHAPTER 7. A NEW TIME MARCHES ON

There is nothing in the world like the day of deployment for a Roman Legionnaire. While there is something to be said for the days of comfort and rest between campaigns, for a fighting man, there is the ever-present need for action. Life at the garrison is a mundane yet balanced routine of staying occupied with trivial duties like polishing armor, training, and, of course, the welcomed revelry on one's off-duty time. Most importantly, though, a soldier needs conquest to stay alive. It is as crucial to him as breathing. Preparing for the march starts the heart pumping and the senses tingling, as one knows that the most coveted trophy of all lay before them—victory. This is something that every soldier knows well, but none has experienced it more or more often than the Roman soldier. It defines him. It is, in fact, the standard by which his very existence will be measured. Victory is his woman and goddess, and he will pursue her with total abandon. There is nothing he won't give or do to possess her. Like an obsessed lover, he will even gladly die for her. Every deployment means that he is getting yet another opportunity to win her. She will once again belong to him. The thought and the thrill of it all is nothing less than intoxicating.

Drusus and his liege, Marcus Maximus, emerge from the altar to Mars after making their sacrifice and devotional to the god who they consider to be the patron of their success. Of course, they have no lack of choices, as there are as many gods to choose from in Roman culture as you can come up with a name or purpose for. Mars, however, is theirs. He is, after all, the *god of war*.

The appearance of the commanders in full battle regalia is most impressive and sends a clear message to the townsfolk everywhere that Rome is alive, well, and fully in charge. It is very early morning, giving the soldiers the opportunity to take advantage of the cool, almost cold morning air. This is a wise move because the brutal daytime sun is only hours away. The troops are assembled and in formation, ready for the command to move out. Drusus mounts his horse, fighting to make it look easy.

General Marcus Maximus whispers with a smirk, "The odds said that you wouldn't pull that off in one try. I'm impressed!"

Drusus, trying to look focused, confidently asks, "Is the word given, General?"

"The word is given, Centurion."

Drusus salutes and takes his position at the lead of his men. He has deployed countless times as a soldier, but being in command this time carries the experience to the highest of heights. He has never felt so strong, so proud, so invincible. He spins his horse around smartly and gives his very first order, "Attention!" The hundred men under his command instantly snap into uniform alertness, raising their banners and shields. *I could get used to this!* he thinks to himself. "Forward!" he shouts with all authority. His battle group falls in line among the other battle groups, and they all step off en masse to the beat of the drums, setting the cadence for the two-day march to the port at Antium. The legion of roughly 6,000 men will then go the remaining roughly 900 miles by sea to Apollonia, Cyrene's main harbor. If all goes well, the force will arrive in about ten days. After a short deployment there, they will be relieved by another arriving legion and then continue the march east to Jerusalem.

As the silhouette of Rome disappears behind them, Drusus notices one of the other centurions riding towards him. He soon recognizes that Gallus, "The Rooster," is the one. He earned that nickname because he is generally boastful and speaks loudly all the time. It is as if he is always crowing. He has much to crow about, in all fairness. He has more successful campaigns under his belt than anyone else in the battle group, including most of the commanding officers. He has cheated death more than once and has kept the gravediggers of his enemies busy. In fact, if not for his tendency to say the wrong thing at the wrong time to the wrong officers, he might be a Tribune by now. Unfortunately for him, tact is not his strong suit. In any case, though, Drusus is secretly looking forward to whatever front-line advice that he has to offer. Besides, they are best friends. Brothers even.

Gallus reaches Drusus and immediately begins ribbing his friend. "So, the little prince has a command! How does it feel?"

Drusus answers with no hesitation, "It's a great feeling, I must say."

"I mean your posterior! How does it feel?!" laughs Gallus.

"Not nearly as bad as yours will feel when I take MY revenge, you weasel!" Drusus retorts, now only partially kidding.

Gallus continues with the barbs., "Now, now, let's not stay sore, ha-ha! Besides, you'll get to be on the dishing-out end one day. Seriously, though, you won't have time to think about it much on this mission." The tone of the conversation changes instantly.

"What do you mean, Rooster?" Drusus inquires, most ready to listen and learn.

"That's right. This is going to be your first time marching into Judea, isn't it? It's a lot different from Antioch, where we were stationed. Let me put it this way: Nothing can prepare you for this assignment. We usually have no trouble from most of the people in the cities that we conquer. Sure, there are usually a few small uprising attempts and a skirmish here and there, but we put them down quickly and make examples of the agitators, usually by crucifying them along the main roads for all to see. Normally, that's enough to control the masses, especially if you terrorize them occasionally just for good measure. They stay afraid, and that works for us. It's better to be feared than respected. The Jews, on the other hand, are religious fanatics. They are defiant and devious. They fear nothing because they believe that their God will ultimately deliver them soon. Our hands are tied most of the time from taking extreme actions due to the politics between the Prefect and the rabbis, which only makes the people even more defiant. They protest constantly. But most of all, you have these Zealots, the 'Long Knives,' as they call themselves, to deal with. Take them very seriously. They will kill you on the spot if they get the chance. They hide and mingle amongst the people and then stage bloody raids, ambushing us when they think we least expect it, especially at night. You really have to watch your back. They know our every move too. Be careful what you eat or drink also. Poisonings are common, so have the slaves or servants taste anything you get first, especially in the brothels."

Drusus nods, "So I've heard. I've also heard about this Messiah character who goes around doing 'miracles.' What's the story?"

Gallus makes a "pffft" sound and says, "There's a new one every week, it seems. This latest one seems to have a much bigger following through. For his sake, I hope he has a better ending than the last."

"The last one?" Drusus asks.

"Yeah, some madman from the desert named John. Crazy King Herod lopped off his head at a party to entertain his guests, I heard. Not much of a legacy for a guy who supposedly had the power to free the Jews and build a new kingdom."

Drusus shares what he knows about the subject, "Marcus Maximus told me that this new one is part of the reason why we're being deployed. His following is growing by leaps and bounds. He doesn't think he's any more a threat right now than other lunatics we've encountered, but one can't be too sure. Many a coup has started this way. Personally, I intend to end any attempts before they begin. It's also my intention to make the General proud of his belief in me. Off the record, though, frankly, I wouldn't mind seeing one of these so-called miracles myself. We don't get much in the way of entertainment in our line of work."

Rooster laughs and spurs his horse, "Ha ha…Wait…just wait!"

Drusus laughs as well and is glad for the momentary diversion of the conversation and even more glad for the content of it. He takes a strong grasp of what he feels is the underlying message from his good friend: Be sure to expect the unexpected. The words are not only wise but will prove to be life to those that heed them and death to those who don't.

Suddenly, he can now see quite easily how the lore of a coming Deliverer could spread so far and so wide, so fast. To the oppressed, hope is all they have, and hope desperately needs a hero.

CHAPTER 8. BY THE SEA

It is often said that there is no such thing as a bad day on the Lake of Gennesaret, also known as the Sea of Galilee. However, today is exceptional. The water is calm, dancing in time and shimmering in the passing noonday sun. There are also more people along the shore than usual. There is a crowd forming, and they all seem to be focused on one figure. In the chatter of the crowd, you can hear him being called "rabbi." He begins to teach them on the shore. However, the crowd grows to be so large that he sees the need to teach from the water to be heard by everyone present. He glances over at the nearby fishing boats.

The young rabbi walks towards two fishing boats, where four men are washing their nets. This is a chore that typically marks the end of a fishing expedition; however, today, there is no catch to show for their efforts. They labor intensely as the sun glistens on their sweat-covered skin. The leader, another named Simon, is on the brink of exhaustion when the rabbi approaches him.

The rabbi smiles and asks, "Are these boats for hire? I wish to go out and do some fishing, as well."

Simon stands up straight, with a glaring look of disgust on his face. He answers in a gruff tone, "Maybe. How much can you pay?"

"It will be more than worth your while, I promise you," the rabbi answers.

Simon sizes up the man and, seeing the fine, seamless outer garment that he is wearing, decides that he might be a man of means.

Besides, he figures that this charter could be some consolation for the wasted night.

Simon heaves a heavy sigh and responds after a moment, "Fine. Let me load the nets and gather my partners—but you had better not be wasting my time!"

The rabbi only stands there smiling. Simon calls out to his compatriots, James and John, and to his brother, Andrew.

"Stow the nets and prepare to go back out. It seems that we have a paying customer."

Their faces all say the same thing. They are tired and disgusted. However, money is money. They obey without grand protest, though some muffled grumblings can be heard. The rabbi climbs into the boat, and they soon push off.

He turns to Simon and says, "Take us a few more yards offshore, and then drop your anchor."

Simon grudgingly does so, still trying to figure out what type of character he has just picked up as a passenger. He does notice, however, that wherever the teacher goes, a crowd follows. Soon, they reach a spot just offshore where the rabbi indicates it is time to take up position. Almost as if on cue, the crowd immediately stops and sits down on the shore, facing them. At this point, the rabbi stands up and begins to speak. Amazingly, his voice carries most clearly. He speaks of his anointing, his mission, the kingdom to come, and the gospel truth of salvation. It is a message of hope unlike any they'd ever heard before. At the same time, it has elements in it that are different to the point of puzzling. Yet, even the four fishermen whom he has enlisted marvel at the power of his words and their stark contrast to anything that they had ever heard from the rabbis of their synagogues.

After a time, the rabbi concludes his message and turns to Simon, saying, "Put out farther into deeper water and let down your net."

Once again, Simon groans audibly but resists the urge to protest too loudly. He reluctantly complies, saying only, "We've been out here fishing all night and have caught nothing. Worse yet, these fish do not gather to feed in the daytime. I don't know what you expect, but I'll do as you ask just to prove my point. Besides, it's your money."

With that, he drops the net and prepares to settle in for a long and futile wait in the hot sun. He looks at his passenger, reclined with his eyes closed and head back, smiling and taking in the gentle breeze. Shaking his head, Simon is about to sit down when, just at that moment, the boat lurches violently and starts listing heavily toward the side of the casted net. Looking over the side, Simon can see that the net is quickly sinking. He begins pulling furiously to raise it when he hears the distinct sound of the net ripping in his hands. He yells out loudly to his fishing partners, James and John, to come quickly and help him. It is all that Simon can do to hang on to the net until they get there. They are met by some of Simon's more colorful language and a full-on fight to raise the net. As it breaks the surface of the water, they gaze with amazement at a harvest of fish that defies both imagination and description. The grimacing men muster all their strength for one last mighty pull. It takes the four of them to bring their bounty in over the side. The cascade of fish spills out onto the deck of the boat and keeps coming to the point where the stern is taking water and fast approaching the point of going under.

"Andrew! Get your boat over here QUICK!" screams a frantic Simon. "Hurry up!" he yells again, adding another round of colorful phrases.

Andrew manages to pull his boat alongside, where they all, including the rabbi, begin scooping up and throwing the flipping and flopping quarry into the second boat. The crowd on shore intently watches and cheers the men bailing their boat of both fish and water at a furious pace. Interestingly, amid all of this chaos, one can't help but notice that the rabbi is laughing with glee, much to the further puzzlement of Simon.

After what seems an eternity, the team manages to stabilize both fish-filled boats and is ready to make for shore. Now, all is silent but for the heavy panting of the fishermen. The experience has left no doubt in their minds that something supernatural has just occurred, especially since other on-looking fishermen's boats are empty. There is no other possible explanation. The catch is more than could have been caught in days of fishing. While all the fishermen stand in shocked awe, it is Simon who is the most deeply affected. The combination of the gospel he heard earlier and the overall sequence of events are serving to convict his spirit. He now subconsciously knows who this rabbi is. He, too, has heard the stories. He looks at the rabbi, and tears fill his eyes.

"Oh, Lord!" he exclaims, falling to his knees atop the fish. "I am an unworthy and sinful man. Depart from me, I beg you! I am ashamed of my behavior before you! I am worthy only of your judgment!"

His voice quivers as he tries to fight back the flow of tears. The rabbi places his hand on Simon's shoulder and says gently, "You are why I am here. Rise up. Do not be afraid. From this day forward, you all shall fish not for fish but for men. Join me now and follow me, as there is much to do to prepare for the soon-coming kingdom."

He helps Simon to his feet and says to him, "From now on, you are no longer to be called Simon. I shall call you Peter, which means 'Rock.' You will serve as the foundation for my church to come, and the gates of hell will not prevail against it."

Up to now, the lives of Simon (now Peter), Andrew, James, and John were backbreaking but profitable. As professional fishermen, they are in a good position on the social ladder of their hometown and live in relative comfort compared to many. Today's catch will bring record-breaking profits and give them a large income boost. Yet, their inner voices are all saying the same thing. They will collectively now choose to give up all that they call familiar, as well as the opportunity of financial gain to follow this rabbi on a journey into the unknown. They cannot help themselves. To be chosen by a rabbi and to follow him is an honor that any young Jewish male would relish, but no rabbi they have ever met is anything like this one. The decision to follow is somehow as easy to make as it is illogical. Something on the inside tells them at their very core that following this rabbi is something that they just must do.

The group finally arrives ashore as the multitude of witnesses and buyers gather around to marvel at the unbelievable sight before them. This is yet another story that will no doubt travel quickly. Peter turns to the rabbi and says to him, "I will follow you. Here I am, giving up everything to follow a man I know nothing about. I don't even know your name, yet I am being compelled to follow you. I don't quite know why. I only know in my heart that my destiny is tied to yours." The others echo the same sentiments. The rabbi responds, saying, "I am Yeshua of Nazareth. Come now, all of you. Leave everything behind, and let us begin."

While the statements from Yeshua are quizzical to them, they do not hesitate to comply. After saying farewell to family and giving their final instructions to the servants of their houses, the five men unceremoniously begin down a road that will become the beginning chapter of a story like no other before or since.

CHAPTER 9. WHEN NOT IN ROME...

The spray of the sea feels good on Drusus' face. Even better, the hazy outline of hills in the distance foretells the eminent arrival in Cyrene. They have been fortunate that the sail has been smooth with no foul weather. That is not to say that some had found the time at sea anything less than unbearable. Seasickness and cramped conditions over the last ten days have literally overcome the intestinal fortitudes of many of Rome's finest, partially due to the salted fish, bread, and olives that is the solitary diet while aboard. After all, for the most part, these men are soldiers, not sailors. Landing ashore cannot not come fast enough for these unfortunates. Drusus, on the other hand, grew up by the sea and is no stranger to sailing. What is hardship for some is heavenly to him. It also tickles him to see some of the very soldiers who had so brutally hazed him just days ago in the throes of sheer agony before him.

Soon, their ship finally reaches the docks of Cyrene's harbor, and the flurry of mooring activities is in full swing. Legate Marcus Maximus dons his full military regalia and shouts out loud and clear, "Form ranks and prepare to disembark!" The order is echoed in relay by the squad leaders so that all stand notified. In true Roman precision, the mass of humanity quickly morphs into clean lines of soldiers standing at the ready. The gangway is dropped, and the cadence of the drums signals the disembarking of the troops. Before long, the legion is fully assembled on the dock, looking just a little less lethal as they try to regain their "land legs." For the spectators at the dock, it is most comical to watch the all-powerful Roman soldiers wobbling like a child's top. For just a moment, they are mere mortals.

The orders are given to prepare to go to the site where they will be setting up camp, but out of mercy and in the interest of morale, the soldiers are given a few hours to acclimate before the next march. There were shops nearby, and Drusus, Gallus, and many more of the officers took this opportunity to be first to seek out the possibilities of finding meat, fresh bread, and wine. As soon as the horses are on shore, they waste no time in being on their way. Rank truly does have its privileges. However, while riding into the village of Apollonia, it is easy to sense that they aren't welcome. The faces of the oppressed residents all have the same look of longing and despair. For some, the look is simply pure unadulterated hatred. For all the marching he has done in his career, Drusus has never really paid attention to the faces before. At that moment, he quickly remembers what Gallus had said. This is the favorite hiding place of the Dagger Men. He snaps into a different state of mind and now eyes everyone he encounters with increased scrutiny. Any one of them is a potential assassin. His focus is only broken by the splendid aroma of food emanating from a small shop just a few paces away. The officers look at each other with glee and quickly dismount their steeds. Tying them up outside, they huddle quickly.

"Let's take a softer approach so as not to create a more hostile environment. Let's see what we're up against," Gallus says. "They'll also surely overcharge us, but for today, we'll play their game—agreed?"

One of the Centurions chimes in, "I'm too hungry to care!"

The motion is carried unanimously. Upon entrance, they find a woman and her presumed daughter minding the store. They are startled to see actual soldiers in their establishment, even though it was no secret that they were coming.

The mother speaks first, "What can I do for you?"

Drusus answers, "We are looking for meat and wine. Bread also, if you have it."

She tells them, "The bread is freshly baked. My husband is roasting a ram in back. I will see if it is ready. Here is a portion to taste while you wait." She turns to her daughter and says, "Give them wine and water," as she goes outside.

The young girl is visibly nervous as she sets the cups in front of the men and begins to pour. One soldier starts to tease her, "You're a pretty thing, aren't you?" grabbing for her wrist.

In a flash, Gallus forcefully grabs the man's wrist, glaring and saying under his breath, "What did we discuss outside? Apologize!"

The response is immediate, and the soldier stands down. "My apologies. I was only kidding around."

No sooner has the encounter ended when a large, brawny man enters the room. He speaks in a tone equal to his stature, "My wife says that you want meat. I can sell meat to you by the plate, or for five denarii, you can take the entire ram."

"Five denarii is robbery! I can buy two rams for less!" shouts one of the officers.

Drusus calmly counters, "Include a barrel of wine plus these loaves here, and we will pay your price, provided that you will extend a discount to us when we come again."

The man looks around the room and grunts his reluctant approval. It is obvious the Romans are merely being tolerated. The shopkeeper's wife and daughter start to package the goods as he goes outside to cut up the meat.

Drusus comforts his comrades by laughing, "Don't worry, my friends. Once the others at the ship smell this, they'll pay us any price we ask for a portion!"

Gallus chuckles, "And the later it gets, the more they'll pay!"

The Cyrenian

Drusus stands up, brandishing his knife, and immediately begins cutting slices of meat sample as an appetizer for each of the men. No words are necessary to express the joy that the succulent morsels are bringing. The looks on their faces are testimony enough. Just then, a young man bursts through the door as if on a mission of high importance. Before he can speak, his widened eyes fall on the soldiers. You can tell that he wants to say something to the shopkeeper but is, at that moment, temporarily stunned into silence. He spins around to leave when Gallus shouts, "Halt!" and walks towards him. "You look like a man with a purpose, yet you saw us and turned to leave. Why?" he says while at the same time sizing up the youth.

From across the counter, the shopkeeper barks, "He can't answer you. He hasn't spoken a word since he was a child. He comes to bring home food for his family. He is harmless. The sight of you frightened him. He has never seen Roman soldiers before."

The shopkeeper puts his hands on the young man's shoulders and reassuringly leads him to the rear of the shop. Drusus pipes up, "It's getting late. We must be heading back."

The soldiers load up their quarry and mount up to head back to the ship.

Drusus turns to Gallus and asks, "What do you think was the real story behind that young man?"

"Nothing I'd be concerned with. I would guess if I'd never seen the likes of us before, I'd be scared too!"

Laughing, they kick their horses into a smart gait and follow the path back down to the ship.

Behind the shop, the shopkeeper has been watching the departure of the soldiers with great focus. Once he is comfortable that they will not be returning, he turns to the young man and says, "You should have waited until they were gone to come inside, Gideon. The less you are seen, the better. I am glad at least that you remembered our emergency code and kept silent."

Gideon says, "I thought that I recognized the horses as being from one of the local farms. I was obviously wrong." He then asks, "Do you have the food supplies ready? They are anxious for my return."

"The Romans bought most of what I had freshly ready, but I have some meat left from a ram I roasted earlier, and I have a few loaves left. I'll get everything ready for you. In the meantime, I am concerned about you Zealots creating deadly trouble for us by confronting and attacking the Romans. We are farmers, not warriors. Moreover, we don't need the kind of iron-handed governing that we've heard about from other regions happening here. Please urge your comrades to let this sleeping bear lie and then pass from us."

Gideon takes a strong but respectful tone in answering, "We don't want trouble any more than you do. We know that we can't take on the legions by ourselves. Believe me, none of us is anxious to be crucified either, especially in vain. But rest assured, we will be watching and waiting in the shadows for the day of our freedom. God will make His hour plain, and when it comes, we will be ready to take His sword into our hands. But be of good courage, we will not move before He does. It will not be long, for we believe that the Messiah has come. We have heard a miraculous word from Galilee that a man who perfectly fits the prophecy is there."

The shopkeeper glares, obviously skeptical. "I dare not let my hopes be lifted again, only to be dashed to bits by disappointment. I've seen enough imposters in my lifetime. I pledge you, if I start to feel any more uneasiness, understand that I will deny all of you and will do or say whatever I must to protect my family. They come FIRST!" he says with an undeniable and blunt seriousness.

Gideon answers solemnly, "I understand all too well, my friend. Thank you for all that you do, especially as you do it out of your heart without compensation."

The shopkeeper replies, "I am a son of Abraham, Isaac, and Jacob. I consider it my duty." He packages up the food, sends the

Zealot on his way, and goes about the duties of closing the shop for the night. Sleep will not come fast enough for him tonight.

Gideon rides with speed up the path to a certain point and then veers off into the fields that will eventually lead him into the high hills. Night is falling quickly, but he knows his route like the back of his hand. Soon, he makes his way through the brush that will take him to the mouth of the cave, which is his destination. No sooner does he dismount and begin to unload the bundles from the shop than a group of men quickly approach him, each holding a long knife. One rushes up behind him and puts the knife to his throat in a menacing yet controlled manner.

"Feed me now or die!" he says and then laughs. "What took you so long?" relaxing his posture.

Gideon spins around, and his face sends the unmistakable message that he is in no mood for games. "The Romans are here and caught they me unawares. They were in the shop, and they looked to harass and interrogate me. Thanks be to God that our shopkeeper was sharp and came to my aid. Our fears are now being realized."

"We fear nothing!" retorts the lead Zealot known as Barabbas, now equally as serious. "They are the ones that should be afraid. The time has come when their fate is in OUR hands. We have the advantage now. We know where they are, and they know nothing of us or this land. They are strong in numbers, but we will quickly pick off their leaders one by one until they are left broken and scattered. If we cut off the head, they will retreat with all speed. Believe me, my brother, they will soon learn what sort of men dwell here. Our actions will send a clear message to Rome that they cannot and will not survive in Cyrene. Besides, God is with us. In fact, the word from Galilee is, God is not only with us, but He is with us in person!"

By now, the rest of the impressive renegade band is surrounding what they know is their supper, and they are all jockeying for position.

Gideon hands over the goods and responds, "All I can say is that you had better be right. I have never seen a Roman soldier before, but after today, I now understand why so many innocents have fallen both far and wide. They are unlike any enemy force that we have ever encountered. I caution you; you had better plan your moves wisely. Something tells me that whatever chance you get…if any…may very well be your one and only."

Barabbas stands firm and repeats, "God is with us!"

Gideon re-iterates his previous response, only this time just in his mind… *You had better be right!*

CHAPTER 10. PACTS AND PROMISES

The familiar bustle and clatter announce that the morning's activities are in full swing in Simon's house. There is an air of both excitement and uneasiness, depending on which side of the breakfast table you are sitting on. Saccius and Aemilius are brimming with keen anticipation, while Simon and Chana are noticeably a bit more guarded in their dispositions than they had been the night before. Nonetheless, they are still ever the gracious hosts.

"I trust that our guests slept well last night," Simon begins, managing to summon his winning smile.

"Indeed! It was impossible to do otherwise, given the wonderful evening that you showed us." answers Saccius, with his partner nodding emphatically in agreement.

"Going home is going to be difficult after such splendid treatment!" Aemilius adds.

"It has been a pleasure to have you here with us," Chana chimes, ever the lady of grace. Breakfast continues and is filled with pleasantries and small talk. Rufus and Alexander finally get the chance to meet their guests as well. They are as smiling and polite as always while at the same time silently forming their own impressions. Soon, they are off to begin their days' chores, leaving the adults to get down to business.

Simon opens the conversation. "Well, I am sure you are waiting to hear our thoughts on your proposition."

Saccius responds, trying his best not to sound too anxious. "I must admit, at times, it felt that this moment would never arrive!" his eyes giving away his feelings. "Please give us your thoughts."

Simon leans forward as Chana sits silently but with full attention. "There was obviously much to consider here. As you know, we have never needed partners to be successful. All that you see is due to hard work and wise decisions. However, while we have not been up to now affected in any way by the changing times, it would be naive to not see that it is only a matter of time before we are all affected to some degree. Admittedly, that is the strongest case for consideration of your offer. At the same time, I must ask you, what guarantee do we have that you and Rome will honor this agreement long-term?"

Chana is glad that her husband has immediately put them on the spot.

Aemilius responds. "We can fully appreciate your concerns here. After all, we are strangers to you, and you have never had to deal directly with Rome before. However, it is to Rome's advantage and, therefore, ours to honor this agreement. Rome needs and wants Silphium. It only grows here, and you are literally the biggest potential supplier in the known world. Moreover, you have succeeded where others have failed or are failing in terms of your ability to make your fields thrive. It would not be prudent to interfere with such a solid situation, especially since we and Rome have no experience in such things. Besides, having you as an exclusive supplier will also increase Rome's supply position by squeezing out the consumer competition for the product. In fact, at some point, you might very well find yourself able to buy out your competitors fully, making you the sole supplier to the world! Think of the possibilities!"

Saccius smiles with approval at his partner's eloquent argument. "Yes!" he adds. "Just think of the House of Simon being the sole

Silphium supplier to the ENTIRE world! In addition, you will also have the complete protection and the rights of passage that come along with being a business partner of the Empire. Rome will fiercely look out for its interests. What better guarantee could one ask for than the guarantee that comes with being under the Roman flag!" Saccius is beginning to feel even more confident that their pitch and closing arguments will, in the end, win the day.

Simon takes a moment to stand and stretch while slowly pacing the floor. The silence of all the parties is deafening. All eyes are on Simon at that moment, and he knows it.

After what seems an eternity, Simon speaks. "Here is what I propose. I think that a trial period for this agreement is in order. This way, Rome, yourselves, and ourselves will be able to better assess the value of our relationship and see at the same time how well it works. I am willing to give it a full season through harvest to see how things pan out. If all goes well and as agreed upon, we will ratify the agreement in its entirety. I think that in the long run, everyone will feel better starting out this way—don't you?"

Saccius, who is just slightly less exuberant but obviously still very interested, asks, "And the percentage?"

Simon answers, "Seventy-five, twenty-five."

Aemilius, obviously not excited at the terms, speaks up, "I don't think that's enough for our end, and besides, I don't think that our Roman counterparts will…"

"Seventy-thirty," Saccius breaks in, grabbing his partner's elbow. All eyes again shift to Simon, awaiting what is surely to be the final offer. Aemilius stands looking puzzled by his partner's outburst but follows Saccius's lead.

After a long but planned pause, Simon declares, "Only on the grounds that you are fully responsible for the transport of the cargo to Rome and that no additional taxes or expenses will be levied upon us. Finally, we are to be paid for all goods before the shipment is loaded. These are my final terms."

The Cyrenian

The deal is as shrewd as any that Simon has had the reputation of making. What he is losing in percentage, he will surely make back by shifting the expense of transport to them. He also knows fully that they will mark up the price of the goods to the end users to increase their profit margins anyway.

Saccius requests that he has a few moments in private to confer with Aemilius, who by now cannot not keep the look of displeasure from his face. They step outside, and no sooner than they have stepped over the threshold, Aemilius opens.

"I think you gave in too quickly. I think that we could have gotten a larger share if you had held out. We don't want to come across as being too eager."

Saccius puts his hand on his partner's shoulder and calmly says, "Fifty percent of nothing is nothing. Besides, Simon is the type who would rather walk away and take his chances than make a bad deal. He's known for it. He's that strong in will, I can tell. We'll take the deal and draw him in closer. We are getting what we want, after all. We must stay focused on the larger picture. Most of all, remember our larger plan."

Aemilius has never seen Saccius so cool and confident before, and they have done many a deal together. He changes the subject and his current perception. "How was my acting? Do you think they were convinced that I was displeased?"

Saccius verbally applauds him, "Absolutely! You could not have done better. Now let's go in and finish this." The two start back into the house.

Chana seizes the opportunity while they are alone inside to praise her husband. "I am proud of you, Simon. You have dealt wisely as always, though I wish we didn't have to do this deal at all. But since it appears that we must, I am glad that it is you setting the terms. Demanding a trial agreement was a brilliant move."

He squeezes her hand and says, "Now, let's see if they bite."

At that instant, the two gentlemen re-enter the room. Saccius extends his hand, saying simply, "Done."

Aemilius takes his turn, shaking Simon's hand, and adds, "You have earned your reputation for driving a hard bargain yet again."

Saccius continues, "We will send the sealed trial agreement and a signet ring by messenger right away. The ring will serve to be your proof seal for every transaction. It is the Roman way. In the meantime, let us toast this most auspicious occasion!"

The goblets are raised in honor of the newly formed alliance, but the act somehow does not possess the same fervor of the toasts from the previous night. Soon afterward, a triumphant Saccius and Aemilius are packed and setting off to meet their ship bound for Italy. As they disappear, Simon and Chana look at each other with obvious uneasiness, yet both try to be positive.

"So, it begins," says Simon.

Chana answers in earnest, "May God watch over us."

Out in the vast and seemingly endless Silphium fields of the House of Simon, Alexander and Rufus join the servants who are cutting the stalks that are ready for harvest and bundling them into sheaves. There is a small army of many men and women working hard at the daily tasks, but the boys participate in the activities with as much energy and focus as any one of them. The workers have the utmost respect for the young men and the family. Simon and his family care deeply for their servants, and they know it. They are treated more like family members than property, and they can always count on Simon and Chana to be there for them in times of need. The stories that attest to these facts are both common and numerous. As for the boys, there is not only any doubt about their respect for the workers, but it is also a known fact that they are willing to do any job that they would ask others to do. Since they almost daily work side by side with their counterparts, they have developed bonds that run deeply on both sides.

The reality is, once you get to know Alexander and Rufus, liking them or even loving them is easy to do. This is especially true for Menachem, the chief steward and overseer, who became a servant of Simon's long before the boys were born. He is more like an uncle or even a second father to them in their minds, and they believe that he would no doubt lay down his life for them if he was faced with making the ultimate sacrifice. The beautiful thing is that the feeling is mutual. Rumor has it that Simon saved Menachem's life once, but the details of the story are a closely guarded secret. As almost by unspoken rule, nobody asks, and nobody tells. He rides his horse past the boys, who are fully engrossed in their labors, pausing just long enough to admire them from afar with father-like pride. There is much to be proud of in both their similarities and their differences.

Alexander is eighteen years old now, which makes him a man in virtually every measurement possible in the culture of the day. He is tall and good-looking, possessing a quick wit and a winning personality. He is also a deep, almost philosophical thinker who is passionate about learning. This is especially true when it comes to the subjects of history and literature. Philosophy is fast becoming his new first love, though, and for a good reason. Cyrene is the home of a very famous and renowned school of philosophy that was founded in the 4th century BCE by Aristippus, a native and a disciple of Socrates. Scholars and students alike from all over the known world come to Cyrene to study and confer. Many will become alums of the school, who are known as "Cyreniacs." Whenever time allows, Alexander finds himself sitting and listening to the debates, opinions, and lessons being openly and passionately shared in earshot of anyone who cares to listen. He can easily spend several hours doing so and has on many occasions. His parents are also very aware of his zeal for learning. In fact, it is Chana's dream that Alexander will follow the path that will lead him to become a rabbi. Simon, however, while respecting the thought and the office, is not overly enthusiastic about the prospect. He sees in Alexander, a protégé, to carry on the family business and has steered him that way. One thing is for certain, though. Alexander is the apple of his mother's eye, and he is very protective of her. Though she respects Simon's choice for their son's future, she never misses an opportunity to send a subliminal message about a more spiritual path, hoping secretly that one day, the seeds will take root and blossom.

Rufus is fifteen and every bit a teenager. His first love is fun, followed closely by mischief. He is the type that will fearlessly attempt tricks and stunts merely for the joy of watching people cringe. He terrorizes girls with creatures and insects he routinely catches and loves to laugh at their rebukes once they compose themselves. At the same time, he has a kind heart and is always willing to help someone in need. He also deeply loves his mother, but his father is his idol. He studies Simon and ofttimes will imitate his dad's mannerisms and favorite catchphrases with perfect accuracy. Even Simon finds himself laughing at the lampoons and Rufus's clowning from time to time. Rufus is also athletic, competitive, and blessed with impressive foot speed. He rarely, if ever, has lost a race and has considerable stamina. He is a natural-born athlete who prefers sports to academics, even though he is also a good student. Many are sure that he will be an Olympian one day.

The boys are fiercely loyal to each other, which is refreshing at a time when most siblings at this age are more rivals than friends. They work well together and genuinely enjoy each other's company. Today is no exception. Rufus stands up and stretches out his back after tying his last sheaf.

"Alexander!" he calls. "How about riding to the beach for a swim?"

"Not today," Alexander answers while finishing what will be his last sheave. "It's kind of late to be starting out. We'd no sooner get there than we'd have to start heading back. I'm hungry, though. Why don't we go up to the house and find something to eat?"

The Cyrenian

"That sounds good." Rufus answers, adding, "Race you!" as he takes off running. Soon, after he realizes that his brother isn't taking the bait, he sits down under a tree and waits for his brother to catch up. Alexander joins him under the tree and heaves a sigh of satisfaction.

"Good job today, little brother," Alexander says while gazing at the vista of their farm before them.

Rufus responds, "You too!"

"Hey, what did you think of the two men that Dad is partners with now?" Alexander asks his little brother while changing the subject as fast as only a teenager can.

"I don't like either of them. I don't trust them at all. Something tells me that they're up to no good, and I wish we never had to see them again." Rufus answers in a serious tone, adding, "Should we tell Father and Mother what we think?"

Alexander leans forward, putting him eye to eye with his brother. "No. Don't say a word. Rest assured that they've already weighed every possibility. Anything that we see, they've already worked out, trust me. To say anything now would only make them feel that we don't trust their judgment. Between us, though, let's make a pact that we'll watch every move and communicate everything we learn or see to each other. And if it comes to a fight to protect the family, you and I must do whatever it takes to do so. WHATEVER it takes, you hear! In the meantime, we say nothing to anyone—do you understand?"

Rufus answers, suddenly feeling more grown up, "I understand."

They shake hands and then suddenly feel the urge to hug each other tightly. Afterward, they straighten up and head for the house. Just then, Menachem rides up and says to them, "Meet me first thing tomorrow morning in the eastern field." This is not an unusual request, as Menachem often gives them their daily assignments.

"We'll see you then," Alexander says as Menachem abruptly rides off. This time, it is Alexander who takes off running toward the house at full speed while shouting over his shoulder to his brother, "Race you!"

The following morning, the boys head down the path to the eastern field, as Menachem has ordered them to. As they walk through the tall grass in the open field, they are suddenly and forcibly knocked to the ground from behind. Before they can utter a sound, they look up to see two masked men with drawn swords pointing only inches from their chests. They had never been so terrified.

"What do you want from us?" Alexander yells, trembling.

Rufus just stares, speechless and wide-eyed, at the imposing figures, breathing at a rabbit's pace.

The taller man says in a deep, put-on, theatrical-sounding voice, "To teach you a lesson!" He then takes off his mask, revealing his identity.

Alexander's eyes fly even wider. "MENACHEM?! What are you DOING?!" he screams, totally confused. Menachem and his accomplice relax their stances and sheath their weapons.

"Today's lesson," Menachem begins, "is that things are no longer the same and life is full of surprises. Therefore, you must be watchful and prepared for any situation, or you may no longer have a life. Starting today and every day forward, you will spend time with me learning the ways of the warrior. You are men now and must learn how to take care of yourselves and your family." The man helps the boys up and walks them to a clearing that has been transformed into a training area, much like one would encounter when training to be a real soldier.

So, it will be from now on. Every day, the boys go through the blood, sweat, and tears of learning the ways of the fighting man. It isn't easy, and they have the bruises and sore muscles to prove it. They have never been stretched so far—or, at the same time, felt so good about themselves. This, after all, is, in their eyes, what real manhood feels like. The boys work vigorously on their new skills, knowing that one day, the focused dedication to these lessons will not have been wasted.

They were never so right.

CHAPTER 11. WINDS OF CHANGE

It has been several months now since Simon and his new Roman partners have been working together under the terms of their trial agreement. So far, all seems to be going smoothly. The harvesting and preparations for shipping of the Silphium to Rome go on as per the daily routine, but now in greater volume and at a faster pace. While it took some adjustments and additional personnel in the fields, Simon has never failed to deliver on his end of the bargain. He is also glad that his counterparts have lived up to their promises as well. They have successfully managed the shipments to their distribution points and have paid him on time and as agreed. While still cautious, he begins to feel more at ease that this venture might just work out well. He also enjoys the peace of knowing that he has the favor of Rome on him during what is turning out to be a time of growing unrest in the world, at least for the time being. Saccius and Aemilius keep him abreast of the latest news upon their arrivals to pick up their shipments, which are averaging at least once a month now. In fact, they are due to arrive again any day.

Another sure sign of the changing times is that the Roman legion that was only supposed to be staying for a short time in Cyrene had set up a more permanent outpost. In fact, even though the legion that was to relieve them has long arrived, Drusus' legion is showing no signs of mobilizing anytime soon. It seems by appearances that

The Cyrenian

Cyrene is to become a key staging center, much to the continued angst of the locals. There are now more Romans roaming the hills and roads, as well as frequenting the various shops and establishments in the city. One would think that this might be good for commerce, but quite often, the soldiers simply take whatever they want or just enjoy goods and services without paying. This is against the Roman rules for a soldier to do, but who is one going to complain to? Moreover, what are the odds that one would be believed over the word of a Roman to another Roman? In the end, it isn't a fight worth fighting, but tensions are building and doing so rapidly. It is a safe bet that something is soon going to give. It must.

Chana and Simon sit on their verandah, taking in the evening breeze. This is their favorite time of the day. Their days' labors are complete, dinner is over, and now comes their time to relax and chat as husband and wife.

"It looks like we'll be sending out another shipment this week," Simon remarks.

"That will make it the second one for the month," Chana responds with just a touch of satisfaction. She continues, "I must admit, as you know, I had serious doubts about this venture. However, it seems to be working out well so far. I only hope and pray it stays this way. A good part of me still doesn't trust either one of them."

"Ah, there speaks my lioness. Always ready to pounce!" smiles Simon. "It seems to me that we all are gaining by this agreement. That's a good thing. There's no reason for anyone to upset anything at this point, especially since we haven't ratified the deal long-term. I am a bit concerned about this Roman occupation, though. There is much discontentment in the air. Fortunately, we have the favor of Rome working for us, but I am hearing a lot of angry sentiments from our neighbors and friends. I am hoping that calm heads will prevail, especially those of the Zealots. An uprising would be all we need."

He gets up from his seat and starts his familiar pacing.

Chana asks, "Weren't they supposed to be headed for Alexandria by now?"

"So I've heard from Saccius, but nothing seems to be happening yet. I just hope that they aren't planning to stay here. It's an accident waiting to happen. One spark from anyone and all of Cyrene might be set ablaze. I'm not sure that even we would go unscathed."

"I want you to keep the boys closer to home from now on," Chana says most seriously.

"They're men now, my love. They must learn to do what men do. Fortunately for us, Menachem also watches over them like they are his own. If I had to put my fate in any one man's hands, they would be his."

"I agree," Chana responds, "but I don't want them down at the port by themselves anymore. Not now."

Simon nods but doesn't verbalize an answer. It's his way of making himself feel that he didn't make an actual promise. While he cannot discount the basis of Chana's fears for the boys, their help at the docks is invaluable. For the moment, though, hopefully, the nod will suffice.

At the Roman camp, General Marcus Maximus is in a briefing with his officers, including Drusus and Gallus. It is time for them to receive their updated orders, and they are more than ready. All are feeling that they have been sitting still in Cyrene for far too long. They are ready for some action.

The General speaks loudly and firmly.

"There is trouble in Judea. There has been growing unrest there for some time, but now there is a full-fledged rebellion beginning to show itself. The emperor is vexed and has ordered that we are to begin our deployment there immediately. We and a second legion will go by ship to Caesarea Maritima and, from there, march into Jerusalem. Rome has completed moving its main garrison from Jerusalem to the new provincial capital of Caesarea Maritima. It has the largest harbor on the Eastern Mediterranean coast. This fact,

The Cyrenian

coupled with its proximity to Jerusalem and Judea, makes it a strong and strategically important base of operations for the province. As for our orders, it seems that the new Prefect, Pontius Pilate, has his hands full. Ultimately, our collective mission is to bring Judea under control. We will, however, be leaving one Centurion and his unit here in Cyrene for security and policing duties. Gallus, this duty as Commander will fall to you," he orders, his eyes fixed on the veteran soldier. Gallus salutes his General in obedience. "If there are no questions, then you are dismissed. Go and make ready for deployment. We move at dawn."

All stand at attention as the General goes to his tent.

General Marcus Maximus is not far off the mark when he states that Pontius Pilate has his hands full. Pilate received his appointment as Prefect of Judea from the notable debaucher, Roman Emperor Tiberius. During his early beginnings in office, Pilate clashed with the local Jews and their religious leaders on several occasions, primarily for defiling the city of Jerusalem and the Jewish Temple in the eyes of the Jews by bringing idolatrous images of Caesar into both. To the Jews, there is no greater insult possible, and it caused absolute chaos between the two sides. This was only the beginning of the tensions. However, this latest clash is far worse than any previous. After forcibly taking money from the Temple Treasury to build an aqueduct, Pilate faced a strong rebellion from the Jewish people. Pilate, therefore, had soldiers armed with clubs, dress in plain clothes, and mingle with the maddened crowd. Upon his signal, the soldiers threw off their disguises and began beating the protesters most unmercifully, regardless of age or gender. Many were either injured or killed. This bloodshed began a new and ugly chapter in the troubled relationship between the Romans and Jews. Pilate was beginning to learn quickly about the stiff resolve of his charges, and Rome was quick to take notice. Tiberius was not at all pleased with his new Prefect, whose career would remain on a rocky road from this time forward. Remember, the emperor demands complete order in its provinces at all costs. For his commissioned leaders, failure is not an option.

Drusus speaks first to his friend. "I can't believe that they are splitting us up on my first mission. Besides, you could better serve Rome in the field rather than just babysitting this place!"

Gallus nods in agreement. "I must have really upset somebody high up to draw this duty. Hopefully, I won't be here for long. I'm jealous that I won't be there to see you earn your first command stripes!" he says, punching Drusus on the arm.

"Don't worry, my friend. By the sound of things, you'll be headed for Judea in no time to help bail out this new Prefect!" Drusus says with a smirk.

Gallus shoots back, "Could be! Well, since this might be the last chance for a while, I think that some wine is in order—don't you?! I think that I have a full wineskin in my tent."

"Lead the way, my friend!" Drusus says as the two friends put an arm around each other's necks and walk into the dusk. Once they arrive at the tent, they spend well into the evening reminiscing and toasting to friendship and good fortune.

The time soon comes for the two to turn in, as they know that morning will come quickly. As they part, Drusus turns and says, "Hey, Rooster, how about this for a pact—I won't let myself get killed before you get to Judea if you'll do the same!"

"Done, my brother!" Rooster answers, "I think you got the worst of the bargain, though. About the only thing to die from around here is BOREDOM!" They laugh aloud once more for the night and go to sleep. As he closes his eyes, Drusus realizes that he was only half kidding in his pact with his friend. He knows well that for a soldier, nothing is guaranteed. Especially not life beyond the moment.

The scene in the harbor the next morning is reminiscent of the day they arrived, only in reverse and sans the seasickness. The sun is just over the peaks of the hills, and the soldiers are packed and in ranks as those who were assigned to the ships were already embarking. The noise of the activities rings through the crisp morning air. Drusus is again on his mount, and the word is given to move out. As the drums pound out the cadence, Drusus and Gallus salute each other one more time in friendship and then immediately re-focus on their duties. The harbor is especially busy today as there are also merchant ships from Egypt docking to bring in their wares for trade. They will be also bringing with them fresh news from the East, including Judea. It will not be long before the recent conflict in Jerusalem becomes the top subject all over the streets and hills of Cyrene.

High on a hill overlooking the port, Barabbas, Gideon, and some of the Zealot henchmen watch as the Romans depart. "This is a good day. A very good day," Barabbas says as he comes to realize that the opposition is now in numbers that will be easier to handle. He is patiently awaiting his moment of opportunity. He will not be disappointed.

There is also a merchant ship about to dock from Rome and Greece. Aboard are Saccius and Aemilius, as expected and right on schedule. They are also deeply engaged in conversation.

Aemilius says quietly to his partner, "Once again, the charade begins. We play the Servant instead of the Master. We settle for a small portion when the whole loaf is before us. Our counterpart Simon, on the other hand, is getting richer with every shipment. The Silphium market grows hotter every day, and we aren't reaping its full rewards. Just as Caesar promised, Roman forces are here permanently and on our side, almost at our command. How long until we rid ourselves of these 'partners' and take full control of our destiny? Surely, we know the operation well enough now to make a go of it!"

Saccius answers in hushed but sharp tones, "Patience! Our timing is crucial. We must wait for just the right moment and situation to present itself. When we move, we must be beyond all reproach or risk being found out by the Cyrenians. Simon has the power of a longstanding good name in this region to his advantage, not to mention his political status and allies. What I am waiting for is the opportunity to neutralize all these things. While we could possibly use the brute force of Rome to achieve our goal, there would be nothing to stop Rome from taking over fully by itself, thus eliminating us altogether. There are many officers and politicians envious of our position. I tell you the opportunity will come, and I—I mean, WE will be ready when it does. In the meantime, as we wait, we are still doing well after our markup of the goods, aren't we? We are also locking our own future market down in the meantime."

Aemilius backs down, hearing the voice of reason once again. "I do understand your reasoning, of course. You know that. I guess my impatience stems from also knowing how quickly circumstances can change from moment to moment. I am hoping that we will be firmly entrenched before either Simon, Rome, or someone else figures this all out and neutralizes us."

"Leave this to me, my friend. Now, put your mask on and get ready to perform!" Saccius says with a tone of evil confidence. Before long, they are once again on their way to the House of Simon to take up temporary residence for a few weeks until another shipment is ready for transport.

CHAPTER 12. THE BROKEN ROAD

It has been several days now since the deployment of the Roman forces from Cyrene. Gallus is now settling into his new assignment as Commander. Ironically, for all his talk of boredom, he is consistently busy. There are security patrols to coordinate, watches to schedule, reports to be logged, and hundred fighting men that must be fed, kept in line, and in a state of constant readiness. All in all, though, he is enjoying the feeling of being in complete command, especially since he already has the total respect of his men. That makes things easy. The time away from battle, however, has left the soldiers few outlets to burn off excess energy. In fact, it will be this very underlying factor that will touch off a sequence of events that nobody can see coming, even though such things are always looming in the back of the minds of most everybody on both sides of the conquest.

The security patrol is going along as normal. While there is no mistaking the resentment of the townsfolk at the presence of the two soldiers on horseback riding along the main road, there are no incidents. The riders are getting close to the end of this watch and are only about a mile or so from the outpost and some time off to rest. Perhaps it is this anticipation that precipitates what happens next.

There is a rise in the road ahead of them, and one calls out a challenge to his partner to race to the top. Without hesitation, both soldiers kick their horses into full-on race mode. Unbeknown to them, there is a group of children playing in the field next to the road on the other side of the rise. The thrill of the race soon turns to horror and tragedy in a matter of moments. While the children chase each other in a game of tag and fill the air with squeals of delight, a little girl darts into the road to avoid being tagged by her playmates. It is at that very moment that the powerful horses come over the peak of the rise at full speed. There is no time for anybody to react. There is only a millisecond of eye contact between the terrified child frozen in her tracks and the surprised riders bearing down on her. The thunder of the beating hooves never breaks rhythm. The shrill scream of the poor child goes silent in an instant as her now lifeless body is brutally trampled by the charging steeds. The shaken riders manage to pull back and stop their chargers some yards further down the road. They stand motionless, staring at the small, broken body behind them as they try to decide what to do.

One soldier says, "This is bad. Maybe we should go back and help."

In the distance, they see the other children running for home as fast as their legs can carry them.

"Help how?" comes the answer. "There's no chance that she's alive. You saw everything. You know that she's dead. I think we'd better just head for camp immediately and let Gallus know what has happened. There will no doubt be repercussions from the locals over this, and he needs to be prepared. He'll know best how to handle this."

They turn and head for the outpost without speaking another word, the awful scene playing out repeatedly in their minds. The grim mental pictures are punctuated only by thoughts of how the parents and people may react or retaliate. There are no good scenarios.

The two riders soon reach the outpost and quickly meet with Gallus to tell him what has transpired. After hearing the woeful tale, Gallus heaves a heavy sigh and runs his hands through his hair.

"While I question the wisdom—or rather the lack of it—that would have you racing on a populated main road, I know that what resulted was not intentional. The issue now is going to be convincing the residents of the same and keeping the peace. These people have been just waiting for the moment to fully condemn us, and you two fools may have just given it to them. I'll have to think on this. Until I come up with a viable solution, the two of you are confined to your quarters. You are dismissed."

The soldiers salute and leave his tent. Gallus reaches for his wineskin, as he now really needs a drink. Of course, the container is empty, and he just then remembers how he and Drusus had finished it off during their farewell.

"Just great!" he grumbles in disgust as he tosses the wineskin across the room. He ponders the situation before him for a while and concludes that the best solution might be to approach the city elders and lay out his case before them. General Marcus Maximus had instructed him before his departure that if the need should arise (and only if necessary), seek out a wealthy merchant and city leader named Porcius as an ally in Cyrene, as he is considered a friend of Rome. Maybe this is the opportune time. He thinks to himself that maybe if he approaches the city leaders first, he might be able to turn down the heat or even eliminate it. It might also not be a bad idea to take the two culprit riders with him to make a formal apology. He might even offer to compensate the family of the dead girl in some way. He could finance the gesture by fining the two soldiers for their actions. It might not be a bad idea to let the leaders know that as well. He is sure that the people will never expect to see such a display of contrition from the Romans. Perhaps this move can work to his advantage by bridging the two sides. After some final contemplation, Gallus decides to pursue this course of action. He calls for the soldiers in question, and the three prepare to go into town.

Meanwhile, the traumatized children have made it home and have sounded the alarm. Being children, especially being children who are upset, there is little attention paid to the language used in explaining the sequence of events. Unfortunately, their words do not roll out in a manner that allows for the possibility of the event being an unfortunate accident. All that they know is that the Roman soldiers—whom their parents have taught them to hate—have run over their friend with their horses. When asked if the Romans came back to try to help, the unanimous answer from the youngsters is no. One does not have to guess the reaction of the adults. An angry mob immediately begins to form and passionately makes their displeasure known amidst the wails of sorrow for the dead little girl.

"These Roman sons of pigs need to be taught a lesson! They steal from us, they insult us, and now, they are killing our children!" says one.

"We should poison them all when they come to us for food or wine!" says another.

Occasionally, a rational voice comes forth. "If we retaliate, it will mean death for many or perhaps all of us. We have no means to stand up against Roman fighting men. Think of our other children as well!"

This seemingly sensible expression of thought pauses the tirades only for a moment. Some even boo his rationale. "May God strike down these swine for us!" one shouts. The throng joins in the anger-driven curse on their enemy as they mass to go and retrieve the battered body of the slain child. As per Jewish custom, she needs to be buried by sunset.

Gideon parts from the crowd and goes to pass on the news to Barabbas and the Zealots in hiding. He knows that this incident might very well be the tipping point for their cause, but there is no way to stop them from finding out. He feels that it is better that the news comes from him, where he might have a chance to keep things under control. Gideon is a sympathizer for sure, but he also knows the realities of the situation. To confront Rome now would be sheer suicide. He doesn't have the answer to the problem, but he knows that conflict now is out of the question. It will be up to him to try to stem the tide of the ensuing anger, though the odds are most definitely against him.

After what seems to him to be his fastest transit ever to the hideaway cave, Gideon finds that he is not nearly swift enough to beat the news. He arrives to find the band vigilantes outside and agitated.

He dismounts quickly, saying, "I take it that you've heard."

Barabbas barks back, "We have heard, and we are about to make somebody pay!"

Gideon starts, "I think it would be unwise to—"

Barabbas cuts him off, saying, "It is time to let the Romans know that they cannot kill our people, especially our children, at will. If they do, we will kill them in kind—starting tonight!"

"How will you do that?" Gideon queries. "There is no way that you can overthrow the outpost. You don't have the numbers or the weapons. Besides, they will see you coming long before you get there."

Barabbas answers with full bravado, "We will wait for the patrol. There will only be two or three of them. If we attack in the darkness, we will have the element of surprise on our side."

"But they are sure to know that we are behind this. They will punish the people for your actions," Gideon argues.

"Not if they can't find the bodies or us. Much can happen to a man in the wilderness!" Barabbas retorts. "Now, either you are joining us on this raid, or you are going back to town. In any case, stay out of the way, my brother. This is what we do!"

Gideon knows now that there is no talking Barabbas down. He reluctantly wishes them well and heads back to town. He doesn't want to get caught on the road tonight. He will be praying with all his might that things will go exactly as Barabbas plans, but at the same time, he knows that after tonight, life in Cyrene will be forever different.

Dusk is approaching, and Gallus, along with the two soldiers in question, arrive in the city center. It is unusually quiet. After gaining directions from a nervous local resident, they go to the home of Porcius, the merchant who the General had told him about. Unfortunately, they find only a servant in the house.

"My master is not here," he says. "He is at the burial for the little girl. Most everyone is there."

Gallus realizes that he has made this trip in vain. He now also has second thoughts about his timing. He didn't realize that they would bury the child so soon, and therefore, emotions will undoubtedly be too high right now for a negotiation. Maybe a night's rest will be of benefit to everybody.

"Please tell your master that we have come in peace and will return tomorrow," he says in a compassionate tone.

"As you wish, sirs," the servant answers, closing the door.

"You two idiots are becoming more trouble to me than you are worth!" Gallus huffs with disgust as they leave the premises. They began back down the road.

Darkness is falling quickly, but a bright, almost full moon is rising, casting its glow upon the landscape. As they know that the Romans will soon be approaching a certain wooded area of the road, Barabbas and his men take up positions in the trees along the roadside and behind the boulders of the embankments on either side. They are still many miles away from the Roman outpost and well outside of the city. Before long, a bird call from one of the lookouts signals that the soldiers are approaching. Each of the raiders waits now in tense but hushed anticipation as their adrenaline and blood pressure reach new heights. The sound of the trotting of the horses helps them to gauge the perfect moment for the ambush in the darkness. At the perfect moment, Barabbas and several others drop from the trees directly above the riders, knocking them off their horses. The Romans are taken completely by surprise, but all manage to draw their swords and begin swinging them wildly in hopes of finding an enemy mark. The two younger soldiers manage to graze a few men, but by now, some of the other "Long Knives" have descended onto the scene with loud shouts of revenge. The Zealot band, however, has underestimated Gallus' prowess. His first swath decapitates his attacker, and he immediately engages a second, mortally wounding him. He manages to rally the other two soldiers, and taking back-to-back positions, the three mount a furious defense. For a moment, it looks like they just might prevail against all odds. But the Zealots on the hillside have now joined their brothers, increasing their numbers by a large margin. Even after this reinforcement, the Romans show their enemies why their fierce reputation is so well founded. Their triumph will only come at a high and bloody price. The Zealots press in hard and eventually manage to overwhelm the Romans at last. They immediately begin mercilessly plunging their blades repeatedly into Gallus and the other soldiers in force. The scene resembles a swarm of army ants atop an unwanted intruder. They quickly complete the bloody assassination despite their casualties. As they stand over the bodies of their targets, shouting in victory like wolves baying at the moon, they fail to notice a small twitch of Gallus' hand. With one last gallant effort, Gallus manages to thrust his sword into the abdomen of a laughing Zealot who is standing directly over him, mocking him. As he falls, the Zealot stabs Gallus through the neck. Though Gallus knows he is dying, in his heart, he still is trying to muster the strength to once again arise, shock the enemy, and single-handedly kill them all. However, as he feels his blood-soaked body begin to grow colder by the second, his final thoughts are of his friend Drusus and the pact they had made. What irony. Not long ago, it was him warning Drusus of the deadly threat of the Zealots and telling him to keep his guard up. *If only I had stuck to just being a soldier instead of trying to be a diplomat. Trying to make peace has killed me...not war*, he thinks to himself as his life slips away and everything fades to black.

Barabbas halts the ensuing celebration abruptly and shouts, "Take our dead and these dead pigs off the road and bury them quickly. We must disappear before the next patrol arrives!"

All hands feverishly comply, and before long, the exhausted but victorious band is headed back to the safety of their hideout in the cave. There will be new stories to tell around the fire tonight. Luckily for them, the road cannot speak.

The much-anticipated Roman patrol quietly passes through the wooded area that had served as a kill zone only a few hours earlier. The soldiers are completely unaware of the deadly chaos that has just occurred in the shaded moonlight. They make their rounds through the slumbering city and find nothing amiss. Satisfied that all is well, they head back to camp.

CHAPTER 13. RED DAWN

The wee hours just before daybreak find Simon thrashing in his sleep, once again a victim of the dream that so often haunts him. Only somehow, it is different this time. While the same crowd noise, dialog, and piercing eyes are as they always have been, the optics are changing. This time, there are actual faces slowly coming into focus. At the usual ending, where Simon normally gets called out, he feels for the first time a force moving him forward into the street. He also notices what appears to be the bloody feet of a person on the ground. But before his view can finish panning up the body to reveal a face, he jumps up in bed, clad once again in a cold sweat. He is startled by an urgent-sounding knock on the door. Chana is also now fully alert because of the knocking and her husband's distressed awakening.

"Who is it?!" Simon shouts in a loud voice while stumbling in the dark, trying to find a garment to put on.

"It's Menachem," comes the answer. "I have some news."

Recognizing Menachem's serious tone, Simon quickly goes outside to meet his trusted steward and friend, hoping against hope that the momentary commotion hadn't caused everyone in the house to wake up. Once they meet outside, they step a few paces away from the house to a nearby tree to talk while doing their best to keep their voices low.

"What is going on?" asks Simon.

The Cyrenian

Menachem answers, "I've just gotten some word. The Zealots killed three Roman soldiers last night in retaliation for the death of the little girl who was trampled by their horses. The soldiers were headed back to their camp after trying to meet with Porcius at his house. It was an ambush."

Simon winces and gasps at the same time. He knows what this means. Blood will only beget blood—and quickly. No one will be safe from suspicion or retribution from here on. Suddenly, there is an undoubted look of puzzlement on Simon's face. "Why were they looking for Porcius, I wonder?" he thinks out loud.

Porcius is not only a powerful member of the Cyrenian ruling class, but he is also no fan of Simon. Moreover, the feeling is intensely mutual. Porcius has long envied Simon's Silphium empire and wealth. He also aspired to be the key supplier to the world but could not find a way to get his hands on Simon's family land. He tried to buy it outright on more than one occasion and even stooped to plotting in his mind ways of having Simon's farm confiscated. Of course, he was unsuccessful on all counts. Porcius' much smaller farm is also one of the Silphium farms that failed over time due to the lack of cultivation skills on his part. The two men have openly clashed more than once on Cyrenian political matters as well, their views being as opposite as East is from West. However, their opposing political influences are virtually equal, only adding to an ongoing power struggle between the two. In addition, Porcius is a friend of many major merchants from all over the known world—including Rome. It is this fact that bothers Simon most of all. In short, he knows that Porcius cannot be trusted and is a dangerous, devious, and well-connected adversary. Complicating matters even further, Simon has no way of knowing just how high Porcius' Roman ties go. After all, why are the Romans seeking HIM out—especially since Rome has not directly influenced Cyrene's affairs to any large degree in recent times? In Simon's mind, whatever the actual reason, it can't be good.

Menachem's voice jolts him back to reality. "I, too, wish I knew why they sought a meeting with Porcius. But be sure, this attack is going to bring Rome down on us all. In the meantime, the Zealots are planning to leave for Jerusalem immediately. It will be easier for them to lay low by blending into the dominant Jewish community there. Things will no doubt be tough here for a while. Hopefully, all will blow over here before too long. We have one small glimmer of hope, though. No bodies have been found. That allows for some small benefit of doubt. Personally, I pray that they are never found."

Simon responds with angst, "While I truly understand the Zealots' motivations, this new breed doesn't understand the full ramifications of what they do to those they leave behind. It's not like when you were one of them, as back in my father's days. More thought was put into the moves they made. They were careful to keep the exposure of innocents to a minimum. I am thankful to God that you are on our side, however. My family and I cannot thank you enough for your loyalty and protection. Not to mention the value of the inside information that you have access to."

Menachem speaks solemnly now, "Your father saved my life and took me in when I was a young and impulsive outlaw on the run. He gave me a new life and a second chance. He asked in return only that I put away my sword forever. To this very day, I have kept that promise. I told him on his deathbed that the only way I would ever break my vow would be in defense of the House of Simon. What your father did for me, I have sworn to do for you and your family."

When Menachem finishes speaking, there is a hushed exchange of hugs and tear-filled eyes that only real, heartfelt family love can produce. Simon thanks him for the news, and they make plans to talk again later in private. Menachem then rides off to his station in the fields, and Simon goes back into the house.

There is only one downside to the quiet beauty and stillness of the dawn here. Sound carries all too well. As Simon goes back inside, there is another, more hushed verbal exchange. Saccius and

Aemilius smile broadly at each other, having heard every word from the window of their guest room. Saccius whispers with all satisfaction, "I told you our opportunity would come if we remained patient! Charging Simon as an aide to a Zealot leader, as well as being a sympathizer and financier, is the PERFECT way to take him down! The best part is that we have *facts* to work with! In our wildest dreams, we could not hope for more!"

Aemilius raises his right hand in a mock pledge and whispers back, "I shall never question or doubt you again, my friend. We have him now!"

Saccius adds, "We only need maintain our composure—and silence—until the trap is set. We cannot let on to anyone that we know what we know, at least not yet. If all goes according to plan, our next trip back here from Rome will be the most triumphant since that of King Ptolemy Apion!" Both men, noticing that their exuberance is beginning to raise their speaking volume, and as if on cue, simultaneously give each other the "shhh" finger over the lips sign. Looking back out of the window, Saccius euphorically decides in his mind that he has never seen a more beautiful sunrise.

Chana, now dressed and waiting, greets Simon as he enters the room, obviously waiting in anticipation for the details of his conversation with Menachem.

"What is going on?" she asks while leading him to sit down next to her on the bed.

"It's bad," he begins as he proceeds to fill her in on the facts. When she has heard all that Simon has to say, it is she that starts pacing the room this time.

"I am afraid for us all, but especially for you," she says. "If Porcius is in any way involved with the Romans, he will surely find some way to use them to make trouble for you."

Simon joins his wife in standing and pondering out loud, "Do you think that our new ties to Rome via Saccius and Aemilius may possibly be of benefit to us in this? I mean, could this deal be a shelter in this time of storm? Having the protection of Rome was a big part of the reason we even considered the deal to begin with. Maybe we should talk to our partners on the subject."

Chana is predictably skeptical. "We're still trying to find out if we can fully trust Saccius and Aemilius. While I do admit that things have gone well so far, do we really want to fully commit to this alliance at this stage? I also find it curious that while Porcius seems to know every major merchant with Roman-Cyrenian relationships, these two have never mentioned him. Do they not know him, or are they just staying quiet?"

Simon smiles at his wife's sharp observations. "You, as always, are making a strong point. I confess that I hadn't thought of that. I must say, I am so blessed that you are MY wife and not HIS! You're right. Let's lay low for now and see how things play out over the next few days. However, I think that it would be wise for us to have an alternative plan should the worst come to pass. I think when our partners head back to Rome, I want you to take the boys to visit our relatives in Judea. It might also be a good time for them to see the Temple in Jerusalem for the first time now that they have come of age. I will join you there before long, but I want to handle things here for now without having to worry about my family being vulnerable, just in case."

"I don't like that idea!" Chana retorts. "My place is by your side, regardless of any situation," she says with a definite flash in her eyes.

"I can't protect you all the way from Judea!" Simon answers back. "And I can't take a chance on my family's safety if things go badly here. If they do, there will likely not be another chance to get you to safety!"

After a brief pause, Simon does his best to cool the moment. "Look, maybe we are creating a situation in our minds that doesn't exist. I just don't want to be wrong on this. I can't lose you or the boys. Look at it as nothing more than a holiday. If you leave while the partners are in Rome, then nobody can track you. Let me work things out here, and I promise to join you as quickly as possible. I also promise to send word from here as things develop. Please, my love—do this for me. I wouldn't ask for this if I weren't sure it was the best possible move."

Silence resounds in the room once again. Chana crosses the floor and embraces her husband. "I will do this for you and for the sake of our children, provided that you keep Menachem around you at all times."

Simon answers, "I will, right after he returns from escorting you to Judea—which, by the way, is a non-negotiable condition."

As much as Chana wants to fight back on the term, she does, at heart, feel better knowing that she will have Menachem as a bodyguard for her and the boys on the journey. While they have the monetary means to travel at the highest levels as passengers, it was not the kind of trip for an attractive woman to embark on alone, even with strong young sons.

"So, who will take care of you while I'm gone, my husband?" Chana asks, only partially kidding.

"You know that Menachem trained me as a young man how to fight, so it will be as if he is still here. Don't worry—I haven't forgotten how," he smiles with confidence.

"You're older now," Chana says coyly.

"Just another advantage, my dear!" he laughs as he kisses her.

The morning meal ritual goes as usual, replete with an above-normal amount of small talk and banter between the hosts and their guests. All sides do an excellent job of not telegraphing their innermost nervousness based on their private conversations from earlier.

Simon pipes up at the end of the meal, saying, "I'm off to the dock to start setting things up to load the shipment for departure tomorrow. I assume I'll see you there later?"

Saccius answers, "Yes, you will, dear partner. We'll be moving the final bales down from the fields shortly. We'll see you then. It has been a good season. We are also very much looking forward to sealing our permanent alliance upon our return from Rome."

Simon says simply, "Yes, we'll talk."

They shake hands, and everybody makes ready to start their day's duties.

For most, the morning will be business as usual. For others, the day will have a much more eventful beginning.

CHAPTER 14. MISSING IN ACTION

There is an unmistakable air of nervous concern in the Roman camp this morning. Normally, Gallus would have called for assembly of the soldiers just before dawn. The sun is rising now, and yet there is no order to muster. Even more concerning is that the night watches report that Gallus and the two soldiers with him have not been seen since leaving for their patrol. Their commander has not returned to camp, even though the next night patrol has returned from their rounds in the city. Theories are flying around the ranks with great speed. Did they get lost searching for the City Elders? Not likely. The road is well established, and the city is easy to navigate both to and from. Could they have been attacked or taken prisoner, perhaps? If so, by whom? Rome isn't currently at war here, and besides, who in this region would want to make trouble with Rome anyway? Surely, everyone here must know that any resistance would be futile—and fatally foolish to boot. Could they have deserted? Highly unlikely, especially for a soldier of Gallus' stature. To desert would mean death by crucifixion if captured and would, at the very least, make them fugitives for life. There would be nothing to gain on any front. Even if the possibility existed, Gallus wouldn't take anybody with him. He would travel much faster alone, and there would be nobody to give him away. Then, there was the possibility of foul play by the Zealots. Even though the soldiers in this unit have heard stories of the Zealots, none but Gallus has ever encountered any. The only conclusion that makes any sense or brings any form of hope to the concerned is the possibility that maybe the three camped out for the night, overslept, and may still arrive. However, unless they arrive soon, this theory, too, will also quickly die. Everybody knows that Gallus' dedication to duty and order is exemplary. As hard as it would be for him to miss even a moment of his assignment, the soldiers are all aware of how hard his new command has been pushing him of late. They certainly wouldn't begrudge him a little extra rest. In the end, though, the men can only hope that this best-case scenario is the correct one.

In the interim, the job of keeping order in the ranks falls to the next man in rank to Gallus, a Captain named Antonius. He is not yet a Centurion but is something of a platoon leader. He is currently serving as Gallus' right hand. He is a good soldier and has seen battle during his career. He is not a seasoned warrior of Gallus' level, but he is nonetheless a formidable soldier. While he has proven his battlefield skills, this is Antonius' biggest assignment thus far in a leadership role—and it is fast becoming a trial by fire. The lower-ranking squad leaders are already turning to him for a plan of action, putting new pressure on him to look and act decisively. He would personally rather wait things out a little longer to see if things work themselves out. However, the optics of perceived indecision could have negative consequences for him, especially if things don't work out. After a little more thought, he makes his decision.

"Soldier!" Antonius barks at one of the squad leaders, who comes running for his orders. "Assemble your squad and begin to search along the road for any possible signs or clues that might explain where or what may have become of Centurion Gallus. In fact," he says while pointing to another squad leader, "have your men work one side of the road while the other squad handles the remaining side. If you find or learn anything, send back word to me immediately. And I want both teams back here by nightfall—understood?"

"Yes, Captain!" they reply in unison as they salute and waste no time in making the orders so. Antonius feels better after saying the words, convinced that his plan is as prudent as any other leader's would be.

Later that day, the squads arrive at the silently infamous wooded section of the road. The men are thankful for the chance to be in the shade for a while after being so long in the hot sun. The trees also present a natural opportunity for the men to relieve themselves. Those who wish to indulge set off to choose their appropriate spots. One soldier ventures into the woods, a little deeper than the others, to find a more private place. As he hikes through the underbrush, he trips over a rock that is hidden under some branches. As he rises, he notices a shiny object before him. There is also a distinct pungent odor being carried on the occasional breeze. He bends down to pick up the object and feels his blood run cold as he recognizes it. It is a silver *phalerae*, or war medal. It is unmistakably Roman and can only have belonged to a veteran soldier.

"Captain! Over here! There is something here!" he cries out in alarm. All hands rush to the scene as the soldier shows the captain his find.

"This is Gallus', I'm sure," the Captain confirms. "I've seen it many times."

Once again, the slight breeze brings about that pungent odor. Nobody misses it this time.

"The smell of death is here," says another soldier.

The Captain commands, "Everyone spread out and start probing the ground. Whatever it is causing the smell isn't far away."

What started out as a search mission instantly became the gruesome task of recovery. It isn't too long before someone calls out, "HERE!" Farther ahead and slightly uphill, a soldier stands over a mound of soft earth. As the Captain approaches, he sees why the soldier called out. Before him is a partially protruding human hand. The ashen flesh is evidence that it hasn't been here very long.

"Dig him out," the order comes.

The men quickly unearth the three bodies. The odor now wages a full assault on the senses of all who are present. The sight before them tells the entire story.

"What would you have us do, Captain?"

"Cover them for now, but mark the graves well," says the Captain. "We'll gather wood to make the funeral pyres and return tomorrow with the rest of our company so that our brothers can be sent off to the afterlife with full honors."

"And then?" the soldier asks.

The Captain answers in a loud voice, "AND THEN? Why, VENGENCE, of course! The murderers will be found and made to pay for this with their lives. Slowly. Painfully. And I don't care how many people we must send to THEIR afterlives to avenge the death of our comrades. Nobody kills ours and lives! I have no doubt that Antonius will do anything less!"

The men cheer at the delivery of the Captain's words. Every one of them can feel their warrior blood beginning to boil. It seems that the war that they have been seeking is now closer than they thought.

The soldiers quickly complete their grim tasks and form ranks for the march back to camp. The mounting adrenaline levels make for a very quick trip. The Captain runs directly to Gallus' tent to find that Antonius is going over some of Gallus' communiques from the General, which include information about the Cyrenian merchant Porcius as a contact. Antonius starts feverishly reading everything in sight, feeling that there may be a need to fully gain firsthand knowledge of every aspect of their mission now, considering Gallus is missing in action.

"Centurion, they're dead! We found their bodies, and they were no doubt murdered!" the Captain breathlessly blurts out as he bursts into the tent.

"WHAT?! Speak, man!" says Antonius, springing to his feet. The Captain then begins to share the sequence of the day's events.

After taking a moment to drink in the full gravity of the situation, Antonius orders an assembly of all the soldiers. He exits the tent to find his men waiting for him in keen anticipation.

"Soldiers," he begins, "You have no doubt learned of the fate of our comrades by now. I am sure that I do not have to express the level of rage within me as I am also sure that you share my feelings. We will march into the city at once to track down the killers. We will begin by confronting the City Elders. If I do not get the answers I seek, we will begin a door-to-door campaign of interrogation of the people. We will apply heavy pressure by instilling fear, but I want no bloodshed—at least not yet. It is more important that we extract useful information. We may even find some cooperatives. Fear is a most effective tool. Use it to your advantage. However, should you find out anything at all that is pertinent, I must be notified immediately before any action is taken. Secure anyone that you need to, but I want these culprits taken alive. Justice will be metered out according to our laws and timing, not theirs. Also, I want no less than four soldiers always working together. Do not allow yourselves to be singled out or outnumbered. Do not hesitate to call out for backup if the need arises. We will work in force by daylight and station multiple full-time patrols in the city at night. We will not rest until we avenge the deaths of our brothers. Is that understood?"

The soldiers shout out in unison, "Yes, Commander!" immediately acknowledging the new rank of Captain Antonius now that Gallus is no more.

His next command is a somber one. "Then let us first go now and honor our dead." Antonius then picks four of his men to meet him at his tent. "I have separate instructions for you four. You will leave for Alexandria immediately. A ship sails tonight on the tide. This way, you are sure to be in Alexandria when the General and Drusus arrive. Let them know what has happened here and that we are requesting reinforcements. There is no telling what may happen in Cyrene from here out. In any case, let them know that we are asking for instructions and return here with the answer as quickly as possible. Understood?"

"Yes, Commander!" comes the answer.

"Go now then with all speed," Antonius says, saluting them back as they leave. Antonius mounts his steed and leads the march toward the place where the funeral will commence, the captain by his side. The afternoon sun is waxing quickly as they begin down the dusty, now notorious road. His eyes are fixed on the horizon ahead. Antonius says to himself, "Now it's a new game."

Ahead of them, within the city limits, Porcius is spending the heat of the day in his wine cellar, sampling one of his prized vintages, when one of his house servants enters and breaks his relaxed state of mind.

"Master, there are two men at the door to see you…merchants, I believe. It also seems that they know you."

Curious and, at the same time, slightly annoyed, Porcius puts down his cup and makes his way to the entrance. "What is it?" he calls out as he approaches the door.

"Now, is that any way to treat an old friend?" Saccius answers back, smirking.

Realizing now who is speaking, Porcius is less than pleased to greet his uninvited guests. "You are more bold than wise in showing up here!" Porcius snarls. "I should kill you where you stand for all that you stole from me the last time we met. In fact, I still might. The only thing keeping me from doing so this very instant is the morbid curiosity that has me wondering what has caused you to make such a stupid move as this!"

"I would like to make amends, old friend. May we come in?" Saccius asks in a most pseudo-humble tone. "Briefly—and I do mean briefly," said Porcius, stepping aside."

"By the way, you haven't met my partner Aemilius," Saccius continues. "Aemilius, this is Porcius, City Elder and one of the most powerful merchants in all of Cyrene. We go back a long way."

Switching the subject, he goes on, "By the way, Porcius, would you happen to have some good wine available? What we've had here thus far has been simply dreadful."

Porcius motions to another of his servants to bring a cup each for his guests. "One cup each. In the meantime, state your business."

"Very well, my friend," Saccius says as he sits down. "We have procured the exclusive trading rights to the Roman Empire for Silphium, and it is a most desirable contract indeed," Saccius gloats.

"If you're not lying again, I would agree, however, it is a worthless fact to me. I am no longer in the Silphium business," Porcius grunts.

Saccius shoots back, "So I've heard. However, would you be interested in getting back into the business—at the top, no less?"

"How?" asks Porcius, his tone changing to one of slightly more interest. "I have no fields, and currently, the man on top is Simon of Cyrene. He is your best prospect, not me."

"Actually," Aemilius interjects, "he is our source. But we have strong reason to believe that he may not be around much longer. We foresee him, shall we say—forcibly retiring from the business."

"How do YOU know this? I've heard nothing of the kind, and if anyone would have heard this, it would be ME!" barks Porcius, glaring at his loathsome former partner.

"Never mind how I know, just that I know," Saccius replies.

Porcius eyes his guests deeply for a moment and then asks, "So why do you feel the need to bless me with this opportunity? It seems that you already have everything you need to succeed."

Saccius replies, "Almost, old friend. Don't underestimate your worth. Your name is widely well-known. We have talked to many of our counterparts in the merchant world, and we have come to learn much about your current position in life. You hold trade agreements to the most lucrative trade routes both inside and outside of the Empire. In addition, you have agreements with some of the most powerful merchants in the known world. Most, if not all, these agreements and relationships are essentially closed to outsiders like

The Cyrenian

us. We wish to expand our business rapidly, so, therefore, your partnership would be indispensable. In addition, as a City Elder of much seniority, you have great influence here in Cyrene as well. Having you as an ally here would also be a most valuable asset. You can ensure, shall we say, a friendly political environment for us all to thrive in, especially where taxes and regulations are concerned."

Porcius scratches his beard, trying not to give away his steadily rising interest by smiling. "It seems that, as always, you've done your homework. I will not argue any of the facts that you have presented here. However, naturally, the next question becomes, what is in this for me?"

Saccius continues, "We would be willing to give you 25 percent of the Cyrene-Rome trade business just for watching over our interests here and guaranteeing our timely shipments out of port. In addition, we would be fifty-fifty partners on all the other routes that you bring in. Does this interest you?"

Porcius stands up, his thoughts racing. "I must admit that you have my attention. However, I want to know more about this Simon issue. I also want you to know upfront that I won't be a part of any murder plots or the like. I will not lose all that I have because of some ill-conceived scheme driven by your greed. If that is in any way a part of your agenda, then count me out here and now. As much as I would relish seeing Simon brought down, I won't go down personally over him or anybody else, do you understand?"

Aemilius now answers, "You needn't worry. Your fears can be put to rest. Besides, we cannot afford to go down any more than you can. We will fill you in fully when the time comes."

Porcius then motions his guests toward the door. "And with that said, we can possibly talk further after Simon's so-called 'retirement.' Until then, I bid you goodbye. And by the way, for the record, you were never here."

The two partners gracefully make their exit, noticeably dejected. As they walk back through the doorway, Porcius speaks up one last time. "Also, for the record, I won't do this partnership for less than 40 percent of the Cyrene-Rome trade and sixty-forty on the rest, and that is only if I to do this at all."

Saccius breaks the rules first by smiling. "Done and done then, old friend. We will see you again when we return from Rome."

"That's not a yes. Not yet. See me when the Silphium fields are yours and not before!" Porcius says matter-of-factly while shutting the door.

Aemilius queries his partner, "What do you think?"

Saccius grins, "That's a yes alright. Trust me. Now let's hurry. We still must get the last of the bales down to the dock before sundown. We don't want Simon to suspect anything."

"Right. You're always right," Aemilius says as the two begin the ride to the port

On the other side of the door, Porcius turns to his servant, who witnessed the entire meeting.

"Gideon," he says, "I hope that you learned something here. Always keep your friends close and your enemies closer. Especially enemies pretending to be friends."

Gideon responds, "Yes, master. I am off now to pick up the meat for the house that you ordered. Will there be anything else?"

"No, just send the Chief House Steward to me. I have some duties for him as well."

Gideon bows, "Very well, my master. I shall return soon." He will do as he has promised, but he knows now that there is one stop he will have to make first. He quickly mounts his horse and rides off.

Gideon soon arrives at Simon's estate and heads straight for the servant's compound. He approaches the door to what is Menachem's quarters. Gideon's knowledge of the grounds is a tell-tale sign that he has obviously been here before. He is about to knock on the door when a nearby servant calls out, "He is not there!"

"Where can I find him?" Gideon calls back nervously.

"He is likely at the main house. Try there," the servant says.

The Cyrenian

"Thank you!" says Gideon, taking the servant's advice straight away. As he rides up the hill, he takes in the view of the seemingly endless Silphium fields, the beauty of which never ceases to amaze him. He is close to the house when he feels a moment of hesitation for the very first time. He wonders to himself if he is doing the right thing by coming here. He is, after all, neither family, friend, nor servant. In addition, what exactly is he going to say? That Simon and everything he owns and everyone he loves could be in danger? From whom? How? In fact, the more he thinks about it, the more he begins to think that maybe he is perhaps premature in his reaction. Maybe it would be best to wait until he can somehow learn more. Yes. It is better to wait. He will tell Menachem later after he has had more time to think everything through. Gideon is immediately at peace with his decision and starts to head back down the hill when he sees Menachem riding toward him and calling his name. There will be no avoiding the subject now.

"I heard that you were looking for me. You know that you shouldn't be here!" Menachem scolds. "What if the Master had seen you? What could be so important that you would disobey me?"

Gideon casts down his eyes and replies, "Forgive me. I have some information that I thought you should know immediately. Something is going on that involves the House of Simon."

"Come back to my quarters now before you are seen. We'll talk there," says Menachem.

The two men ride back down the hill and to Menachem's quarters. Once there, Gideon explains what he has witnessed earlier at Porcius' house. Menachem stands in sober silence for some time after hearing the tale.

"I knew that those two jackals were no good and not to be trusted from the very beginning. I knew that their true colors would show sooner or later. It seems that it's more sooner than later, after all. Did you get any hint at all as to how they plan to take Simon down? Think of every detail that you can remember—no matter how small!" Menachem says sternly.

"I don't think that they plan to kill him, but there is definitely some kind of trap being set. Porcius said he would not be a part of any murder plot, and they told him not to worry. They told Porcius that Simon would be 'forcibly retiring' from the Silphium business soon, whatever that means. Saccius said that they will all meet again after they return from Rome. They leave tomorrow," Gideon says with much angst in his voice.

"Alright then," Menachem responds. "At least there is a little time to work with. Get back to Porcius quickly so that you are not missed. Come back tomorrow after Saccius and Aemilius leave for Rome, and I will take you with me to speak with Simon. He needs to hear all this straight from you."

"Are you sure? You have always warned me to stay away from here—that I can never be seen under any circumstances," Gideon says with great concern.

Menachem looks out the window and says, "There is a season for everything. Apparently, a new season has begun. Now go."

Gideon rises to leave when Menachem grabs his shoulder. He says softly, "You did the right thing in coming."

Gideon smiles and answers, "Thank you, Father."

"Go in safety now, my son," Menachem whispers as he closes the door.

CHAPTER 15. SANDS IN THE HOURGLASS

This morning comes quickly for the Roman camp at Cyrene. Many in the camp didn't sleep at all due to the anticipation of this day's coming events. The sights, sounds, and smells of the funeral rites for their fallen brothers the day before are still burning in the minds of all who were in attendance. Burning even hotter than the flames of the pyres is the desire for revenge being felt by all. The morning assembly fast becomes the stepping off for the march into the city. Every man is determined to personally be the one to bring the murderers to Roman justice and will not rest until the mission is accomplished. The hardest part of the job will be exercising restraint during the process. That is not where one's emotions are at this moment. Antonius is especially focused this day, as it will be his first test as Commander. Even without the rank, his motivation would be at its highest level ever. Failure is not an option. That especially includes the duty of maintaining order during what will no doubt be a highly charged environment. At the same time, he can't help but dream a little. After all, success here could very well bring him the coveted Centurion rank that he has spent his career thus far so fervently pursuing.

As the soldiers approach the city, the residents are already well into their daily routines. They watch with great concern the show of force coming steadily towards them, knowing full well that such

The Cyrenian

Roman presence cannot mean anything good. Most move quickly out of the way to avoid any form of contact, while some others stand still as if frozen, watching the scenes unfold. There is still much fresh and fervent resentment among the people over the horrible death of the little girl under the hooves of the Roman horses, but what is looming larger is the fear of reprisal for the murder of the soldiers at the hands of the Zealots. The news of the clash has spread throughout the city, but true to form, nobody in Cyrene will chance willingly saying anything within earshot of the Romans. The last thing they need or want is more soldiers being deployed to the region. Everybody knows of the Zealot existence in the city, but up to now, there has never been an issue to be concerned with. Cyrene has been, up to now, more of a hideout than a hotspot. Besides, since many of the residents have strong Jewish ties and lineage, there is a quiet appreciation of the Zealot mission. However, the current situation is yet untried ground.

Antonius raises his hand to signal a halt to the march as the force reaches the edge of the city. He relays his next directions, "We will first go to the Temple and seek the Elders there. Keep tight ranks and look sharp!" There is good wisdom in his strategy. Antonius figures that by arriving in force, he will send a clear message that Rome means business. Hopefully, putting this psychological pressure on the local leaders will result in enlisting their direct cooperation in extracting the desired information from the people. He is counting on their strong desire to avoid the carnage that will surely follow if the Romans are defied. He is gambling that the Cyrenians will surmise that if the Romans can accomplish their goal without conflict, it will be better for all the Cyrenian parties involved.

Antonius and the soldiers now make their way to the magnificent and awe-inspiring Temple of Zeus. It houses the seat of the Cyrenian government, as well as its banking, in addition to its primary spiritual role. Antonius feels sure that he will find the leaders he seeks here. His instincts prove to be correct. The Elders are present and engaged in an emergency meeting to discuss the current tense situation that they now find themselves in. Antonius is met on the steps of the impressive marble building by several priests, including the High Priest himself, who is the first to speak.

"Greetings to you. How may we be of service?" he asks, trying purposefully to set a peaceful tone for their conversation.

Antonius replies, trying his best to be authoritarian but not overly menacing—at least for now, "Three of my men, including a Centurion, were murdered just outside of the city two nights ago. I believe that the killers are here in Cyrene. At the very least, I believe that someone here knows who and where they are. Zealots, first and foremost, are highly suspected. We wish to speak with the leaders of Cyrene to get them to assist us in our search before we take matters fully into our own hands."

The High Priest responds with a bow and says, "The key officials are here, and I am sure they will grant you an audience immediately. Please allow me to go into the Temple and announce you."

"That won't be necessary," Antonius says as he signals for four soldiers to escort him inside. "They'll know I am here in a moment."

"At least grant my request that you keep your swords outside of the Temple itself. It is a holy place of peace," petitions the Priest.

"Not a chance!" Antonius retorts. "I will, at best, promise to keep them sheathed until we are given a reason to use them. Consider this act one of great favor. What happens henceforth is completely up to you." He and his escorts resume the climb up the steps, along with the now agitated but silent priests.

After winding through the majestic columned halls, the parties enter the large chamber where the meeting of the Elders is in session. Simon is also in attendance, as he too is an Elder.

The High Priest announces, "Good Sirs, these gentlemen wish to speak with you on a matter of great urgency."

"Thank you, High Priest," says Porcius as he rises to his feet, surprisingly calm about the sudden appearance of Roman warriors in their hallowed halls. Looking at Antonius, he says, "We have expected that we would meet you before long. Please take a seat and join us."

"I'll stand if you don't mind." Antonius responds, adding, "Let me get right to the point." Antonius repeats his case to the leaders, leaving them no doubt as to his position and intentions.

Another Elder speaks, "We sympathize with your loss and your subsequent feelings. As I am sure you know already, we lost an innocent daughter at the hands of Roman soldiers just days ago. We are also great believers and protectors of justice. Without it, society cannot thrive. Your request, however, is not an easy one to fulfill. Finding anyone who knows anything of the Zealots, as well as being willing to talk about it, will be difficult. Moreover, it will take time to do so. You must understand."

Antonius' brow furrows.

"Results are directly proportionate to the methods used and the efforts expended. You have your ways to achieve results, and we have ours. Shall we put them all to the test and see who is more effective?" Porcius again speaks.

"Let us assemble the people and start our probe. I assure you that we will find what you seek. Give us three days to work at this before you make any further moves. We will be most diligent. You have our word."

The other Elders eagerly verbalize their concurrence.

Antonius replies, "I give you two days, after which we will begin our own campaign. Make sure that your people understand that it will be best if they face you rather than us. As a physical reminder, we will be encamped on each side of the city. No one will be allowed to enter or leave without being searched and identified. Be sure, resistance on their part will be most foolish and costly. I will return to you in two days. Do not disappoint me." Antonius scans the faces before him. After he is satisfied that his edict has achieved the desired results, he and his escort about-face and depart. As the sound of cadenced steps fades into the distance, the inevitable chatter begins.

One Elder stands up and pounds his fist on the table, saying, "These Romans are a curse! They will destroy this city and everyone in it as they have so many others. We must find the answers they seek immediately! It is better to sacrifice a few than to have the entire city wiped out!"

"The impetuous actions of the Zealots are at the root of this problem. We have turned a blind eye to them for so long that they have become emboldened to the point of our own detriment," says another.

Porcius breaks in and chides, "Look, we all know that we have hidden and supported the Zealots for many years. We all share the same dream that one day, this Roman tyranny will end. We all hold out hope that these patriots will speed that day in coming. Unfortunately, this recent attack was badly miscalculated. However, I believe that the best course of action is to get the Romans looking elsewhere for their quarry. The story we use will have to be believable and thoroughly convincing. We do know that Barabbas' murderous reputation is common knowledge both far and wide. In fact, this deed is no doubt his handiwork, in my opinion. It's no secret that he has been here. It is also not a secret that he has caused us much trouble before as well. In addition, his ability to evade capture is also legendary, as proven by the many bounties on his head. I am thinking that the mere mention of his name as the culprit will get the attention of the Romans for sure. We can say that we have heard word from the people that he has fled and headed for Egypt. I am sure that I can get a merchant friend or two to say that they have encountered him on the run. In any case, if we can make the story stick, perhaps we can appease the Romans enough to get them searching elsewhere, taking the pressure off Cyrene."

There begins a definite buzz in the air as the leaders explore the plausibility of the plan amongst each other. It is not long before the decision to vote on the subject is made.

Simon then stands and speaks up, "There is much cunning and dark brilliance in your plan, Porcius. However, to do this will also be a betrayal to the Zealots, who are dedicated to fighting for our freedom. We may very well be sending Barabbas and his followers to their deaths. How does this sit in your heart?"

Porcius answers, "They have already vowed to die for their cause. Truth be told, most, if not all of them, expect to end their lives that way. The subject is already settled in their minds. They are risking death every day of their lives. On the other hand, no one in Cyrene should have to die for something that they did not do. In my opinion, it is better to protect the innocents here and let the Zealots take their chances."

Once again, Porcius' logic wins over even the most skeptical of the Elders. Even Simon seems to be satisfied with Porcius' rebuttal. The plan is put to the vote, and the results are unanimous. At least for the moment, it appears that much bloodshed may just have been avoided. Now, they must hope that the Romans buy the story. Everything is riding on it.

Simon adds one last thought. "We should still follow through with an assembly of the people, though, if not for any other reason than the optics of it all. If the Romans witness such a gathering, it might make the new-found 'information' more believable," he says with his gaze fixed on that of Porcius' equivalent stare.

Porcius answers most facetiously, "That is a wise observation, Simon. It seems that you are quite capable of 'dark brilliance' yourself."

Before Simon can fire another verbal counterstrike on his rival, the High Priest calls out, "Let us adjourn this meeting and work to assemble the people before sundown. The sooner we start the process, the better."

The men leave the chamber and proceed outside. As they start down the steps, Porcius bluntly asks Simon, "So, how is your new partnership working out?"

Simon looks at him with a quizzical expression on his face, wondering what has prompted the question. He certainly hasn't discussed his business dealings with Porcius, or anybody else other than Chana and Menachem, for that matter. In a flash, he deduces that there must have been more truth to Porcius' rumored secret meeting with Saccius and Aemilius than he realized. He answers in a casual tone, "It's not a partnership. Simply a supplier-buyer relationship. Nothing more."

"I see. Maybe I got my facts wrong. Good luck, nonetheless. However, should you decide that you might want a better deal to consider, let me know," Porcius says flatly as he sets off in the direction of his home.

Giving no acknowledgment to the comments, Simon picks up his pace as he begins his walk home, his head spinning. What "facts" is Porcius talking about? Why would HE be offering "a better deal"? All he can be sure of is that Saccius and Aemilius are involved. Simon's insides are getting an all-too-familiar feeling of discomfort. It is a feeling that he has learned over time to never ignore.

Chana sits dumbfounded as she listens to her deeply concerned husband explain in detail everything that has transpired since he left home this morning. He ends his report with an admission that he feels is best said by him before his loving wife says it.

"You were right, Chana. Saccius and Aemilius have had an agenda from the beginning. It seems that Porcius is in on it as well. Whatever their ultimate plan is, I can feel the walls closing in."

Chana responds with a strong, while at the same time nervous tone, "As much as it would be easy to say that I told you so, you must know that this is something that I'd hoped to be wrong about, as did you. They are seeking to destroy us, Simon. I believe that they are planning some way to eliminate us and take our land. My fear

The Cyrenian

is not knowing how far they will go to get it." Simon starts pacing now, a sure sign that a plan is about to be unveiled.

"We have no choice," he begins. "We must take our fallback position and go to Judea. I will immediately arrange passage for you, the boys, and Menachem to Caesarea Maritima on the earliest available ship. From there, you will get to your family in Capernaum within two days by caravan."

"What about you?" Chana asks.

Simon says, "I will be staying behind tying up things here and follow shortly behind. For our safety, I want our move to look more like a holiday than an exodus. Nobody will question me for staying behind to conduct business while my family takes a trip. This way, I will not only be able to cover your escape, but I'll also know exactly what is going on here in real time."

"Then there's Porcius and the other two. It's too dangerous for you to wait here until they return. Whatever the trap is, I am sure they won't wait too long to spring it," Chana says, laying out her concerns.

Simon reassures her, "If all goes well, I'll be long gone before Saccius and Aemilius return from Rome. In the meantime, you must start making ready. I am going down right now to speak with Menachem. Fill the boys in when they return from the field. Make sure that they know that nothing is to be said to ANYONE about our intentions."

"I will take care of everything," says Chana, making plain her level of commitment.

"As you always do," Simon says, kissing her forehead.

Almost at that very moment, the sound of beating hooves can be heard coming towards the house. Looking out, Simon immediately recognizes the lead rider as being Menachem. The second younger rider, however, is a stranger to his eyes. They come up to the door, and Menachem hugs Simon as he always does. Menachem then turns Simon's attention to the young man.

"This is Gideon. He has some vital information to share with you about Porcius and your partners."

Simon responds with exuberance, "Your timing is impeccable! Come in quickly and tell me what you know."

As they come through the door, Chana's eyes fly open wide as they meet those of the young stranger. She drops the bowl she is carrying, which breaks with a resounding crash as it hits the floor. "YOU!" she shouts, visibly shaken. "You are the one who accosted me in the marketplace some time ago! You warned me about strangers and told me to trust no one. What are you doing here? Simon, this is the man I told you about!" she calls out toward her husband.

Simon rears up, questions coming out of him at a rapid-fire pace. "What is the meaning of this? Menachem, what is going on? This man left Chana terrified!" Turning to Gideon, he says angrily, "Who are you to scare her that way?" as he reaches out to grab the young man.

Menachem steps forward between them and bars Simon, saying, "Wait!"

All motion stops in an instant, and Menachem's voice lowers. "Gideon is my son."

"Your SON?" Simon says in a shocked state. "I—we never even knew that you had a son!" he continues.

Menachem goes on, "It was for your own protection, Simon, as well as his. My son has ties to the Zealots. Several of his closest boyhood friends have long joined the cause, but he has chosen not to become an active participant. Killing isn't in him, especially after learning firsthand what can happen. Gideon has seen friends killed in conflicts. He is more of a support for them in the way of delivering messages, bringing them food, and the like. Virtually no one outside of his circle of Zealot friends know his real identity. I would rather that he stays away from them altogether, but I do understand his feelings. I have even shared my Zealot past with him in hopes that he'll remain a non-member. Things are getting more and more dangerous, as you well know. I figured that by keeping him a secret, if something should ever go wrong, there would be no chance of anything coming back to you via me. You would always have plausible deniability on your side. Naturally, keeping his ties a secret will be crucial to protecting his life as well. He works for Porcius' house as a servant, which is why he is here now. He has important information for you that I want you to hear straight from him."

Simon is reeling from this new revelation. It is becoming difficult to keep up with all of the changes of recent days. Nonetheless, he and Chana sit down, totally fixated as Gideon's story unfolds.

After finishing his testimony, Menachem breaks the looming silence. "What are your thoughts, Simon?" he asks.

After a long pause, Simon answers, "Well, at least I now clearly understand who and what I am dealing with and what their goals are. I also know now how little time we have."

Chana asks, "How do you see our odds for success?"

Simon answered, "We have one thing in our favor. We know their plans, but THEY don't know that we know. I think we can use that fact to our advantage. One thing does puzzle me, though. The deal we have with Saccius and Aemilius is working. Obviously, the only way that they would stand to do better for themselves would be to either literally eliminate me as a partner or otherwise find a way to take the land out from under us. Eliminating me wouldn't do them any good because we only have a basic trial agreement so far, which doesn't include a death clause. By law, if anything happened to me, the obligations of both parties would end immediately. The agreement would be rendered null and void, and the estate would remain with the family. Besides, the trial agreement ended with the shipment they had just left with. Therefore, only the second possibility exists. But what could they possibly use to cause me to forfeit our estate? We own it outright. By Roman law, I would have to have committed a crime against the State and be found guilty of the same to have our land taken away. But surely, I've done nothing that could possibly be construed as a crime, especially one of that degree." Simon ponders.

Gideon speaks up. "Would harboring or aiding a Zealot or Zealots qualify as that type of crime? I mean, let's say the Romans decide that their soldiers were killed by Zealots and that you are somehow involved in helping them either survive or escape. Would that be a crime against the State?"

Simon stops dead in his tracks. "Yes, it would. It would be a capital crime because it was murder. Worse yet, it was the murder of Romans, which would now bring Roman justice into the equation. That would have far-reaching effects. Deadly effects. The Elders would be glad to turn us over to the Romans to end the situation peacefully. Not to mention the fact that our land would go to the highest bidder. That would be right up Porcius' alley because it would be impossible for anyone else in Cyrene to outbid him. What made you think of that, Gideon?"

Gideon replies, "It was something that Saccius said. He said that you would be 'forcibly retiring' soon. The way he said it made me sure that he had a plan. I just didn't know what it could be."

Menachem then asks, "Do you think that they shared these ideas with Porcius?"

Simon said, "I don't think so. I know Porcius well. He would have moved on me be now, like a hound on a wounded deer. If he was going to move against me, this would be the perfect time for him to do so. With Saccius and Aemilius already in Rome and the Romans already here and eager for revenge, he could have pulled this whole thing off within a day, cutting both out completely. The other two are also probably trying to set up funding and Roman support to take their chance. It would be best for them if Porcius didn't know. But I still can't figure out how they would be able to prove my involvement. I have no Zealot ties—other than the story of my father and you, Menachem. Nobody knows anything about your secret past but you and I."

After a moment of silence, it is Menachem's turn to feel his blood run cold. A reality flashes through his mind. He speaks up, his voice quivering with a frightening realization, "They must have heard us! They must have heard us talking that morning outside the house! They were here that morning. There is no other possible explanation. They had to have heard me telling you the story!"

Simon nods his head with reluctance. "I agree. It all fits. Again, I still don't think that Porcius knows. However, time is of the essence now for sure. We must move quickly now. I must decide what my best move is from here. Our inevitable exit must be smooth and beyond suspicion. I must keep Porcius under control but, at the same time, keep his scent off the trail. The question now is how best to do that," he ponders.

"By giving him what he wants," Chana says with steely conviction, her eyes speaking to his.

Simon thinks for a moment and begins laughing out loud. "You are a beautiful, wonderful genius! Exactly!" he gushes as he embraces her.

Menachem, feeling somewhat foolish for not getting their meaning, says, "I don't understand. Give him what?"

Gideon has suddenly figured it all out and blurts out, "The estate! Of course! Sell it to him, and he gets everything without any risk or effort! It solves everything, and no one gets hurt—except Saccius and Aemilius, who deserve a much worse fate than that!"

Menachem reclines in his seat, gazing with wonder at his son. "Who knows that you have grown up to be so wise!" he marvels.

"Who knew that his father was such a wise and great teacher!" Gideon says with pride.

For the first time in a while, there is laughter in the House of Simon. After a few moments, though, Simon brings everybody back to the new realities of the day.

"We all now know our assignments. There is much to do. Let's get started. Remember, time is not our friend."

CHAPTER 16. SUMMITS AND SUMMITS

A rider approaches the Roman camp on the edge of town where Antonius has established his command center. The City Elders have sent him to invite Antonius back to the Temple for the sharing of their new information. They have collectively decided that things will look better if they approach Antonius before his deadline the next day.

After hearing the message from the courier, a satisfied Antonius remarks to his officers, "It is amazing how quickly results can be acquired when the proper methods are applied." Turning to the courier, he says, "Tell your Elders that we shall arrive there shortly."

The courier bows nervously and makes a rapid exit, most glad to leave the intimidating scene. He considers himself lucky that he is bearing good news. Couriers have often lost their lives for bringing unwelcome news.

Antonius begins to quickly don his armor, eager to hear what reward his tough stance will yield.

"Do you think that they have anything of real value to tell us?" asks one of the squad leaders.

"They had better!" Antonius huffs as he puts on his helmet and goes to meet his escorts. In his mind, though, he is trying to come up with a solid plan for any possible scenario. The best situation will be that they either already have the culprits in custody or at least know where and when they can be apprehended. If things go that way, he will be able to publicly make an example for all as to what happens should Rome be crossed. That will go a long way in establishing not only law and order but also a healthy fear of planning any form of insurrection in the future. However, Antonius knows from experience that things rarely work that easily. He also knows that people under duress will say almost anything. The key now is to not fall for false information. To be fooled would seriously undermine his position on many fronts. He vows to himself to be more focused and discerning than ever before. While he needs to apprehend the true perpetrators, he knows also that his angry men need only scapegoats. Their thirst for blood and revenge must be satisfied. One way or another, Antonius is resolved to giving them what they need. He is in command, and he plans to keep it that way. He soon finds himself once again in the columned halls of the Temple of Zeus and before the Elders. As before, Porcius takes the lead in speaking. Simon sits in deep and focused observation.

"Greetings, Antonius. We are pleased that we can share with you the results of what has been a productive investigation. Will you sit down with us this time?"

This time, Antonius decides to accept the offer. "Go on," he says.

Porcius continues, "As you know, we called the people of Cyrene together and explained to them your position in the same terms as you explained it to us. We are glad to say that we got almost instant results. First, we have learned without a doubt that your hunch is correct. Your colleagues died at the hand of a roving band of Zealots. Moreover, they are not just any Zealots. These are the band headed up by perhaps the most notorious Zealot leader of all. His name is Barabbas."

"Barabbas!" Antonius exclaims, springing to his feet.

Porcius senses and seizes this rare moment of Roman emotional outburst perfectly. "So, you know of him?" he says most innocently.

"Know of him!" Antonius continues. "Every Roman legionnaire is on his trail. His head will fetch a tidy sum, not to mention lifetime notoriety for the one or ones who capture him. It has been some time since anyone has heard anything having to do with him. The rumors are that he has fled to some faraway land since he has been so successful at evading capture. Now you say HE did this? Who told you this? I want to speak with him here and now!"

There is a new-found fire in Antonius' person. This is exactly what Porcius is counting on.

"They are here," Porcius motions for two men in the room to come forward. "These two men are merchants who were part of a caravan from Egypt. They encountered Barabbas and his accomplices in the desert. I know them and will personally vouch for their integrity. Gentlemen, please tell the Commander what you have experienced," he says, turning the attention to them.

One begins, "We were a part of a caravan making its way here from Alexandria. We were bringing spices to trade here for Silphium to take back to Egypt. While making camp about four nights ago on the desert road, some men on horseback approached us, asking if we could spare any food and water as they were trying to get to Alexandria. They said that they could pay for it. I asked them how they came to be there and where they were from. I said that anyone who has made that journey before would be aware of what supplies they would have to have as a matter of life and death. It was a most curious situation."

The other merchant chimes in, "He said that his name was Barabbas and that they were Jews being pursued by the Romans. He said that they were wanted for killing some Romans. We guessed that since he could see that we were Jews, he felt safe revealing himself. He was probably also sure that we would help him once we knew the story. We did sell him some supplies, but we had no idea what they had done. We did not want to know the details, and we didn't ask. We also didn't know that they were Zealots. We helped them strictly as a humanitarian gesture as well as out of Jewish brotherhood. Once we arrived in Cyrene and found out from the Elders what had just happened here, everything made sense. That is why we immediately came forward. We want no trouble with Rome."

The two men bow deeply and step back, nervously awaiting judgment. One of the other Elders comes forward and asks Antonius, "Does this information please you, good Sirs?"

Antonius takes a very long time to answer. "How do I know that these men—or you, for that matter—are telling the truth and not just trying to save yourselves?"

Porcius once again steps in. "Commander, we would not risk Rome's wrath in a futile attempt to fool you. There are too many lives at stake, no doubt including our own. We're too wise to do that. However, if you are truly aware of Barabbas' exploits, you must agree that he is no doubt your perfect prime suspect."

The silent standoff between the two sides seems to last forever. There is not a brow in the room that isn't moist. Each man in the room is convinced that the next voice to speak will be the losing one. Porcius calculates the risks and decides that graciously letting the Roman off the hook by speaking first was a winning move. If Antonius was going to dismiss their argument, he would have done so by now—or so he hoped.

"Please give us your thoughts, Commander," he says.

Antonius answers, "While I am not completely convinced that you would not lie to me, there is some reasonable substance to your account. I believe that a flight to Alexandria makes sense. The crime itself completely fits Barabbas' style of attack, and your timeline is plausible. We have a legion on the march to Alexandria as we speak. At the same time, we have a squad from here traveling to catch up with them to bring them news of the killings and bring back instructions. They should intercept your Barabbas somewhere between here and the legion's position. In any case, I will allow things to stay as they are until our squad returns. What happens after that will depend on what they tell me. In the meantime, our men will stay posted here as they are. The rules of ingress and egress to and from the city shall also remain in force. Is that understood?" All the Elders agree, sensing that, at least for now, their plan has brought about a stay of execution. Antonius and his men make their exit in typical military fashion, leaving the Elders to drink in all that has just transpired.

The sound of breathing as well as renewed flesh tones return to the room. "Thank you, Porcius," Simon begins, breaking the ice. "It seems that your plan was the right one."

Porcius answers, obviously relieved, "Thank you, Simon. I think we all played our parts to perfection today. The victory, if there is one, is ours collectively."

Simon moves close to Porcius' ear and whispers, "I would like to speak privately with you when and where we will draw the least amount of attention.

Porcius, his interest aroused, answers, "I'll let you know when. Now, it is time for wine. It tends to get people to focus elsewhere."

"Bring wine!" Simon calls out to the servants, following Porcius' lead. "We've earned it." There are no dissenting votes on the proposal.

By the next hour, the wine is taking effect on its patrons. Porcius walks over to Simon and says quietly, "Follow me." Simon gives him a few steps as a head start and does exactly as he was instructed. They join up in the corridor and quickly head off to one of the courtyard gardens. Once they find a suitable spot among the splendid botany, the conversation begins in earnest.

"So, Simon, what is on your mind?" Porcius begins.

Simon answers in a most serious and business-like tone. "I am strongly considering a new business venture. An opportunity has just presented itself, but the window of opportunity is small, and a decision must be made almost immediately. The biggest consideration that I must deal with is that the venture would require me to move my base of operations from Cyrene. It is a most difficult decision to make, but one that I must make. As you know, I have done very well for myself here. That said, I have decided to sell my Silphium business, along with my estate. You have expressed your desire to buy me out on many occasions. Therefore, I thought to approach you first."

Porcius cannot believe his ears. He has dreamed of hearing these exact words for longer than he can remember. Now that he is hearing them, it seems almost surreal. "I am grateful that you have approached me first, though I must admit that I never expected to hear you say this to me," Porcius responds. "What type of business are you looking to get into? It must be quite a lucrative situation for you to be considering such a drastic change of life. Personally, I'd fully expected that you would be buried on the property at a very ripe old age, with your sons becoming the new Masters of the House of Simon."

Simon adeptly avoids answering the question. "Now you know the rules. No prudent businessman will reveal the business or the location until all is in place and his advantages locked. Surely you understand."

Porcius admits, "I cannot dispute that. I wouldn't do it myself," all the while trying his best to mask the overwhelming excitement within him for this possible good fortune. "Naturally, there is one factor that will decide everything. What is your price?"

Simon is fully prepared for the question. "In anticipation of your possible interest, I have prepared this agreement, which states the price and terms of the transfer. This is my firm price, and I will not be granting any further discounts. The combination of the business, my trade agreements, and the estate will easily fetch this amount. Perhaps more with the Silphium demand being what it is."

Simon hands Porcius the scroll and stands aside to allow him to read it uninterrupted. At the conclusion, Porcius says, "This is a sizeable sum, but at the same time not outlandish. However, I am not sure that I can raise all your price at one time. Would you consider holding a note?"

Simon knows that he has him now. His assessment of his adversary proves true. In all actuality, it is an offer that Simon calculates that Porcius cannot and will not refuse. Porcius does have the financial means to do the deal then and there, but if he can get Simon to agree to the note, it would mean more working capital at his disposal. Simon gives Porcius the "planned pause" and answers, "I am willing to take seventy-five percent now and hold a note for the balance, payable one year from now, with interest. You need only one full season to make that happen."

Simon is Porcius' match when it comes to financial shrewdness. The seventy-five percent down payment will be enough for him and his family to live on anywhere they choose at virtually the same level of lifestyle that they are accustomed to for a reasonable time. Even more so if they choose to build a new life outside of the larger cities. It will also provide seed money if he does indeed decide to engage in a new venture. He calculates that he will likely never see the other 25 percent and, therefore, has adjusted his pricing accordingly. After all, he has no plans or desires to return to Cyrene once he makes his flight anytime soon.

Porcius inwardly revels in the realization that he will not only finally possess this most coveted prize but, at the same time, lay waste the ambitions of Saccius and Aemilius. It is almost too good to believe. Perhaps it is this thought that prompts Porcius to ask the next question.

"I am curious about one thing. Saccius said that he suspected that you would be somehow retiring soon. How much does he know of your plan? Is he involved?"

Simon straightens his stance. "You said that to me once before, and it struck me as most curious. I have not spoken to him or anyone of my plans, nor would I. The fact is that this opportunity has only recently come about. My only guess is that they possibly overheard me speaking to my wife about it while staying in our home. I see no other possibility. If it is true that they know, they may very well be making plans of their own. I put nothing past them. In addition, our temporary agreement for one season ended with the last shipment. That is even more reason for them to be shoring up their finances now to work their own plan."

Simon hopes that introducing this new sense of urgency will push Porcius over the edge. It does. Their mutual distrust of Saccius and Aemilius trumps their mistrust of each other. Porcius extends Simon his hand, this time smiling.

"Done then," he says. "We will meet at the Mensa (bank) at business opening tomorrow and have our *Argentarii* (commercial banker) handle the transactional duties. You will have your 75 percent via bill of exchange by the end of business tomorrow."

"Done," Simon answered. "Bear in mind that I will need several weeks to handle moving out. Also, note that my servants are all free men under contract with me. They are to stay that way—agreed?"

"But of course. The estate is only as good as those working it," Porcius replies. He is only saying it, though. Having slaves is a much more profitable way of doing things, and they are also actually valuable financial assets. However, he will play along for now. He realizes well that the skills that Simon's servants possess for running the farm will need to be transferred to his new personnel before he can afford to let them go. In any case, he will soon be Master, and Simon will soon be gone. There will be nobody to contest him. "As for moving, take whatever time you need," he adds.

"Until tomorrow then," Simon says as the two men part company.

"Yes, until tomorrow."

It is said that the greatest deal is one where both sides get exactly what they want. In this case, nothing could be truer.

CHAPTER 17. THE EYE OF THE STORM

A little more than a week has passed since the Elders met with the Roman commander Antonius, and so far, all is well. While the military presence looms large in Cyrene, life is going on as usual. By all appearances, it seems that Antonius is living up to his word as he gave it. It is cautiously optimistic to say that the gamble of the Elders is working—at least for now. Simon is probably the most relieved individual in the city based on the current climate. His deal with Porcius has gone through without a hitch. Since then, one would easily believe that they have been lifelong friends, judging by the appearance of their new relationship.

Today, Simon is busy putting his plans in motion. While he is enjoying the slightly lower stress levels, he is ever mindful of the fact that this condition of relative calm has a time limit. He calls the family and Menachem together for a conference and fills them in accordingly.

"I have completed your travel plans to Judea," Simon begins. "Your ship will leave on the tide tomorrow for Caesarea Maritima. It is a merchant ship that has a cabin at the stern. It was very expensive to get since cabins on these ships are rare, but I don't want my family to have to ride and sleep on the open deck, especially for the expected ten-day trip. It will be safer and much more comfortable for you. Fortunately for us, Silphium has value to virtually everyone, even ship's captains. Menachem will guard your cabin entrance at night and rest during the day. Alexander and Rufus, I expect that you will never leave your mother unescorted. In addition, go no place alone, ever. While you are in a better position than the other passengers by having a cabin, take no chances. Be respectful if approached by strangers or crew, but the less said to anyone, the better. In addition, show no fear so that you don't become a target. Travel can be hazardous, depending on who is aboard. I will also have some long knives stowed in your travel bundles for your protection. Keep them accessible but hidden, as they are not allowed aboard if you are a passenger. Menachem, you will be allowed to carry a sword as you are traveling in a guardian capacity. You will have all your own food, water, and supplies as well. You will be completely self-sufficient. Once you arrive, you will be met by a caravan being led by the Sheiks of Midian. Their leader will introduce himself to you once you arrive. You will travel with them for the final two-day trek to Capernaum and your relatives. Are there any questions?"

Alexander speaks up, "Father, when will you join us?"

Simon answers, "I will be close behind. A week or two at most, I would say. I must complete the final Silphium shipment obligations that I have before I can officially turn the business completely over. When the last shipment is loaded, I'll be on the first ship to Caesarea."

Rufus now voices his concerns for his father's ability to trust everyone who he has described.

Simon does his best to assuage them. "Son, I know them all, and they all know who I am. You'll see, as I will be sending you off personally."

Menachem reassures the family, saying, "Don't worry. You know your father. He has everything taken care of. Trust in him."

Simon shares in his confidence. "And my trust is in all of you, especially you, dear friend. You have my life's treasure in your care, and I wouldn't do this with anybody else."

"My life is yours, as you well know, Simon," Menachem replies. "Gideon and I are forever in your debt, and we are both looking forward to this fresh start."

Chana rises, feeling a need to hug each of them tightly. "I will go to the market now. Tonight will be our last dinner together in this house, and I plan to make it very special. Boys, go and help your father prepare the shipments. Gideon, you can accompany me—now that I know who you are!" she jokes.

"Glad to!" he answers, laughing out loud. Suddenly, the reality that they are leaving for good hits home. Chana's eyes began to well up with tears. Simon hugs her instinctively, trying to console her.

"It's all right, my dear. Now, let's get busy. I'm looking forward to dinner!" he says, trying his best to redirect her thoughts. She smiles with gratitude at his efforts and goes to make herself ready.

Not too far away, Porcius walks along his roof terrace, taking in the inspiring views and gathering his thoughts. His vista includes the waving Silphium fields of his new property off in the distance. His anticipation and excitement are punctuated only by his concern about the reaction of Saccius and Aemilius upon hearing the news that their deal is no more. It could go well, and perhaps even a new deal can be negotiated, though Porcius isn't particularly interested in sharing the wealth. After all, he has his own large and well-established distribution network. He is also sure that he can find a way to cut his own deal with Rome. Worst case, he can simply offer them some money to make them just go away, he figures. Now, he is in complete control of his destiny and can easily make his offer a "take it or leave it" situation. On the other hand, there is always the chance that things could go very badly once his counterparts grasp the reality of their new and unexpected situation. It is this possibility that concerns him the most. He is all too familiar with the ruthlessness of his soon-to-be-former business associates. While they likely can do nothing to him legally, it is the other options he must consider. Nothing will be off the table with these two. At the same time, Porcius is still, deep down, somewhat looking forward to the satisfaction of informing them that he has just pulled the rug out from under their feet. He will be laughing last and best, even if only on the inside. He momentarily amuses himself by trying to imagine their facial expressions upon hearing the news. Admittedly, he is looking forward to the moment for many different reasons.

Morning finds Simon and his family at the dock, awaiting their chance to board the ship. The previous evening had been the wonderful and bittersweet affair that everyone expected. There was laughter, and there were tears. There was keen anticipation of the near future as well as fears about the same. There were stories and memories. There were well wishes and goodbyes to and from the servants, who are each also every bit a member of the family. As far as they were told, the family is going on an extended vacation. This narrative has been set up for the safety of all. However, those who are closest to Simon and Chana know in their hearts what is really going on, especially when the moment came when each was given a financial bonus for their service. Simon plans to give his inner circle more to go on once the time comes to introduce them to their new Master.

The supplies are loaded, and eventually, the captain comes down to greet his new first-class passengers. "We welcome you," he says. "You may now come aboard, and I will see you to your quarters. We will be departing shortly."

Menachem, sensing the need for the family to have a private moment, declares, "Gideon and I will take the last of the bundles aboard. May God watch over you, Simon."

The two shake hands, and Simon answers, "May God watch over all of you as well. I know that you will take good care of our family. I will see you soon."

Menachem and Gideon follow the captain aboard, leaving the immediate family to each other.

"The days will pass quickly," Simon begins, holding Chana close.

"No, they won't," Chana says, her voice quivering ever so slightly. "I will be worried sick about you until you arrive. Please be careful and trust nobody. If anything looks the slightest bit wrong, leave here right away. Promise me this."

Simon reassures her, "I promise, my love. Put your mind at rest; I'll be fine. Do you have the Bills of Exchange and documents from Porcius that I gave you in a safe place?" he asks.

"On my person at all times," she answers.

"Alexander and Rufus," he continues, "you are the men of the house now. You must guard your mother and each other at all costs. Be strong and courageous. Let nothing and no one come between you—ever. I also want you to obey any instructions that your mother and Menachem give you without hesitation. They know what they are doing. Promise me this."

"We will, Father," Alexander answers.

"Count on us, Father," Rufus adds. "We will not fail you or the family."

"You have always been good boys. Now you are good men," Simon says with great paternal pride.

After one last exchange of embraces, Chana and the boys make their way aboard the ship. It is not long afterward that they are waving to Simon on the shore as the large ship heads out to sea. As they fade from sight, Simon breathes a sigh of relief, as well as one of anxiety. He decides that he will stop at a shop for some wine before heading back to the empty house. Today, the decision to do so is one more of necessity than desire.

CHAPTER 18. CAESAREA MARITIMA

The Roman garrison is alive with activity, as is the usual. Drusus is in the midst of overseeing the training of his men when a soldier runs up to him and salutes.

"Centurion," he begins, "the General wants you to report to him in his quarters immediately."

Drusus replies authoritatively, "Thank you," and turns to a squad leader, commanding him to take over. He quickens his pace to meet the General, wondering what would be behind such an urgent request for his presence. He reaches the doorway of the General's quarters to find him there, along with four other Roman soldiers who look vaguely familiar.

Drusus salutes, saying, "Reporting as ordered, General."

"Come in and take a seat. These soldiers have brought news from Cyrene," General Marcus Maximus says in a most serious tone. In that instant, Drusus realizes that he knows these soldiers. They are Gallus' men, which would explain the feelings of familiarity. The General nods at the lead soldier, signaling for him to repeat his story. He begins again. "There has been an ambush, which has resulted in the assassination of three Roman soldiers, including Centurion Gallus." Drusus winces at what he has just heard, the news coming as a huge shock and a full assault on his mentalities. True to veteran soldier form, his reaction lasts only a millisecond before his brow furrows and his jaw stiffens.

"Do you know who did this? Have you found or killed them?" he questions, now without any filter on his anger.

"Based on the information that we have at this time, we suspect that the act was committed by a band of Zealots." Once again, the reputation of the Zealots amplifies the news. "They have been a thorn in the side of Rome for quite some time now. It is time to remove it once and for all," says the General.

"Do we know where to find them?" Drusus queries.

The soldier answers, "We have no information other than it appears that they have fled from Cyrene. Commander Antonius is actively hunting for them. He is requesting reinforcements and instructions from you, General. We are under orders to return to Cyrene with your answer."

Drusus interjects forcefully, momentarily forgetting proper protocol. "General, I would like to request your permission to take my battle group back to Cyrene to assist in the search efforts. My request is admittedly also one of a personal nature. Gallus was my best friend," Drusus explains, visibly upset by the new developments.

The General replies, "Permission is granted, and you are given full discretion in the completion of your mission. I know how close you two were, Centurion, but I warn you, be mindful not to let your personal feelings cloud your judgment. Feelings can be a dangerous thing. That is why you must work to purge yourself of them. Use them to drive you, but do not let them rule you. Many a good man has been lost that way. Understood?"

"Yes, General. Thank you for both your permission and your advice," Drusus answers.

Turning to the four soldiers, the General says, "You have done well. Get some rest now and prepare to leave with Drusus and his force by ship the day after tomorrow. You are dismissed," commands the General.

After the soldiers leave, the General takes the opportunity to further instruct the new young Centurion. "These Zealots are a bane. They are ruthless and most elusive. There is one leader who goes by the name of Barabbas. Remember that name. He and his henchmen have the blood of many Roman fighting men in many territories on their hands. He is highly wanted by Rome, preferably alive, so that an example can be made to all that would dare to follow his lead. In any case, I would make him your prime suspect unless you get information to the contrary. Somebody out there knows something. He can't hide forever. If you can find him, you will be able to cut off the head of the snake, so to speak. We will be doubling our efforts between here and Jerusalem. We know that the Zealots have a strong presence there as well."

Drusus takes every word from the General to heart and emblazons them in his mind. He vows to himself that he will be the one to bring this outlaw and his cohorts to justice. Even more so, he also vows not to rest until he can avenge the death of his friend. Nothing else matters to him now. This mission has just become his sole purpose in life. While he has only just arrived in Caesarea and has yet to regroup physically from the journey from Cyrene, he is now eager to make his way back to begin the hunt for his quarry. "I thank you again, Marcus Maximus," this time addressing the General as a family friend in their privacy. "I will look forward to accomplishing my mission quickly so that I can rejoin your command."

The General places his hand on Drusus' shoulder and says, "I promised your late father that I would do all I can for you. May the gods be with you. I will have your orders prepared and sealed immediately. Good luck, young Drusus."

Drusus spends the rest of the day and into the night seeing visions, which are his memories of "The Rooster." He can't get their final pact out of his mind. He wonders if things might have gone differently had he been there. The thought will haunt him for a long time to come. While he will never be able to change the past, he is determined to shape the future *his* way. For the first time since hearing the news, he allows a tear to escape and roll down his cheek. "They will pay, Rooster!" he pledges to the spirit of his friend as he finally drifts off to sleep. "I will make them pay dearly, I promise you."

Down at the perpetually busy dock, there are two more arrivals to Caesarea Maritima. A merchant ship from Rome is disembarking. Saccius and Aemilius step off the ship, stretching and allowing their "land legs" to find their way back. As they stand amid the beehive of activity, they talk at length about their reason for being in Caesarea. Aemilius says exuberantly, "The timing of our arrival is good. The *Mensa* (or bank) should be open now. Once we can arrange our Bill of Exchange and loan guarantee, we will have all the funds we need to take over the Silphium business. Our plan is working well. I can't believe our good fortune. Our tree is about to bear fruit!"

"Yes," Saccius says with cautious confidence. "Once we do that, the next thing we need to do is to begin the process of eliminating Simon from the equation. That is why we must meet with the Roman Command at the garrison. If all goes well, the Romans are going to handle that for us!"

After the completion of their financial transactions, the two begin making their way to the garrison, rehearsing their upcoming presentation as they go. They want to make sure that they deliver every line perfectly. The Romans have no tolerance for inaccuracy. They soon arrive at the main gate of the imposing outpost. After stating their business and making a request to see the Commanding Officer, they are allowed to wait inside for a response. The fact that they are Roman citizens gets them an immediate audience, as well as the assumption of credibility. They are led to see a board of officers, including General Marcus Maximus.

A Tribune says, "State your business."

Aemilius starts. "My lords, we have information about the murder of three Roman soldiers in Cyrene." All eyes and ears are immediately fixed on the two gentlemen as the word of the murders has reached virtually everyone at the post.

"Go on," Marcus Maximus says with particular focus in his voice.

Aemilius continues, "There is a man named Simon in the city of Cyrene who has long and deep ties to the Zealots, who are suspected of carrying out the deed. It is believed that he is harboring and protecting them. He is a very prominent citizen and a City Elder. He has both the power and the means to secretly hide and assist them. His chief steward, a trusted family friend, is a former Zealot himself—if there is such a thing. If you are looking for a place to start your investigation, he would be the logical choice."

The General answers, "We are dispatching a force to Cyrene tomorrow. Do you know where to find this man?"

Saccius responds with zeal, "We do, General. We have been involved in a business with him, which is how we have come to know what we know. Of course, our loyalty is first to Rome. That is why we are here. We wish to assist in any way that we can."

The General stands up and says to the two men, "You will accompany our force to Cyrene and lead us to this Simon. We will then get to the bottom of this."

Saccius bows his head in respect, saying, "It will be our honor to serve you. However, if I may be allowed, I wish to make a request. Our business and, therefore, our livelihood are tied to this man. Should he be arrested as an enemy of Rome, we will suffer a devastating financial loss."

"Are you asking me for compensation then?" the General asks with more than a hint of skepticism.

"Only that we be allowed to solely and legally take over the land and the business according to Roman law," Saccius answers.

The General's response is gruff. "If what you say proves to be true and we can capture this man and his Zealot friends, then I am sure that something can be arranged. However, should your information prove to be worthless or untrue, you will be swiftly and accordingly dealt with—do you understand?"

"We will not disappoint you, General," says Aemilius.

"Very well then," the General says in a full military tone. "You will stay here in the garrison and depart with the force under the command of Centurion Drusus on the morning tide. I will see that he meets with you. In the meantime, you will be always kept under our watchful eyes."

At the General's command, Saccius and Aemilius are led to their temporary quarters, unmistakably nervous about their unexpected sequester. At the same time, they try to take comfort in the belief that they can deliver what they have promised and thus complete their plan. They are one step closer to becoming the masters of their destiny. At least, they hope so. Their very lives just may depend on it.

Caesarea Maritima's busy port, with its constant bustle and throngs of people, offers an advantage for some—protection from detection. One can easily hide in plain sight. It is this factor that gives Chana and Menachem a small degree of comfort as they join their caravan and prepare to leave the city for Galilee, totally unaware of the very near presence of their enemies. Conversely, their enemies don't know that their targets are literally right under their noses. All through the journey from its beginning, the prayers of Chana have been for Jehovah's protection for her and her loved ones. Unbeknown to her, those prayers are being answered in ways that she cannot even imagine.

In stark contrast, while she and Menachem are stoic about their experience thus far, Alexander and Rufus are enjoying it to the fullest. They have never seen camels before, and the two are absolutely awed by their size and stature. One of the sheiks notices their boyish exuberance and approaches them, asking, "Would you like to ride one?" Their eyes widen with delight as they turn to their mother. "Mother, may we?" they ask while bubbling over with excitement. The fact is Chana's first impulse is to say no as her natural maternal instincts kick in. But after seeing her boys' faces glowing with joy despite their ordeal, she gives in to the moment. "Just be careful!" comes the answer that the boys hoped for. She almost recants her approval as she watches the two huge beasts kneel to take on their new riders. The boys grin from ear to ear as the camels spring to their feet with a lurch. Even Menachem finds himself smiling at the sight. He turns to Gideon and says, "I suppose you want to join them, don't you?"

Gideon surprises him with his answer. "Maybe later," Gideon says while trying to hide the fact that he is a bit intimidated by the animals. He decides in his mind that he'd rather wait and see how the ride pans out for his new friends first.

Before them all lay the vast and beautiful Plain of Sharon, which will be their landscape for the last leg of the journey to Capernaum and the promise of a new life.

CHAPTER 19. MILE MARKERS

Simon stands on his verandah and gazes out at the beauty of the fields in the morning light, as he has done almost daily for so many years. However, today there is a different feeling within him than the peace and satisfaction that a moment like this normally brings. Today, he will go down the pathway that he has traversed to and from this ancestral home his entire life for the very last time. He will be turning over the House of Simon to his rival, Porcius, and leaving it forever.

As he stares out transfixed on the horizon before him, the tapestry of his life plays out in his mind's eye. He was born in this house, and he can see himself running through it as a child, trying to evade being captured by his father, who is hot in playful pursuit. He watches himself rolling down the hill in the tall grass and laughing gleefully as he keeps falling from dizziness while trying to walk back up the hill. He sees himself learning how to care for the animals and then working the fields at his father's side as a young man. He remembers the love and pride in his mother's eyes as she took care of the beloved men in her life. He also vividly remembers the deep sorrow that he felt when she fell ill and died at a young age. He can still see his father wasting away as he would deeply pine daily for his lost love. He was never the same. It wasn't very long before his father, too, passed away from what Simon truly believes was a broken heart. But he didn't die before imparting every possible life lesson to his son. He taught Simon that wisdom, hard work, honesty, and family were everything. He stressed to his son that everything else in life might fail, but those would be the anchors that would sustain him always. With these thoughts in mind, Simon finds himself fixated on a particular tree in the nearby beautiful meadow, under which he laid them both to rest side by side. His mind then quickly turns to the memory of bringing his new bride to the house for the very first time. She hated it. It was too "Manish," she said. She was right. In his years as a bachelor and a businessman who traveled often, the spartan and oft-neglected interior most definitely cried out for a woman's touch. She was the perfect one for the challenge. Before long, Chana transformed the house into a real home, one that would soon become iconic to the many guests who would be fortunate enough to break bread under its roof. Nothing made it more of a home, though, than the sound of the first cries of his newborn sons. Now, these chapters of their lives have ended.

Solitude is not something that Simon is unused to. He has spent countless days alone in his life traveling as a merchant. It is essentially a way of life for him. It never really has bothered him. He always has the details of the upcoming deals at the forefront of his mind to focus on. Afterward, he either has the thrill of victory to savor or the disappointment of a deal gone bad to contemplate as he heads for home. In any case, coming home is always a comfort. He can always look forward to his arrival here to be a source of deep-seated happiness. He can always count on that. He is, after all, an immortal hero at home. While he is sociable, he doesn't get to socialize very often. That doesn't bother him either, as he prefers to spend his free time with his family whenever possible. Nothing makes him happier.

However, even with all Simon must be thankful for, today, some new and unfamiliar feelings are beginning to rear up in his spirit. For the first time in his memory, he begins to feel a cold bitterness creeping into his heart. After all, he had no plans of ever leaving or selling the home and business that was both his history and his legacy. He has worked hard and had a payoff coming. He was looking forward to the joy of future marriage celebrations. He was looking forward to having his grandchildren reared here. He had always envisioned that somewhere in the distant future, he and his beloved Chana would go to their eternal rest in the beautiful meadow under the same tree that peacefully shades his beloved parents. But now, he is leaving it all behind. Forever. Without a choice. Why? To save himself and his family from ruin and possible death at the hands of evil, jealous and devious men who want to convict him without merit or fact and steal all that he has built. His only crime, as far as he can see, is working hard and being honest, just as his father had taught him. Now, he and his family are essentially fugitives, fleeing from people who are willing to destroy him for doing just that. Simon is, by nature, a man slow to anger. However, spark is progressing quickly to flame. He is being forced to deal with the reality that, no matter how far he may run, he will be forever looking over his shoulder and waiting for the sword to strike. He will no longer have a full say on the direction that his life or those of his family members will take, at least not in this lifetime—a lifetime of building, all wiped out in no time by a couple of jackals. The lives he has saved or changed by his benevolence count for nothing. The battles that he championed for the sake of others as a City Elder are now meaningless as far as he is concerned. Who fights for *him* now? His wife, his boys, and he are now unjustly and forever branded outcasts. Worse yet, he will never know from which direction his enemies may come. Increasingly, he feels deeply that life is not only unfair, but it is a cruel hoax—a bad joke. Somebody needs to pay. He deserves the chance to get even. He deserves justice. Who can argue the fact? Who wouldn't take such a matter into their own hands? Yet, the true fact of the matter is that his priority has to be

The Cyrenian

escaping his nemeses, at least for now. The thought only fuels the fact that Simon is angry. Very angry. Angry enough to kill.

He thinks about what Chana might say at a moment like this one. Her father had been a rabbi from the tribe of Levi. She grew up in the shadow of generations of high priests. She would surely remind him of the lessons from the Holy Scriptures and the Commandments that they were raised to keep. While Simon has deep respect for his wife's heritage and his parent's Hellenistic-Jewish roots, he is not one who is personally deeply convicted when it comes to an unconditional belief in God. As far as he is concerned, if God truly is God and the Jews His "chosen," then the trials and tribulations that he sees and lives through daily shouldn't exist. The Jews would rule always and be free always. He has heard his share of stories, prophecies, and promises; in fact, he is surprisingly well-versed in the scriptures as well. He has seen more than his share of people dying in despair, clinging to this "desert prophet hope" amid lives of bondage and oppression, leaving him even more jaded. This is even more true now that Rome is their conqueror. As if another cruel trick is being played on him, Rome is the reason that he finds himself on the run. Making his case for skepticism even more strong is the fact that he is a successful man of business. As such, he truly believes that you make your own luck in life. Your choices and work ethics are where your faith belongs. In his mind, wise choices and shrewd moves are the order of the day. The power to succeed in life is inside one's own self. This is the only thing that you control and the only thing you need to know. He has lived it. He has proven it. As far as he is concerned, anything else is a myth, a tale, something for the gullible losers to cling to out of desperation; or use as their excuse for their failures. After all, they need to find SOME reason for living—right?

Speaking of the gullible, Simon is also well-versed in the money-exchange business. He sees every day how the moneychangers set up shop in the very Temple where the Jews believe God has His residence. He also knows very well how these same "men of God" rob other men as well as the poor by manipulating exchange rates and prices for sacrificial animals to make a profit for themselves. Worse, they are making that profit on the backs of people. Poor people, who are obligated to spend what they don't have to gain atonement for their "sins." The whole thing has left him quite jaded. All told, in Simon's mind, God is either a myth or asleep. He has decided that he will take his own chances and follow his gut on things. This philosophy has worked best for him so far, so why change it?

Simon takes one last, long look around and tries his best to center himself. He mounts his horse and rides the full expanse of the property one last time, stopping to bid farewell to his servants as he goes. Once on the road to Porcius' house, he promises himself not to look behind him. It is a promise he keeps.

Simon and Porcius complete the final formalities of the sale quickly. Simon must meet his ship, which will be sailing that evening with the tide. Porcius manages to get him to tarry for a final toast.

"I wish you well in your new venture, Simon. I only wish you would clue me in on it, though. It must be quite lucrative for you to leave everything behind you! I admit, my curiosity has got the best of me," he says to Simon, raising his cup in tribute.

"Maybe when I return to collect my remaining 25 percent payment on the property, I'll have something else to entice you with!" Simon jokes, all the while knowing that it is money that he will likely never see.

They drink their cups, and Simon prepares to leave. He says to his now-former adversary, "The estate is a grand lady. Treat her and all who work for her well, and she will do the same for you. I wish you good luck also, Porcius."

As the two men part company, each momentarily wonders in their minds how and why they waited so long to make peace between them. Even though they have spent almost their entire relationship at odds and in distrust, there is a strange mutual feeling that they will both somehow miss the game. Somehow, in a curious way, they are a part of each other.

After meeting the servants waiting at the dock, Simon oversees the loading of his possessions aboard the ship that will take him to Caesarea Maritima. Unlike the passage that he arranged for his family, his journey will be far less comfortable. This ship does not have a cabin like the one that ferried his loved ones. He will have to live and sleep on the deck along with the crew and the other passengers. He has done this before, but he is less than enthusiastic about spending the next ten or so days in the cramped and noisy environment. If he had had more time, he could have booked passage on a better ship. But unfortunately, time is a luxury he doesn't have. Besides, it is getting close to the end of the travel season on the Mediterranean. As fall and winter approach, storm conditions prevail, making safe transit all but impossible. Most every vessel will soon be putting into ports until the spring, shutting down the sea-going highways. Simon hopes that he will get in under the wire and avoid rough seas on this trip. For a moment, he even considers praying about it.

Simon bids the last of his servants a fond farewell and goes to stake out his claim on the best possible spot-on board. Fittingly, the weather is stellar, as if Cyrene is giving a final tribute to her native son. As the ship sets sail, Simon fights back the urge to yield to his inner emotions and let tears flow. Instead, he chooses to let the sun, the ocean breeze, and the passing scenery minister to his troubled soul.

CHAPTER 20. NEW ARRIVALS

The nearly three-day trek to Capernaum is almost over, the end of which for Chana and the family cannot come too soon. The hot days, the cold nights, and the general discomfort of sleeping on the hard, earthen floor of their tents has taken its toll on the bodies and the dispositions of all the parties involved. However, there is a definite lifting of the moods as the village of Capernaum and the glistening Sea of Galilee come into view.

Alexander queries his mother. "How will we find your cousin once we get there?"

Chana replies, "We will find her through the Synagogue. We have a standing pact that we will always find each other that way whether we come here or she comes to Cyrene. The rabbi will know where she is."

Rufus then asks, "Will she remember you? You said that it has been many years since you have seen each other. Before we were born even!"

Chana laughs, "You were both very small, but you were here. Besides, I haven't changed THAT much! I am sure that she hasn't either."

Menachem opens up, "Will she be able to accommodate Gideon and myself, or should we look to find an inn once we arrive?"

The Cyrenian

Chana replies in an assuring manner, "She is married to the main steward of King Herod Antipas. She lives very well, indeed. My guess is that her home outside of the palace will be large and most accommodating, which is why she has sent many an invitation for the entire family to come for an extended visit on several occasions. We have always had a standing invitation for Passover, so I assume we'll all be just fine."

Before long, the group finds themselves on the shores of the sleepy fishing village. How different it is from the city that they have just left behind. It is smaller by far and much less active. However, the quiet calm is, at the same time, a welcome change of pace. In addition, the natural beauty of the area is very easy to fall in love with. The gentle lapping of the waters invites one to rest and regroup. But first things first.

"Menachem," Chana calls, "come with me to the synagogue. Boys, stay here and watch our belongings until we return."

The boys acknowledge and proceed to walk cheerfully into the waters without a moment of hesitation. The synagogue is close by and easy to spot as it is taller than most of the houses. Chana and Menachem are greeted by the rabbi as they enter the tall and imposing doorway.

"How may I help you?" he asked.

Chana answered, "We have arrived just now from Cyrene. I am Chana from the House of Simon. My lineage is of the tribe of Levi. This is Menachem, my steward, guardian, and family friend. We are here seeking your help in locating my cousin Joanna, whose husband Chuza is the chief steward to King Herod Antipas. She told me that you would know where to find her."

The rabbi nods his head. "She is well known to us and has often spoken of you. You are just as she described you. She lives not far from here in Gennesaret. I can arrange for one of our young men to escort you to her house if you like."

"I would greatly appreciate that," Chana replies with gratitude.

"Very well then. Rest yourselves while I fetch him," the rabbi says with a smile. Soon, they depart with the young man, Benjamin by name, in the lead. He is a friendly type and is eager to learn more about his charges.

"Have you been here before?" he asks.

Chana says, "Not in many years. This is the very first time for my sons."

Benjamin smiles, "I have lived here all my life. I've always wanted to see Cyrene. I've heard so many stories from the merchants as their caravans pass through. Is it as fabulous as they say it is?" he asks.

"It is a fabulous city indeed, steeped in rich culture and history. You must visit someday," Menachem answers.

"I will someday soon, for sure. Who knows, I might even move there! So, what brings you to our little village? Stories of the rabbi from Nazareth, perhaps?" Benjamin asked.

"Who?" Alexander queries.

"Yeshua of Nazareth. He is rumored to be the Messiah that was spoken of in the book of Isaiah. I'm not sure about all that part, but he is unlike any man I've ever seen or heard of. He has done things that defy understanding. He has healed multitudes of sick people with a mere touch of his hand. He has made a well-known local paralyzed man walk. He has even cast unclean spirits out of tormented people."

"Rubbish!" exclaims Menachem. "I've heard of these types of magician's tricks before. Every time, the people would make the same claim that 'the Messiah has come,' and then, in the end, more evil than good came out of these encounters. My advice to you is, don't get caught up in the hysteria." Benjamin falls silent for a moment as he didn't expect Menachem's reaction. In Capernaum and all over Galilee, Yeshua's fame is the talk of the town. In a town this small, there is no hiding these kinds of happenings. Everybody knows everybody as well as their situations, so it is hard to discount the claims.

"I know some of the people that were healed. I know that these things really happened, though I can't explain them," Benjamin retorts, trying hard to be convincing while at the same time polite as he does so. "Humph" is Menachem's last word on the subject.

Benjamin leads them through the marketplace of Gennesaret. It is bustling with buyers and sellers and full of some of the finest produce that Chana had ever seen. Her instinct to want to start shopping takes some willpower to keep in check. She makes a mental note of the best booths for future reference while they pass by. As they reach the end of the main street, they approach a comfortable-looking home sitting alone on a nice patch of property. They can also see some livestock grazing in the field. While a bit smaller, it reminds Chana and the boys of home. Benjamin points to the house and says, "Joanna lives there."

As they draw closer, a female figure appears in the doorway. In an instant, the figure begins running toward them.

"Cousin! Dear sweet Cousin!" she cries with glee.

"Joanna!" Chana yells, now running as well. They embrace and, losing their balance, fall to the ground in peals of laughter. Alexander and Rufus had never seen their mother in such a playful state and find themselves laughing out loud as well.

"Boys, come and meet your cousin!" Chana says as she brushes off the dust and tries to regain her composure.

"Boys? These are full-grown men!" Joanna exclaims, throwing her arms around both. As they look at her, they marvel at the family resemblance. She is about the same age and stature as their mother and almost as beautiful. Menachem and Gideon catch up and introduce themselves. Menachem is doing his best not to let on that he finds Joanna quite attractive. It isn't often that he's had the luxury of just simply admiring a woman. Suddenly, he realizes that he has been single for a very long time. Nonetheless, he shakes off the feeling and bows respectfully to his new hostess.

"Come in! Come in!" Joanna continues. "I can't believe that after all these years, you are finally here! Where is Simon?"

Chana answers, "I expect him to arrive anytime in the coming weeks. He's just handling some final business at home. How are things at the palace?"

Joanna stops smiling for the first time. "It's a long story, but Chuza and I are no longer husband and wife. He divorced me almost two years ago. I'll fill you in later. In the meantime, let me show you where you can clean up, and I will start supper. You must be starving!"

"Yes, we are!" pipes Rufus.

"Don't mind him, he's always hungry!" Alexander says, rebuffing his brother.

"Good!" said Joanna, now smiling again, "I'm always cooking!" The rest of the evening is filled with good food and good stories. The night is filled with good sleep. No rolling ships or desert floors. No schedules to keep either. Just a deep and most welcome night's sleep.

The morning finds the men off exploring the village, leaving Chana and Joanna with time to catch up without interruption. Chana does her best not to open the conversation with the questions that are burning inside of her since the day before. When the opportunity finally arises, though, she wastes no time.

"So, tell me, Cousin," she begins. "What happened between you and Chuza? Why the divorce?"

Joanna draws a sigh and begins. "It's rather complicated. I will try to explain the best way I know how. We were fine, and Chuza was thriving as Herod's right hand. He ran everything in the king's household. We had it all. Money. Power. Position. The highest social standing there was. There were many times that Herod would even actually consult with Chuza on matters of state. In time, Chuza also became Herod's envoy, speaking for him to other leaders. His word

The Cyrenian

carried the full authorization of the king. The rewards and benefits were beyond my wildest dreams. After all, I was just a young maiden when Chuza met me. I was enthralled with him, and he was smitten with me."

Chana sits in wonder and asks, "So what went wrong?"

Joanna hesitates, then continues, "I was being tormented by demon spirits. I mean REAL demon spirits. As time went on, it got worse. I couldn't function as myself anymore, and there was no hiding it. It went far beyond just my sanity. I said and did things that were not of this world. Worse, I was powerless to do anything about it. I heard stories of things that I had supposedly done that I had no recollection of whatsoever. Eventually, Chuza kept me out of the public eye—locked away in our quarters as a madwoman. I was no longer seen in court, and I felt like I was dying. Well, one day, a servant disguised me and got me out of the palace. She took me to see a man. He was surrounded by a large group of people, all of whom had various kinds of maladies and illnesses. As I stood watching, he healed every one of them. I mean, healed them completely! I was in disbelief and speechless. My servant said to me, 'You need only believe in Him, and you will be healed as they have been.' I didn't know what to think. Then suddenly, he looked at me. It was more like he looked INTO me. The demons inside me rebelled. I heard shrieking voices in my head, and I felt the heat of a thousand fires. I never knew such pain. He softly touched my head and looked into my eyes with a degree of caring that I had never seen before. To this day, I cannot find the right words to describe it. Then, with a voice as soft as his touch, he asked me, 'Do you believe that I can heal you?' I said yes. Then he said, 'Do you want to be healed?' Again, I said yes. He held onto me and said, 'Your faith has made you whole. You are loosed.' Instantly, I fell to the ground as if struck by lightning. He reached out his hand and raised me up. I had never felt so strong. I never felt so at peace. I never felt so free. He looked at me, smiled, and said, 'Follow me.' My life would never be the same from that day forward. I didn't even know who this man was, but I knew there and then that I would never leave his side. I have followed him virtually every day since."

Chana sits dumbfounded. She has never heard such a story. But somehow, in her heart, she believes it. After a few moments, she asks, "So how did Chuza take all of this? I would think that he would have been glad to have his wife back."

Joanna responds, "I did too. However, there were major political forces at play. You see, Chuza was torn. This man, Yeshua of Nazareth, was becoming larger than life. The Pharisees and Jewish ruling class saw him as being dangerous to the status quo. Extremely dangerous. In addition, the Romans weren't going to tolerate any disorder from the Jews, so everything needed to stay quiet. Herod had put up with Yeshua and the folklore up to now as it wasn't causing any direct harm, at least not yet. In addition, he was struggling with the fact that he had ordered the execution of another man of God, John the Baptist, while in a drunken stupor. He was manipulated into doing so against his will by his wife and stepdaughter. Chuza witnessed the whole thing. Deep down on the inside, Herod was afraid that God was going to punish him for the evil deed and might do so through this man, Yeshua. He even feared that Yeshua was John the Baptist, come back to life. These thoughts haunted him perpetually. Moreover, he could not let his feelings be known, for his own safety. Any sign of weakness could and would be exploited by his detractors. Chuza was deeply concerned for his own situation. My illness was no secret, and some in the court thought that I might be cursed. Even Chuza thought the same at first. In addition, once I was healed by Yeshua, the problem became that he had to choose what he would publicly claim to believe. Then, add to the fact that I was now going to become an open follower of this man. Overall, as much as Chuza loved me and deep down was glad to see me healed, he feared for his now vulnerable position. Herod could flip his opinion at any time, and there was no shortage of courtiers who would gladly take Chuza down to elevate themselves. He shared his feelings with me one night. He was a tortured man. So, out of love, I set him free and asked him to divorce me. It was the most logical solution. I had a ketubah as part of our marriage agreement, so I have a very substantial amount of money that has been passed to me to use as I see fit. I also gained this country property that you see here. Now, I use my means, my connections, and my finances to support Yeshua and his ministry of love and healing. Not only do I not regret doing so, but I've never been happier. The best part is, I'm not alone. I am one of several women who share a similar story. Oh, Chana, I cannot begin to tell you about the wonders that I have seen and the lives that have been saved and changed forever. I have never felt more complete!"

Chana's head is swimming from all that she has just heard. One thing is for certain, though. She wants to know more. "Can I go with you to see these things for myself? I need to experience this firsthand."

Joanna holds her hand and says simply, "Come."

CHAPTER 21. REVERSAL OF FORTUNE

Saccius and Aemilius find themselves once again on the road to Cyrene from the port of Apollonia. This trip, however, is much different than the previous ones by far. Firstly, they have never been escorted in such a way. Even though they are technically free men, they hardly feel so. They are being marched among the Roman battle group as if they are part of the ranks themselves. It is an intimidating and sobering experience. First, they find it remarkable just how quiet the soldiers are on the march. No conversations or idle chatter. Just drums and feet beating out the cadence. Under the circumstances, the two men find themselves having to be as quiet as the soldiers. On the inside, however, there is a heightened sense of anxious anticipation. There is much to contemplate. They are about to spring their trap on the unsuspecting Simon, which in the end, will make them the apex predators of the Silphium trade in the Roman world. The nearness of it all is titillating. However, they also know that they must execute their plan perfectly. The Romans made it clear to them what the results will be if their claims don't yield the desired results. There will only be one chance for success.

Drusus sends a rider ahead to inform Antonius of his impending arrival. His stomach is tightening as well, but for much different reasons. His anger and need for revenge for his best friend's death is a beast that is becoming hard to control. He will not be wasting any time getting his search underway once he gets to the camp. He is counting on the accuracy of Saccius and Aemilius' information in a huge way to speed the achievement of his goals, thus bringing this chapter to a successful close. He dares not even allow himself to think about the possibility that these men might fail him for fear of what he might do in response. He then remembers what the General had so pointedly told him about not allowing his feelings to cloud his decision-making. He draws a deep breath and calms himself down.

Before long, the battle group arrives at the Roman camp, and Antonius greets Drusus with a hearty salute and bids him welcome. "It is good to see you again, Centurion. I am also glad to see your troops. The reinforcements will be a big help in both the search and in keeping order."

Drusus responds in kind. "I commend you for the job that you have done in keeping order here under the circumstances, Commander. I know that your increased duties came unexpectedly." Turning to Saccius and Aemilius, Drusus continues, "These two men say they have information that will hopefully expedite our efforts in finding the killers. They say that a City Elder named Simon is in league with the Zealots suspected of perpetrating the ambush. They were supposedly led by the one named Barabbas. We will be seeking Simon out immediately."

Antonius' face contorts in puzzlement. "I've met this man Simon, and I must say that I am a bit surprised. His reputation is impeccable, and he in no way strikes me as being the plotting or murderous type. Are you sure?"

Saccius jumps into the conversation, saying, "People are often not who they appear to be. We know this information firsthand." It is hard to decide whether the tone of his voice is one of annoyance or of fear.

Drusus continues, "I have also been told about Barabbas. Whatever the case, we will seek Simon out at first light. In the meantime, let us get our men fed and situated. Saccius and Aemilius will share a tent with the soldiers. I want them watched at all times."

"Understood," Antonius salutes.

True to his word, Drusus, Saccius, Aemilius, and the morning Roman patrol are on the road to the former House of Simon at the crack of dawn. Saccius and Aemilius are thankful that they are on horseback this time, at least. As they tie up their horses and approach the door, they are met by one of the servants.

"How can I serve you?" he asks.

Saccius speaks first. "We wish to speak with your Master," he says.

The servant answers, "Master Porcius is not here. He is at his home in the city."

Saccius and Aemilius gaze wide-eyed at each other in confusion and shock. "What do you mean by Master Porcius?! We wish to see your Master, Simon! Where is he?" demands Aemilius, with unmistakable shock in his voice.

The servant lowers his head further. "Forgive me, Sirs; you have obviously not heard. Master Simon is no longer the owner of this estate. He has sold it to Master Porcius. Master Simon and his family left Cyrene weeks ago. We all now belong to the service of Master Porcius and his house."

Terrified at the ramifications and the possible repercussions of this news, Saccius flies into a violent rage as Aemilius stands staring in dazed horror.

"Liar! Liar!" he cries, grabbing the servant by the throat and slapping him in the face repeatedly. "You shall pay for your treachery! You are hiding him!" he screams. At that moment, Saccius reaches for the sword of a soldier standing next to him but is stopped cold in the attempt by Drusus himself. He draws his own sword and orders Saccius to stand down. Then he turns to the servant and, after giving him a moment to compose himself, calmly asks, "Where did your Master Simon go?"

Trembling, the servant stutters, "We know not where he is. He did not tell us where he was going when he bade us farewell. His family left before he did, on holidays, he said. He thanked us for our service and made us pledge to serve the new Master as well as we had served him. That is all any of us knows. I swear this truth on my life. Please, have mercy on me, good Sirs!"

The shaken man falls to the ground in tears, not knowing what to expect next. Drusus then turns to Saccius. "It seems that your suspect has fled. Or perhaps, your story is exactly just that—a story!"

"Centurion, we know this man Porcius very well. We also know where he lives. We will lead you there. Then we can all get to the bottom of this!" Saccius answers with all the conviction that he can muster.

Drusus replies coolly, "For your sakes, we had better." He orders that the servant be let alone and for all to mount up for their departure.

There is no doubt in Saccius' and Aemilius' minds that they have been had. What they cannot figure out is how Simon played them so perfectly. And so quickly. They have no reason to suspect that Simon suspected anything. Mere coincidence? Possibly but highly unlikely. Wouldn't it have made more sense to just make an offer to sell if he truly just wanted out of the business? More even than that, he wonders how and why Porcius has gotten involved to this degree. Is he the mastermind of a larger plan, perhaps? Curiously, in their last conversation, he showed little interest in getting himself involved in their plans. Now suddenly, he has beaten them to the punch on every level. Either he is an incredible strategist, or he and Simon were working together all along. Perhaps both possibilities are true. In any case, both Saccius and Aemilius now know that they are in serious trouble if they can't deliver Simon or the Zealots. Worse yet, under the current circumstances, they cannot have their conversations with Porcius privately. The underlying truths, if revealed, will only serve to paint them as frauds, trying to use the Romans for their own personal gain. Porcius would see things the same way as well, and he could seal their fate very easily. After all, getting the two of them out of the picture would work out very well for him. They will have to play this next encounter very carefully. If not for the Romans, the prudent move would be for them to cut their losses and move on. It seems that now, the option no longer exists.

They arrive at the House of Porcius to find him readying himself to go and inspect his newly acquired Silphium fields. He is surprised by the arrival of Saccius and Aemilius in the company of the Roman military. While he had expected the two men at any time, he certainly wasn't expecting their escorts.

"Gentlemen," Porcius begins, "to what do I owe this unexpected pleasure?"

Drusus speaks first, as he is now becoming tired of small talk. "I understand that you now are the owner of the House of Simon. Is that correct?"

Porcius nods, "That is correct, Centurion. The sale is completed, and the deed recorded as the law requires. Why do you ask?"

Saccius then pipes up, "How did this come to be? We are his business partners, and he said nothing to us of any interest or plans to sell his business or property. I would think that he would have approached us first." There is no mistaking the angst in Saccius' voice.

"I cannot speak for the thoughts or motivations of your former partner," Porcius responds. "He approached me on the subject. He told me that your contract with him had expired and that he was looking to sell his estate to get involved in a new venture. Therefore, we pursued an agreement, which obviously we reached."

Aemilius interjects, "This all seems to have come up rather suddenly, don't you think?"

"Again," Porcius re-iterates, "I cannot speak for Simon."

The Cyrenian

Drusus again takes control of the questioning. "Do you know where to find him?"

"No, I don't." Porcius answers, eyeing his associates warily. "He said that he was going to meet his family who were away on holiday, and that is all I know. He would not tell me where or what his new venture is. Frankly, I don't care though I was initially curious. However, I do owe Simon one final payment on the estate. It is due upon the end of the next harvest season. I am quite sure that he will come back then to collect it personally. Is there anything else?"

"We are also trying to locate the Zealots who murdered our soldiers here. There is one by the name of Barabbas. What do you know of him?" Drusus asks, now agitated.

"Nothing except the stories that have been told locally through passers-by. It seems that he is something of a folk legend. I, for one, would not risk my good name or my fortune by associating with such men. On the other hand, I have known Simon for many years. We've had our differences and had many an ideological clash over the years. However, if you wish my opinion, his view and philosophy regarding Zealots is the same as mine. I am sure of this. He's no murderer, nor would he be a party to it."

In that very moment, it suddenly becomes very clear to Porcius just what Saccius and Aemilius had meant by Simon's impending "retirement." Simon is being framed by them. He has figured it all out. He never thought that he would ever in life find himself cheering for Simon, but this very feeling is welling up inside him. He is also glad that, at least for now, Simon is a few steps ahead of them. He realizes that his two former cohorts are no longer an issue. Porcius knows now that they can do nothing to him personally without risking their own necks. He is only sorry that his wish didn't come true as he wasn't present at the very moment that they learned of the change of the estate's ownership. That would have been priceless.

Drusus, realizing that this "hot" lead is anything but, decides in his mind to withdraw—for now.

"I thank you for cooperating, Porcius," he begins.

"However, I want you to know that from now on, you are under surveillance. You are also not to leave Cyrene under any circumstances without notifying either myself or the Roman Commander in authority. Any breach of these rules will result in you being considered a fugitive from Roman law. As such, you will be dealt with accordingly. You are also to notify the same authorities immediately should Simon or any of his family come to you, especially since he has a payment to collect. Again, you will be held accountable for any disobedience. Is this understood?"

"Completely," Porcius replies gruffly. "Now, if you'll excuse me, I must attend to my business. May the gods guide you in your search."

Drusus mounts his charger and says in parting, "Remember, I expect to hear from you *immediately* if you hear anything at all. Do not disappoint me."

"You have my word, Centurion," Porcius nods in acknowledgment.

The Roman party rides off to return to the camp, and Porcius heads for the Silphium fields. As they ride, Drusus flatly says to Saccius and Aemilius, "Your value to me is rapidly beginning to diminish. That is not the position that you want to be in."

Trying his best to seem unshaken, a nervous Saccius answers, "Rest assured that the condition is only temporary. Simon is obviously on the run, but we will find him."

Drusus retorts without even turning to make eye contact, "I admire your dedication because the two of you aren't going anywhere until we do."

While he is seething inside over the overall failure of his grand plan, Saccius is mentally working overtime trying to figure out exactly how it came to its demise. Moreover, his current state of sequester is going to make any operation or retribution plan difficult, if not impossible, to execute. More crucial yet is the unknown variable of the length of Drusus' patience. The underlying fact of the matter is that they need a new plan, and they need it fast.

CHAPTER 22. THE HOME STRETCH

Simon is especially uneasy today, for a few reasons. First, there is no way for him to know if his beloved family has arrived at their destination safe and sound. He knows well that the best-laid plans are in no way a guarantee of success. He is only able to find solace in the fact that he was able to get them out of Cyrene before the walls started closing in. Then there's his own case. He goes over every nuance of the events prior to his departure repeatedly, trying to reassure himself that his permanent flight and his final destination are safely under wraps. Even as he fights to resist the onset of paranoia, he finds himself scrutinizing the movements and eyes of everyone on board the ship for any tell-tale signs that would indicate that they suspect or are tailing him. It's difficult to discern the facts though, since being a passenger on a merchant ship, he already stands out as a natural curiosity.

All of this, however, falls behind his number one concern now—the weather. The dreaded storm season on the Mediterranean Sea is soon to begin. If today's worsening conditions are an indicator, it may have just arrived. The winds and waves are quickly rising. The skies are turning ominously dark, and the light chop has now turned into ever-present whitecaps. Anyone who has experienced the fury of an angry Mediterranean knows that these are signs that are not to be taken lightly. Countless many have not lived to talk about it.

The Cyrenian

There is no mistaking the nervousness of the crew as they begin to secure the cargo and clear the decks. What makes these encounters so terrifying is how suddenly they come up. What appears to be a promise of calm sailing can become a matter of life and death in no time at all. No matter how seasoned a sailor or traveler one might be, battling a storm on the open seas is something that elicits the same levels of terror each time the situation presents itself. Adding to their woes, there are no ports between the ship's current position and Caesarea Martima. The shoreline is also a long way off.

Simon anxiously scans the deck, trying to discern the best possible place of refuge should bad come to worse. This is the primary disadvantage of being aboard a merchant ship without cabin accommodation. He tries to quell the butterflies in his stomach by thinking about the fact that he is only a day away from safely reaching the end of this harrowing experience. He also tries to convince himself that the storm will pass without coming to full strength. While walking the deck, he finds a length of strong rope that is yet unclaimed, and he tucks it into his tunic. He figures that he can use it to lash himself to the ship somewhere if necessary. After all, something is better than nothing. The captain orders the ship to be turned to take the waves head-on over the bow. To be hit by a rogue wave broadside would be disastrous, as the ship could easily capsize. Unfortunately, the move also means that they will be heading even farther away from the shore. This only diminishes the chances of survival should the worst come to pass. Simon takes a moment in the midst of the commotion to take a look in the ship's cargo hold to see if there is any safe room to spare. While he sees a few spots, he observes that the cargo is moving about according to the gyrations of the ship. To hide here would mean that he surely would be crushed by the sliding payload. He will have to take his chances on the deck like everybody else.

A couple of hours have now passed, and there is no mistaking the fact that the worsening conditions have reached a frightening new degree of intensity. The chaos on deck is now at a fever pitch as the yelling and cursing of the scrambling crew would testify. The huge mainsail is flapping out of control in the gale, and the sailors have no way of getting it under control. Even if they could grab the lines, they would be launched into oblivion by the force generated by the incessant wind. The scales are fast tilting away from the favor for those aboard. Nature is now fully in control, and her assault on the senses makes that fact undeniable. The stinging rain and spray have made clear sight all but impossible. The howling wind and the booming thunder are the only sounds that one can discern, except for the heavy creaking of a ship writhing in agony. It is progressively becoming impossible to stand as the ship is beginning to rise and fall at angles that are not meant for walking. Taking in the full scene, Simon decides that now might be a good time to secure himself. He pulls the rope he found from his tunic and spots a place along the railing that just might work for him. Bracing himself against the wind, he works the rope around the rail and subsequently around his wrist and lower arm. Unfortunately, the rope is only long enough to be used in this way. He would have much rather wrapped it around his waist if he could have. But again, something is better than nothing.

The waves are breaking hard over the bow now, and their force is sweeping the crew along the deck as if they are small twigs. The intermittent and dazzling flashes of lightning are the only way to momentarily get one's bearings or see the realities on deck. Simon, for an instant, can make out the grimace on the face of the captain as he is fighting with all of his might to keep the ship on course. His focus on the figure at the stern keeps him from noticing the wall of water headed toward him from the bow. In an instant, the ship dives deep, and Simon is hit squarely from behind by a wave with a force like none he'd ever felt before. It lifts him off his feet and over the deck rail leaving him still lashed and completely submerged at the same time. The unexpected wave has caught him between breaths,

The Cyrenian

so now he is choking and in danger of drowning. Simon feels the panic inside of him grow as he is being held underwater for what seems to be an eternity. The bubbling in his ears is all he can hear above the sound of his pounding heart. He thinks to himself, *Is this it? Is this what all my life comes down to? All the work...all the pain...all the joys and sorrows...all the victories and losses...my family...my memories, everything I've built and fought for—all snuffed out in a moment? What was it all for? What was the point? This is like some cruel joke.*

At that very moment, Simon is violently jerked upwards, and he feels an excruciating sensation as if his arm is being yanked out of its shoulder socket. As he flies over the rail, the rope that he has lashed himself to the ship with draws fully taut around his wrist and holds fast. It is both a blessing and a curse, for while he is not swept out to sea, he cannot escape his predicament. He can draw a deep breath as the ship reverses its angle and plunges into the briny waters again. Simon nervously wonders how many times he can survive the fierce, repeated dunking that he is being subjected to. He knows whatever the number, it won't be many. Simon once again endures the cycle of diving and rising while doing his very best to time his breathing to coincide. All the while, he fears that he might be separated from his arm at any moment. Another plunge and another violent rise. This time, he rises higher than ever before, his stinging eyes transfixed on the furious black heavens. A huge flash of lighting illuminates the boiling billows. For a millisecond before diving again, Simon can see the flailing forms of several unfortunates who have been washed overboard, their fates surely sealed. He has no doubt in his mind that the same waits for him. His strength is fading fast. So are his hopes. His heart sinks at having to accept the reality that he will never see his love Chana or his boys again. He wants so much to be angry, especially with God, at this moment. However, as he gets ready for what he resolves will be his final plunge, all he can do is cry out to Him, "If it is not Your will that I live, please let my family live!" The harrowing cycles continue, and Simon knows that the end is near.

The ship once again faces into the deep, this time having risen with more force than any time previous. Simon hangs weightless in space for a moment, followed by his body, then tumbling back over the deck rail again as the ship descends. The somersault ends with a solid thud as Simon lands flat on his back upon the deck. Choking and gasping, he feels himself being washed over by another wave, and he is scared that he might go overboard again. Should that happen, all will be over, as the now exhausted Simon surely will not be able to fight anymore. Simon's body is numb with cold, while at the same time, he is completely wracked with pain. He cannot move his still-lashed arm. He lifts his head in time to see a very large wave rising. He closes his eyes and stiffens up in anticipation of another huge impact. Suddenly, he feels the strength and weight of a body lying on top of him, shielding him from the fury. He cannot *not* make out a face, but the tall and powerfully built figure remains solidly in place, seemingly more than able to fight off the ferocious waters. "Who are you?" Simon cries out. The man does not answer but continues to be Simon's human shield. Finally, the physically and emotionally spent Simon can no longer remain conscious.

While in his semi-conscious state, Simon begins to experience his dreaded recurring dream. It plays out as it always does. The angry mob. The crowd noises. Most of all, those piercing, intense eyes. He hears that voice again, yelling, "YOU!" Only this time, it is different. It is louder and more repetitious. "YOU! YOU!" Simon feels something strike his leg. He wakes up with a start to find the captain staring down at him and kicking his leg to awaken him.

"So, you're alive after all," he said, his face bearing the scars of his battle with the elements. He continues, "I need every available hand to start bailing out the cargo hold! We are listing badly to one side, and we can sink if we take on any more water. We also need to hoist a new mainsail. The storm destroyed the one we had on the mast."

Simon responds, saying, "I'm afraid that I won't be much help. I believe that my arm is out of place."

He moves to get up and finds that his arm is in perfect working condition. He looks at it and moves it again in disbelief. "I was lashed to the rail, and I went over. I nearly drowned before I was thrown back onto the deck. If not for the fact that I had lashed my arm to the rail, I would have been lost!"

Simon then notices that there are no marks on his arm either. He is most definitely sore everywhere else, though. The captain gives him a most skeptical look and then says, "I only wish that some of my crew had been as wise as you were. I've lost six good men to the storm. In any case, you look well enough to get to work."

Simon's head is spinning, trying to process these events. Has he been dreaming? Perhaps he was struck by something and rendered unconscious. Then he remembers.

"Wait!" Simon started. "Someone helped me stay alive on the deck. Very tall. Very muscular. He held me down and kept me from being washed away. Does anybody here fit that description?"

The captain sneers, "If you find him, you owe him your life. In the meantime, get to bailing if you want to get to port!"

Simon does as he is told, all the while eyeing everyone aboard, hoping to spot his possible benefactor. He questions a few men who look as if they could have been capable of the deed but to no avail. His rescuer remains a man of mystery. As time passes, he plays the events over and over in his mind. Looking again in disbelief at his fully functional and unscarred arm, Simon seriously begins to wonder if the entire encounter was, in fact, all just a figment of his imagination. Maybe he simply passed out and dreamed the entire thing. There is no way that he shouldn't be severely injured after the violent ordeal. Then he thought about his prayer during the storm. A new theory begins to form in his mind. "Was the man who saved me actually a man after all?" Simon whispers to himself. The thought makes him shudder. Sure, he knows of many stories and tales about divine interventions and visitations, but he is having a hard time applying that possibility to himself. Simon has always been most skeptical about "miracles," and he knows that he will be pondering this question for a long time to come. Despite his belief in God's existence, his philosophy has always been that fate is fate, and the only variables are the moves that you make yourself. In any case, for now, it seems that God wants him to live long enough to get his destination, at least.

CHAPTER 23. SIGNS AND WONDERS

Chana is busy helping to clean up after the morning meal when she notices a handsome young man running through the pasture towards the house. She calls out to Joanna, "I believe that you have a visitor!"

Joanna comes to the front of the house to look and then says, "Oh, that's John, one of the followers of Rabbi Yeshua. They are camped nearby out in the field at the foot of the hills on the far side of the pasture."

John bounds up onto the front porch, barely even breathless from his long run. "The Master has sent me to tell you that we are to prepare to go to Capernaum this morning to heal and preach to the people. He wishes for you and the other gracious women to come as well."

Excited, Joanna looks over to Chana and says, "Now you will get your chance to experience firsthand what I have been trying to explain to you!"

Turning to John, she says, "Tell the Master that we will meet Him on the road shortly. By the way, I wish for you to meet my cousin Chana. She and her family are moving here. She and her sons will join us today."

"It is wonderful to meet you, Chana. Welcome to you and your family. We will be honored to have you join us!" John says with a most radiant smile. "I will inform the Master of your plans and see you on the road later. Blessings!" says John as he starts his jog back to camp, running just as fast as he did when he arrived.

"How pleasant he is!" remarks Chana.

Joanna answers, "They are all very nice and, at the same time, so very different from each other. But if you think that John is nice, wait until you meet Yeshua."

Chana smiles, saying, "I look forward to meeting him most of all."

Shortly after, a party of women carrying baskets arrives at the house. They all embrace Joanna and introduce themselves to Chana. While the women are all memorable, there were two from this group who stand out especially. One is Mary, who they call Magdalena, and the other is named Susanna. Mary is especially memorable, not only for her beauty but for her demeanor. She is a born leader; strong, wise, and confident while at the same time compassionate. Her "take charge" attitude is unmistakable, as is the level of respect that she garners from the other women (and some men) in the group. The story is told that Yeshua cast seven demons out of Mary. From that day forward, she has become one of the rabbi's most loyal and trusted confidants. Joanna once again formally introduces Chana to the other women and then immediately gets down to business.

"We must immediately prepare to leave. We are to meet the Master on the road to Capernaum."

With almost military precision, each woman takes her assigned place and sees to staging the necessary supplies for the trip. They have no doubt done this before.

Mary turns to Chana and asks, "Can you cook?"

Chana, almost laughing at the irony of the question, answered, "Can't we all?"

Mary, however, is surprisingly flat in her response. "While we all can cook, not all can cook WELL," she says.

"Don't worry—I can," Chana responds, desiring to convey her own subliminal message of both confidence and strength. It works. Mary gives a smile of approval that makes it clear that Chana is now in the fold.

"In that case, let's get you started. You can help in cooking the fish. The others will start baking the bread. These men will eat more than you can ever imagine, so we all are tasked with keeping the meals coming. Believe me, it is no small feat."

Chana gives a smile of acceptance and says with warmth in her voice, "I'll feel right at home then!" She takes her place at the fire with Susanna and wastes no time in getting the fish cleaned, skewered, and cooking. During their culinary duties, there is time for the women to talk and get to know one another. There is no doubt something special about this band of women.

It turns out that Susanna has much the same story as Mary and her cousin Joanna. She was healed by Yeshua from a deep, debilitating depression that began after her husband was killed by robbers a year earlier. He was a very wealthy merchant, and she is, therefore, now also a woman of means. Susanna is also a very secure and friendly type. Like Joanna, she has decided to dedicate her life and her resources to the ministry of the young rabbi. She has witnessed many a miracle in her travels with Yeshua and his followers already. She exuberantly expresses to Chana her heartfelt joy and conviction about the path that she has chosen. Chana's desire to meet this man and see these things for herself is growing by leaps and bounds. She admits to herself that if the peace and joy in these women are real, it is something that she is beginning to want for herself more and more.

Before long, the voices of Alexander, Rufus, Gideon, and Menachem can be heard as they return to the house from their meanderings in town. The smell of wood smoke, fish grilling, and bread baking has the men's senses running wild.

The Cyrenian

"When do we eat!" shouts Rufus as he hugs his now fish-entrail-covered mother, much to his repulse and surprise.

"Later, when everyone else eats my most ravenous son!" Chana says, laughing.

"There is a fig tree over there. See what you can find."

The boys run off to do just that, leaving Menachem behind, curiously scanning the scene before him. Chana knows exactly who he is looking for and giggles to herself.

"She's baking bread over there!" she says while pointing to the group of women at the baking fires. Menachem is startled by Chana's comment and tries his very best to save face after realizing that she is completely onto his interest in Susanna.

In a desperate attempt to cover his tracks, he says, "I am merely getting a lay of the land for security reasons."

Chana laughs and says, "I'm sorry. Forgive me!"

Menachem knows that he has been correctly analyzed and walks towards the women with all the dignity that he can muster. After only a couple of steps, he hears Chana call out his name. He spins around to meet her eyes. She says in a half whisper, "I think she likes you too!" Menachem finds himself smiling to the point of blushing and then abruptly wipes it off his face in order to not give away his feelings. Chana, on the other hand, laughs out loud and says, "Go on!" waving him forward towards his quarry.

Before long, the women pack up their savory wares and begin the journey to the rendezvous point and then onward to Capernaum. The weather is exceptionally beautiful and perfect for the walk. There is much excitement in the group today as the twelve chosen disciples have just recently returned from their first journey without Yeshua. This is a momentous occasion, as the rabbi endowed them with his power and authority to cast out demons and heal the diseases of those that they would encounter in their travels. The men went from town to town doing just that, as well as preaching the gospel. The townspeople, for the most part, were awed, and many became followers of this new ministry of hope and wonder. Yet there were others who viewed the twelve chosen as being demonic heretics and rejected them fully—even to the point of violence. In any case, everyone in the group is looking forward to hearing the stories that the disciples are sure to be regaling them with on this trip. Storytelling in this culture is, without a doubt, the number one form of entertainment, and these will be stories unlike any other.

The traveling bands soon meet up on the road to Capernaum. There is an infectious feeling of love and joy in the air as everyone embraces each other. As Chana, her sons, Gideon, and Menachem observe the glad reunion, the disciples all approach them to introduce themselves.

John comes up first and greets Chana again. "Chana, allow me to introduce the other followers of our rabbi to you and your family." He proceeds to move them down the reception line, where they meet Peter, his brother Andrew, John, his brother James, Phillip, Bartholomew, Matthew, Thomas, James, Son of Alphaeus (who we will call "the Lesser"), Simon the Zealot ("Zeoletes"), Thaddeus and Judas Iscariot. Chana thinks to herself, *Joanna is right. They are all so very different, yet somehow the same.* As she reaches the end of the line, her eyes meet the most warm and compassionate eyes she has ever seen. In addition, there is a smile as radiant as the afternoon sun that they are walking in. He needs no introduction.

"Yeshua," she says, finding herself irresistibly compelled to fall to her knees. She feels a gentle yet at the same time strong hand take hers.

"Rise up, daughter," he says in a voice even warmer than the eyes she has just beheld. "I am the one who is privileged to meet you!"

Chana finds her footing while never breaking eye contact. "These are my sons Alexander and Rufus and our dear friend Menachem and his son Gideon," she continues, her voice quivering ever so slightly. He proceeds to hug the boys.

"You are all fine young men. Your parents can be proud."

The Cyrenian

Alexander replies, "Thank you, rabbi, they are."

Yeshua laughs and rustles Alexander's hair. Turning to Menachem, he says, "You are a mighty man of valor. You are also a most loyal friend. You would lay down your life for them, wouldn't you?"

Menachem, amazed by the rabbi's confident insightfulness, replies, "I would, without hesitation."

Yeshua touches his shoulder and says softly, "There is no greater love."

As the rabbi turns to continue greeting his followers, he once again stops to speak to Chana. With no back story on Chana or her family, he says unexpectedly, "Don't worry, Chana. Your husband is safe and well. You shall see him soon," he says with a smile of reassurance before moving on.

Chana is taken aback. *How could he know that I was thinking of Simon at that very moment?* she thinks to herself. *This man is unlike anyone I have ever encountered.*

As if on cue, Joanna whispers in Chana's ear, "He leaves you rather speechless, doesn't he?!"

"And then some!" she says in a voice of sheer amazement.

Joanna laughs and says, "Just wait. You haven't seen anything yet! We'll be in Capernaum before sundown, in time for Shabbat. He will preach in the synagogue tomorrow. It will truly be an experience."

Chana replies, "I can't wait."

As Joanna predicted, the traveling party arrives in Capernaum during the afternoon. There, the group finds a multitude of people awaiting them, as if an announcement of their pending arrival has been broadcast to the entire region. There are shouts of adoration from the people as Yeshua and his followers make their way into town. It is a most warm welcome indeed. The disciples instinctively take their positions, surrounding Yeshua to keep him insulated from the crush of humanity, wanting to in some way touch or embrace him as they clamor for his attention and favor. As they move forward, a familiar face makes it into the rabbi's line of sight. His name is Jairus, who is the high priest of the synagogue and a high-ranking member of society. He knows Yeshua well and allows him to preach at the synagogue whenever he comes to town. Jairus is convinced of Yeshua's anointings beyond any doubt. Today, however, he is visibly shaken, and his face is one of deep distress. As he reaches Yeshua, he falls at his feet, weeping bitterly.

"Yeshua!" he cries. "My daughter is dying! She is only twelve years old! Please come to my house and heal her, I beg you!" he sobs.

Yeshua raises him up, saying, "I will come."

Jairus thanks him, adding, "We must hurry!"

The disciples are now pushing through the crowd to make a way for Yeshua to pass. Just to the side of them stands a woman who is obviously not well. She has, for the past twelve years, suffered from an issue of incessant bleeding. Her clothing is stained and matted from the odorous and clotted blood flow. In addition, she is now indigent, having spent all her money on physicians who were helpless to cure her. She has resolved to herself that the only way that she can be healed will be by the touch of the young rabbi. But alas, he has just passed her by, and the movement of the crowd is threatening to cut her off from any possibility of contact with him. In an act of sheer desperation and determination, she lunges at him with all her might. As she falls to the ground, her outstretched and straining fingertips manage to brush the trailing tail of his *taleet*. In an instant, she feels a rushing jolt of supernatural energy course through her body, which stops her rampant blood flow instantly. At the very same moment, Yeshua stops dead in his tracks.

He asks in a loud voice, "Who touched me?"

The din of the crowd falls to a hush. The people begin to look around at their peers, each denying their own culpability while at the same time waiting to see who the culprit might be. After some minutes, Peter says to Yeshua, "Master, in a crowd like this, being touched is inevitable. How can you be surprised or even ask who touched you? Maybe even one of us brushed against you."

Jesus says, "You do not understand. Somebody specific touched me, for I felt the energy leave me as they did."

His eyes then fall to the ground, where the woman is still lying. Those standing within Yeshua's gaze follow his stare and focus on the woman who, up to now, has been completely unnoticed. She realizes that all eyes are upon her. Trembling and shaking in anticipation of the Masters' response, the woman speaks up for all to hear. She is also afraid as it is both forbidden and punishable for an "unclean" person to touch a Jew, especially a rabbi.

"People, please hear me," she begins. "It is I who touched the rabbi. I have spent the last twelve years suffering with an issue of blood. I have spent these twelve years being cruelly mocked and ridiculed for this affliction for which I have no answer or cure—an affliction not of my own doing. I have been branded 'unclean' and spurned by anyone and everyone. I have been relegated to a life of sorrow, solitude, and exile. Love and relationships are things that have been forever denied me. I have had to live through a daily existence filled with unkind stares and hurtful talk that nobody thinks I can hear. I have been called cursed and accused of sins that I have never committed. I have been forced to live alone, with my only company being the constant thoughts of ending my life and, therefore, my torture. I have lost all my worldly assets, earnings, and substance in hopes that the promises of physicians and false healers might finally bring an end to my illness. But all of this changed when I heard the words of love from this rabbi. For the first time, I have real hope that my life can be different; that redemption and healing can be mine if I believe. I knew in my heart that if I could touch even just the hem of his garment, I would be healed. Please, Master, have mercy on me!" she cries, her tears falling like rain.

The hush of the crowd is deafening as everyone present awaits the rabbi's response. He kneels and, drying her stained face, softly says to her, "Daughter, be of good cheer. Your faith has made you well. Go in peace."

Yeshua continues to speak with the woman, and the mesmerized throng starts to raise their voices in praise when a man runs up to Jairus and speaks into his ear. Jairus recognizes him instantly as one of his house staff. The look in his servant's eyes strikes terror in his heart as he knows what was about to be said.

"My lord, your daughter has died. There is no longer any need to seek or trouble the rabbi. It's too late. Forgive me for having to bring you such sad news!"

Stunned and broken, Jairus looks at Yeshua, who has also just been informed of the news. Yeshua softly says to Jairus, "Don't be afraid. Just believe, and she will be made well."

The whole group continues to the door of Jairus' house. Chana and the other women seek to enter the dwelling and do what the women would normally do under the circumstances. Yeshua blocks the door. He says, "She is not dead. She is only sleeping."

Some in the crowd who have been a part of the vigil erupt in angry protest. "How can you say that?!" says one.

Another yells, "What kind of fools do you think we are? Don't you think that we know death when we see it?!"

Yet another spouts, "You are a cruel man to give the family false hope at a time like this! You are not a man of God!"

Chana fears what might happen next, but the other women seem strangely calm. Yeshua turns to the parents and says, "Come with me." He also instructs Peter, James, and John to follow also. Then he commands the rest, "Stay here." The crowd continues with the ritual public wailing that is customary upon the death of one of their own, especially a child.

Yeshua, the girl's parents, along with Peter, James, and John, enter the dark room where the beautiful little girl lay. He gives a loving look to the parents and then turns his attention to the motionless child. He takes her by the hand and says, *"Talitha cumi,"* meaning, "Little girl, arise." To the absolute astonishment of her parents, the little girl immediately begins to stir. She sits up and smiles brightly at Yeshua. After he hugs her, he turns to the awe-struck parents and says, "Give her something to eat, and tell no one what happened here."

With that, the young rabbi joins his disciples and leaves the humble abode. Though they have seen scenes of such wonder before, the disciples cannot deny their own feelings of awe that come along with each miracle, every time. As they leave the house, Chana asks John, "Does she live?"

John replies, "What does your heart tell you?" winking as he does so.

The group goes on to set up their lodging for the night. Chana is mentally reeling from all the days' events, trying her best to comprehend all that she has witnessed. As they turn in for the night, she asks Joanna with all sincerity, "What kind of man is this?"

Joanna answers, "Every time I think I can describe him, the description gets bigger. I only know that he is the man that all of mankind has been waiting for."

Shabbat morning finds the disciples and the townspeople in the synagogue once again being inspired and awed by the words of the young rabbi. Chana has heard many a sermon in her time, but nothing like this. Never has she come to understand the powers of love, faith, hope, mercy, compassion, and forgiveness in such depth. Yet, for all the intricacies of these subjects, they have never seemed so easy to understand and natural. Yeshua speaks to her heart in a way that makes her wonder why she has ever spent even a moment being confused about any of life's questions. Chana is moved and lifted to spiritual heights and a peace like none she has ever known. She is convinced to know Yeshua is to know God. He has never felt closer. She isn't alone in her beliefs. The faces of her family and the others in the congregation tell her so.

Now more than ever, Chana can't wait for her husband to return. She realizes that they have found even more than just a new home.

CHAPTER 24. ONE AGAIN

The next few days come and go quickly for Yeshua's group, aided by the fact that his ministry is perpetually in motion. As per the daily routine, Chana is going back to her work of grilling fish when she feels a strange sensation come over her. She felt the same thing in the marketplace in Cyrene when Gideon stalked her. She feels strongly that someone is watching her. She looks towards the road, but all she can see is smoke. She continues to stare until there is a break in the haze. Her heart swells as she sees the familiar form of her beloved Simon coming towards the house along with an ox cart and some bearers carrying his cargo.

"SIMON! HUSBAND!" she screams as she accidentally drops her newly prepped fish directly into flames. Susanna rescues it before it is totally ruined and watches the sweet reunion, her eyes moist with tears. Chana is running as fast as her legs can carry her, and Simon is standing before her, his arms outstretched to catch his beautiful wife after her anticipated leap. As if in a perfectly choreographed dance, the two connect in perfect stride and spin around and around in heavenly bliss. The cascade of kisses is abruptly interrupted as the smell and residue of raw fish upon Chana's person make themselves known.

Laughing, Simon quips, "Let me guess—fish for lunch?" while holding his nose.

Chana playfully beats his chest and says, "How did you guess?"

The hugs and kisses resume in earnest just as Alexander and Rufus come running to join the joyous scene.

"FATHER! FATHER!" they shout with unbridled glee. They all embrace in one giant family hug and then almost simultaneously break into tears of joy. For a few moments, words give way to touches and glances of pure love.

"We have been praying for your safety every day since we parted," Alexander begins. "God has answered our prayers. We knew that nothing could keep you from us!"

Simon looks lovingly at his now-entering-manhood son and answers, "Believe me, many forces tried. Everything from treacherous 'partners' to the very Mediterranean herself. There were many days and moments I sincerely believed that I would never see my beloved family again. There is so much to tell you. I, too, prayed for your safe passage in what seemed to be every minute of every day. I prayed that even if I didn't make it here myself, you would."

Menachem then steps into the picture along with Gideon and says, "That was never in doubt, my brother," as he embraces his friend.

"I promised you that on my very life." Simon smiles.

"Yes, you did. As always, I knew I could count on you."

Chana takes her husband's hand and speaks in a most calm, convicted tone, "We also had it on divine authority that you would arrive safe and sound."

Simon asks quizzically, "On DIVINE authority?"

"Yes, my husband," she continues. "We have come to join the ministry of a young rabbi who I believe—no, I KNOW, is the Chosen One of God. He foretold your soon, safe arrival."

Simon's face cannot mask his skepticism. "Okay, here we go. If we had a shekel for every one of these 'chosen' men, we would be rich indeed. Look, I realize that our circumstances could naturally make anyone vulnerable to anything or anyone that represented hope. However, I'm sure that he was just trying to be supportive to you based on what was obviously a conversation about me."

Chana responded, "That's just it. He has never met me or any of us before, and there was no conversation whatsoever about us or you. He just looked into my eyes and spoke about you out of the blue as we were introduced for the first time. You had to be there to totally grasp what I am trying to tell you. And there is so much more. He heals the sick and even raised a dead little girl back to life. Moreover, when he speaks, it is to your very soul, as if you are the only one in his presence. You can feel his connection to the Father."

"Wait now—hold on," Simon bristles. "This man sounds to me more like someone to be feared than trusted. I want to meet this man who has cast such a spell on you. It sounds like I've arrived just in time!"

"It is all true, Simon," Menachem chimes in, along with the vocal backing of the three boys. "This man is like no other you or I have ever encountered. Chana is telling you the truth—understating it even. I am an eyewitness to everything she is describing to you, as are our sons. There is definitely something supernatural at work in him."

Simon is taken aback by the strong display of solidarity and conviction before him. He also knows that despite the appearances and facts in question, Chana and Menachem are nobody's fools. They are not easily convinced or taken in. Admittedly, he is now becoming deeply curious, if not concerned, about this rabbi.

Chana, seeing an opportunity in the silence to break the tension, breaks in. "My dear love, there will be time soon enough for you to meet him as well as his disciples. I promise you that when you do, you'll understand. In the meantime, you have just arrived from a most harrowing trip, and we are all together again. Let us rest now and celebrate God's goodness. After all, we can now start our new life! Come and greet Cousin Joanna and meet the other ladies who are now a part of our family. They have taken such good care of us from the moment we arrived."

Simon sighs and relaxes his position. "Yes, my love. Let's do that," he says, finally smiling again. Simon must admit, he cannot help but notice the calm and genuine peace on the faces of every one of his family members. As the day progresses, that same sense is felt by him every time he meets another member of Yeshua's group. Not to mention the fact that all of the stories told by them about Yeshua and his works are always consistent.

Simon is deeply happy to find his loved ones in such a wonderful state of mind. At the same time, he is now more eager than ever to encounter the source of their new-found joy. He soon finds himself caught between wanting this rabbi to be all that he has been told and what Simon is needing him to be. Nonetheless, Simon vows to himself that he will not be an easy mark. He considers that to be his duty. In his mind, if this man is truly the Son of God, he shouldn't mind the challenge. In fact, he should welcome it, shouldn't he? Simon hopes so. He's waited a lifetime to ask God some questions. He starts to think that this might finally be his chance to get some real answers, making him even more eager to meet this rabbi.

CHAPTER 25. PIVOT POINT

Drusus is pacing back and forth inside of his tent, his temper rising higher with every step. It has been many weeks now that he has been on this fruitless mission, and the frustrations associated with goals unrealized are starting to show.

First, he is a new officer who was on his way to his first major deployment alongside generals, commanders, peers, and friends, all of whom he reveres. He is looking forward to laying groundwork for his career to rise to the top as a part of an elite collective. It now seems that his first major decision to request this mission is turning out to be a mistake. He gained some points for having had the character and loyalty to want to find the killers of a fine Roman officer and dear friend and avenge his death. Accomplishing this task, especially if done quickly, would have been a quick and solid launch for his aspirations. However, the success of his quest has been hung on the promises and claims of two swindlers who are beginning to look like they are more talk than substance. Instead of being valuable assets to his plan, thus far, they have been much more a liability and a drain on his time, energies, and resources. Worse, Saccius and Aemilius could very well end up being a permanent monument to his current immaturity in decision-making as an officer after having fallen for their empty assurances. In addition, this unproductive chase of Barabbas and of Simon has had Drusus and his division

The Cyrenian

marching and riding over the entire expanse of the region, chasing shadows while the operation takes its toll on supplies, manpower, and assets. Moreover, Drusus also has to maintain the appearance of dominance and control to the locals of Cyrene. It is fast becoming impossible to justify these elements in the eyes of those under his command. Morale among the soldiers is starting to wane, which can be a dangerous threat to both a young officer's career and sometimes his very life.

Finally, the moment comes when Drusus cannot take it anymore. He calls to the sentry outside of his tent. "Soldier!" he shouts.

In an instant, the guard presents himself. "Yes, Centurion!" he shouts in proper fashion.

"Bring me the two jackals from the prisoner tent IMMEDIATELY!" Drusus barks, obviously agitated.

"Yes, Centurion!" he shouts back as he bounds off in the direction of Saccius and Aemilius. In no time, they stand before the seething Centurion, their hands and feet bound in all of their trembling sweatiness. He moves them to the outside and calls the soldiers together in general assembly. Now pacing before a captive audience, Drusus faces the two men and begins his tirade.

"The two of you have promised me much and have delivered to me NOTHING! Therefore, I have decided to give you one last chance to save your wretched lives. You will give me your final plan here and now as to how to find and capture the Zealot Barabbas and Simon of Cyrene. If what you say pleases me, I will let you live to carry it out. If what you say displeases me, I will make sure that it will be the final time that you will ever have the chance to do so again. Agreed?"

Both men swallow hard as Drusus draws his sword and moves towards them. After a few moments of silence, Drusus looks at both men, who are now looking at each other, dumbfounded.

"WELL?" Drusus yells, raising his sword to the two of them.

"I have a thought, noble Centurion," Saccius stutters.

Drusus levels his sword against Saccius' neck and says, "Speak!"

Now sweating profusely, Saccius begins. "It occurs to me that if Simon has truly sold his property, then his Bill of Exchange must have reached the bank here in Cyrene by now for him to receive the funds from the transaction. Also, the harvest season is upon us, and Porcius said that Simon would have to return in person to collect the final payment from him for the property. I say that we approach the bank here in Cyrene. They should also be able to tell us where Simon is forwarding the money to, therefore giving us his location as well. Once we have him, we can squeeze him to get to Barabbas."

Saccius closes his eyes and awaits the verdict. Aemilius can only stand speechless, quivering uncontrollably. After a long moment of silence, Drusus stops his pacing. He gazes at the two men before him with steely eyes. Slowly, a smile comes to his face.

"Well, now!" he starts. "Was that so difficult? It's amazing how brilliant a man can be if given the proper motivation, isn't it?!" Drusus begins to laugh and to sheath his sword. The soldiers all join their commanding officer in the moment of levity and break the tension by adding to the laughter. Relieved, to say the least, so do Saccius and Aemilius. Suddenly, in a split-second flash so fast it is virtually undetectable, Drusus' sword once again leaves its sheath at blinding speed. Saccius can feel the breeze from the blade upon his skin and can clearly hear it piercing the air. He turns to his partner just in time to see Aemilius's still smiling face falling backward in a shower of crimson, his body still momentarily standing erect. His cleanly severed head hits the ground just as his body succumbs to gravity and follows suit. The collective gasp of everyone present carries far and wide. Drusus walks up to Aemilius's still blood-letting corpse and cleans his sword on his victim's outer garments.

He turns and looks at Saccius and says without any emotion, "Since I only heard one idea, I've decided that I only need one of you. Congratulations. You've bought yourself a little time. I emphasize the word 'little.' We will go to the bank together in the morning. You had better be right." With that, he orders that a very pale and shaken Saccius be taken back to his prison tent and Aemilius's remains buried.

Drusus retires to his own tent, satisfied that he has just made a major statement to Saccius and to any man in his ranks who might be wondering about his mettle. He thinks about how his act may have just solved several different issues for him.

What a difference a blade makes! he muses. He also can't help but notice the complex feeling growing inside of him. Aside from the bodily shaking brought on by the natural adrenalin rush of the moment, there is something else. His taste for blood and the power to satisfy the need for it has just grown exponentially. He realizes that he has now truly graduated to the rank of an Alpha Leader. He has, in one swift stroke, set his mark and firmly established his command once and for all. He looks at his sword with the kind of admiration one might show to a close friend. The fact is, from now on, it will be just that.

Morning breaks, and Drusus is looking forward to the trip to the bank. Hopefully, he'll get the information he needs that finally gets his mission back on track. If not, he might just have to take the opportunity to make the moment another teachable one. In fact, he may do that regardless. He'll see what happens. In the meantime, a very nervous Saccius is brought out to mount a horse for the trip into town. Drusus starts to say something to him but then decides that silence will serve to heighten the pressure and possibly yield better (or even additional) results. After assembling a squad of five other soldiers, Drusus and Saccius set off to the bank in the Temple of Zeus. He gazes across the road while passing the spot where his friend, "The Rooster," met his demise, as he has done repeatedly now during his time in Cyrene. His spine and resolve tighten up every time.

Before long, the party reaches the Temple, and they dismount to head inside to seek the scribe who would be keeping the bank records. Sure enough, he is there doing his accounting, and he looks up, startled by the imposing figures before him.

Standing up, he asks, "What service can I be of to you, my lords?"

Drusus pushes Saccius forward and says, "Speak!"

Saccius begins, "I need to confirm a Bill of Exchange issued to a man known as Simon of Cyrene by you for the sale of his property to Porcius of Cyrene. We want to know if it has been presented to another bank for the release of funds. You would have had to confirm and record the transaction, wouldn't you?"

"That is correct, good sir. Give me the timeframe of the transaction, and I will look for the record for you," the scribe answers, his eyes skittishly darting back and forth at the faces of the men. Saccius complies, and the scribe goes to another room to seek the information. The keen anticipation of everyone present rises steadily as the minutes seem to hang like hours over them. After what feels like an eternity, the scribe returns with a ledger in his hands. Drusus and Saccius both silently see this as a sign of good news. It is.

"I show here that we have recently sent a confirmation for release to the exchange in Jerusalem," the scribe reports. The hearts of Drusus and Saccius leap as both men feel as if they have just been rescued.

"How long ago did you send it?" Drusus asks, stepping forward briskly.

The frightened scribe answers, "It cannot have been very long ago since travel on the Mediterranean has been only recently resumed. In fact, they may have not yet received it in Jerusalem."

Drusus' face shows that he is satisfied with the answer. Saccius' face was one of agonized relief. The men quickly depart and head back to the camp.

Looking straight ahead at the road, Drusus says to Saccius, "You must be a real betting man. The odds as to what was going to happen to you today were not in your favor."

Saccius tries his best to reply in a relaxed and confident tone. "I was sure that we would get the answer we got."

Drusus looks over at Saccius and begins laughing out loud, "Of course you were. I could tell!" he says most sarcastically. "In any case, you might just live long enough to tell the story."

Saccius swallows hard. He asks his captor, "Now that you know where to look for him, can I be allowed to go back to Rome?"

Drusus' face morphs into one of steely conviction. "I'll decide that once we catch him and I verify that what you have told me is the truth. Until then, put the thoughts of Rome out of your mind. Be of good cheer, though, my friend. After all, you are about to get a change of scenery!" he says mockingly.

Drusus goes back to focusing on his thoughts. All in all, he could not have gotten a better answer from the scribe under the circumstances. Now that he knows that Simon is somewhere in the vicinity of Jerusalem, his search area has narrowed immensely, and his chances for success have just gone up significantly. Better yet, he can now rejoin the legions at Caesarea Maritima and operate with not only the unlimited power of the Roman forces behind him but do so with his beloved General Marcus Maximus in observance. When his moment of victory comes, the General will be there to see it firsthand. In addition, he will arrive with a budding reputation, some strong stories to tell, and a prisoner to boot. Things are decidedly starting to look up. What looked like a failure and wasted time only this morning is now starting to look more like major progress.

Saccius is deep in thought as well. He is desperately trying to figure out how to work himself out of the deep hole that he has dug for himself. He had initially hoped that he would easily be able to set the Romans off on a wild revenge-driven hunt for Simon and Barabbas, allowing him and his now-dead partner to succeed in confiscating the coveted Silphium empire, complete with Rome's blessing. Instead, he is now a captive whose very life depends on finding a man he has falsely accused, finding a murderer he has never seen, and proving that his lying account is true to the satisfaction of an officer of the most ruthless, powerful, and deadly force on earth. For a moment, he contemplates the thought that by going to a large city like Jerusalem, an opportunity to escape and disappear into the crowd may present itself—if, in fact, it is possible to escape the eyes and arms of Rome. He can only hope that what has so far been for him a charmed life stays that way.

The squad arrives at the camp, and Saccius is immediately led back to his place of incarceration. Drusus takes time to meet with Antonius privately to brief him of the upcoming changes. Afterward, he calls the troops to general assembly. After explaining the new conditions of his mission, he calls Antonius to his side and makes an announcement that he is surprised to hear.

"I am transferring complete and permanent command of this unit to Captain Antonius. I am also raising his rank from Captain to Centurion via field promotion. He has earned it. You will serve him as you would me. My unit and I will deploy to Caesarea Maritima on the next tide."

The men cheer their approval. Drusus grins at his newly promoted officer and announces to the troops, "Tonight, you may initiate your new Centurion as you see fit! Make it count, as this will be your one and only opportunity!" The order is met with howls and jeers.

Tonight, the men will enjoy a night of relaxation and revelry—something they have not done in some time. Drusus also feels that, for the first time in a long time, he has something to celebrate.

CHAPTER 26. TRUTHS BE TOLD

The sky is still dark in the early morning hours of the day when Simon and Chana hear a knock at their bedroom door.

"Who is it?" Simon calls out.

"It's Joanna. May I come in?" comes the reply.

Simon sits up and does a quick toss of his head to try to smooth his disheveled hair. "Come," he says.

Joanna enters the space, looking as fresh as someone who has been up for hours. "I just want to let you know that we have been given word that Yeshua is going to be healing a great multitude today. I and the other women, along with the disciples, will be accompanying him. I thought that you might want to join us."

He looks at Chana and can clearly see the desire and excitement on her face. He answers, "Yes, of course. I have been eagerly looking forward to meeting the rabbi, as you know. It will be most interesting to see him in action."

Joanna smiles her approval. "We leave in a few hours. You won't be disappointed, Simon," she smiles as she exits. Chana knows that she'll be needed to help with the preparations. She also wants to make sure that her boys, Menachem, and Gideon prepare as well. This is going to be the family affair she has been praying for.

The village fishermen arrive with the overnight catch right on schedule, and the daily routine of cooking begins. Chana is baking

The Cyrenian

bread today, which, for her, is a welcome break from being covered in fish essence. Before long, the food baskets are packed and ready for the trek. The sunrise reflects the morning dew and shines brightly upon the approaching rabbi and his disciples as they arrive at the house. There are the usual greetings and hugs as the groups come together. Before long, they reach Simon's end of the receiving line. Peter greets Simon with the firmest of handshakes.

"Greetings and blessings, Simon of Cyrene. I am always glad to meet another Simon, though now I am known as Peter," he says in his gruff but friendly voice.

"Greetings and blessings to you, Simon-Peter. The pleasure is mine," Simon answers while trying to equal Peter's grip. He continues to smile as he meets each disciple one by one. Curiously, however, the man he is most looking forward to meeting is not among them.

He asks without hesitation, "Where is Yeshua?"

Andrew pipes up, "He is still in the foothills praying. He spends a lot of time communing with his Father, especially when he is ready to travel and heal. He sent us on ahead, but he'll be joining us shortly."

John adds, "By the way, we thank you for sharing your wonderful family with us. You can be proud of them in every way."

Simon responds, "I am blessed indeed."

The chemistry between everyone present makes Simon feel surprisingly at ease. It is just as Chana had described in that he feels as if he has known these men all his life, though he can't explain why. It is amid exploring his new fellowship experience when he hears the disciple known as James, brother of the apostle John, call out, "Master!"

Simon spins around quickly and stands face to face with the one he has so much been longing to meet.

Yeshua immediately hugs him and says, "Blessings, Simon, on both you and your family!"

Simon instinctively puts his arms around the rabbi and feels a warmth from him like he has never felt before.

"I look forward to our walk today!" says a radiant Yeshua to Simon as he squeezes his shoulder.

"As do I," he answers as he processes the growing wave of feelings inside him.

Once again, Chana's previous descriptions of the rabbi ring true in his mind. This promises to be an amazing day. Simon returns to helping Chana. The look on his face tells her all she needs to know.

"It seems that He is as you said He would be," says Simon.

Chana answers, "Just wait."

The group begins its journey to the village of Tiberias on the southwest shore of the Sea of Galilee, approximately a half day's travel. As is the cultural norm, the men walk together ahead of the women, giving them time to fellowship and talk about manly things. As if the journey is perfectly scripted, Simon finds himself walking directly beside Yeshua in such a way that they can hold a one-on-one conversation.

The young rabbi begins, "You have been through much recently. You have had to sacrifice much to be here."

Simon is taken by the unexpected depth and insight of the rabbi's opening statement. He questions, "How can you know that?"

Yeshua smiles, "You cannot be a disciple or travel as one without sacrificing much, if not all, that you hold dear. It is required. For instance, not long ago, I went to my hometown of Nazareth, where I was raised. One Shabbat, I stood in the synagogue and read to the congregation from the scriptures where the prophet Isaiah wrote of the Messiah's arrival and mission. I then said to them, 'Today, this scripture is fulfilled in your hearing.' While they marveled at the words, they didn't believe in me because they had seen me grow up there. For that reason, they would not accept that the promised Savior could possibly be me. Ironically, those in Nazareth always bragged to the world that the Savior would, in fact, come from among them, though nobody else would believe them. When I attempted to enlighten them by quoting Scripture, their wrath was kindled to the point where they took me to the edge of a cliff and prepared to throw me off. God intervened and allowed me to walk away through their midst, as my hour to die was not yet. Learn this well, my brother, no prophet is accepted in his own country. Foxes have dens, and the birds of the air have nests, but the Son of Man has nowhere to lay his head."

Simon immediately seizes this opportunity to open a debate. "Why would such sacrifice be required by God in order to follow? We are born and raised as men to provide for our families and their futures. In fact, we are considered lower than the lowest Gentile if we fail to do so. We are even measured by this. Our status in society is determined by this. Can one not follow and serve God while enjoying that which he has worked for and wisely invested for? Is poverty and solitude the price of God's favor?" Simon queries, feeling good about his own opening remarks.

The rabbi responds in a soft but convicting tone, "One cannot serve two masters. Where your desires are is where your heart will be. One focuses on that which is most important to him. If his earthly desires are the most important, that is where his heart and mind will be. If the things of God are the most important to him, his heart and mind will be there, also. The kingdom of God is come and will last forever. If a man seeks the kingdom first, everything else will be added to his life. But the things of this world that we so desperately seek to possess will pass away. So, I ask you, which is truly of more value? What good is it if a man gains the entire world, but he himself is lost?"

Simon, in that very moment, finds himself measuring his own motivations against the words he has just heard. To his dismay, he doesn't quite know how to answer. He knows what answer sounds right, but he cannot honestly say that he fully understands the full depth of the question.

After a long pause, Simon responds, "I know that the scriptures say that one day, a Messiah will come and establish His eternal kingdom here on earth. Until then, however, this world is all we know. Is it not reasonable to suggest that a man dedicated to living a good, honest, and generous life has done well in the sight of God, especially if he labors long, takes care of his family, and helps people? Are you saying that such a man can still find himself falling short in the eyes of God, even if he keeps the Commandments given to Moses? If that is so, he cannot possibly please God, so why bother trying? It seems that his fate is already pre-destined."

Yeshua looks deeply into Simon's eyes and says with a smile, "Think of your own personal experience. Can a drowning man save himself?"

Simon is dumbfounded. The question immediately conjures up memories of the storm when he was aboard the ship to Caesarea and his near-death experience. In a millisecond, he re-lives the moment when the mysterious man saved him from drowning. Is this what the rabbi is referring to? Does Yeshua know what happened to him?

He looks down and whispers, "No…He can't."

Simon now finds himself physically shaking out of sheer wonder about this man who seems to know him in ways that can't be possible. For fear that he might be wrong about his conclusions, however, Simon resists the urge to ask the rabbi why he asked that question in particular. He fears that if it turns out that he is reading too much into the conversation, he'll look seriously foolish.

Yeshua breaks the silence, puts his hand on Simon's shoulder, and says softly, "You are carrying much within your heart. You are hungering for answers. You shall be filled. Follow me."

Still dazed, Simon looks at the rabbi's face and nods, unable to stop himself from doing so, and says, "I will follow."

"Good," says a smiling Yeshua, who then slaps him on the back and runs to the front of the pack to join his disciples. At that

The Cyrenian

moment, Simon thinks to himself the very same thought that every member in this party has thought at some time about the rabbi, even now: "What kind of man is this?"

The group arrives at their destination to find themselves facing a great multitude of people from all over the land, waiting to greet them. It is unlike any scene that Yeshua's followers, old or new, have ever seen. Most have come by boat from the eastern shore of the Sea of Galilee. There are men, women, and children of every description and creed moving toward Yeshua in a massive crush of humanity. Many of them are afflicted with diseases and ailments. There are also many who are being tormented by unclean demon spirits. The arriving disciples hardly have a moment to take in the beauty of the hillside they are standing on that overlooks the reflection of the blue sky on the lake. Simon and Menachem both are a little nervous as they watch the giant mass of bodies moving ever closer to them. The crowd of thousands surrounds Yeshua and fills the air with their praises, petitions, and wails, each one vying for even one glance or touch of the rabbi. He calmly but firmly stands in place and allows every person present to draw near to him so that they can receive their healing. Simon and Menachem look at each other in total awe as they watch cripples walk away without the need of aid. They watch as the blind are made to see and lepers are healed completely. Those who were carrying on like madmen due to their demon possession instantly are restored to placid normalcy. Whatever the malady, Yeshua heals them all. Never has anybody witnessed such a scene. When the healing is over as if by command, the crowd simultaneously sits down on the hillside facing Yeshua in hushed silence. They are waiting with keen anticipation to hear the message that the rabbi is about to impart. He raises his hands and begins to speak.

"Blessed, filled with joy, and endowed with divine favor and protection are you who are poor in spirit, for yours is the kingdom of God. Blessed are you who are meek, for you will inherit the earth. Blessed are you who hunger and thirst now for righteousness, for you shall be filled. Blessed are you that weep now, for you shall laugh. Blessed are you who are merciful, for mercy shall be shown to you. Blessed are you who make peace, for you shall be called the sons of God. Blessed are you that are pure in your heart, for you shall see God. Blessed are you when men hate you and when they exclude you. Blessed are you when they revile you, destroy your reputation, and cast out your name as evil for the Son of Man's sake. I tell you, rejoice in those days and leap for joy! You are suffering the same wrongs your fathers did to the prophets, and like them, your rewards in heaven are great! You are the light of the world. No one lights a light just to hide it under a basket. It is put on a lampstand so that everyone in the house can benefit from it. Do likewise and let your light shine by letting men see your good works. By doing this, you glorify your Father who is in heaven."

Simon finds himself hanging on every word that the rabbi speaks, even if the complete meaning of some of these ideas escapes him. They are ideas so different and so foreign. Never would he ever have thought of being poor, hungry, sad, and persecuted as being a blessing or even an advantage. He listens intently as Yeshua continues, his tone becoming more serious.

"But woe to you who are rich and are obsessed with being so. You've already received all that this world can give you. You will only seek consolation in your riches and possessions, for they will be what you trust first and turn to most. I say to these, woe to you who are full now, for you shall hunger. Woe to you who laugh now, for you shall mourn and weep. And woe to you when all men speak well of you because your fathers did the same to the false prophets."

Yeshua pauses for a moment to allow these unconventional ideas to settle. Simon also can't help but notice how clearly Yeshua's voice can be heard, regardless of one's proximity to Him. It almost seems, though, like he is hearing more from within his head than through his ears. The feeling is most uncanny. At that moment,

The Cyrenian

the rabbi speaks what might very well be the most radical concept Simon could ever imagine.

"Listen well, all who hear me. I tell you today, love your enemies. Do good to them that hate you. Bless those who curse you and pray for those that spitefully use you. If someone should strike you on one cheek, offer the other one also. If someone takes your cloak from you, be willing to give him your tunic as well. If someone steals your possessions from you, do not ask for them back. As you want men to do to you, you do likewise to them. It is no credit to you if you only love those who love you or those who do good to you. Even a sinful man can do that. When you do as I have told you here, you will become sons of the Highest because he does these things. He is kind to the thankless and the evil. Therefore, be merciful, as he is. Love your enemies, as he does. Do good and lend, expecting nothing in return, as he does. Do this, and your rewards will be great."

Simon's mind is reeling from all that he has seen and heard today. He ponders most, though, the concept of loving and forgiving your enemies. He must admit to himself that deep down inside, he is still very bitter about all that has happened to him at the hands of Saccius and Aemilius. Simon finds himself going over the list of wrongs he has most recently suffered. He has had to flee his home and the very property that has been in his family for generations. He has had to forfeit a business that he has spent the better part of his life building into a most successful enterprise. He has had to uproot his precious loved ones and subject them to every anxiety he has ever fought to shield them from, including risking their lives as well as his own in getting here. His enemies have destroyed his reputation on a falsehood. They have reduced him to a vagabond and an outlaw, with the forces of Rome now likely in hot pursuit. Almost everything that an enemy can possibly do to him has been done to him. He can't imagine anyone who would blame him for harboring bitterness towards those who have wronged him to this extent.

How could anyone not understand his burning desire for vengeance and restoration? Is he not justified in his feelings? Isn't he the one in the right? Isn't HE the VICTIM here? Yet, this young rabbi has just told him to rejoice and be glad about these injustices. He says that he should bless these agents of evil and be prepared to yield to them even more—even to the point of helping them, if need be. Simon also finds it curious and unsettling that every time the rabbi speaks, it is as if he is speaking directly to him and his particular set of circumstances. It is obvious to Simon that much more pondering and soul-searching is on the agenda for him.

Simon is not alone in his questionings. Two of the disciples, Simon Zeoletes ("the Zealot") and Judas Iscariot, are also mulling the words that they have just heard.

"I do not understand him," Judas begins in a tone of somber concern. "I thought that the Messiah is supposed to come and quickly vanquish his enemies once and for all, then set up his kingdom. Yet, instead of giving us the hope that we are about to defeat our oppressors and be forever liberated, he gives us instructions on how to be even more subservient. We don't need lessons on how to be better subordinates and slaves. We don't need to learn how to live as a conquered people. We've been living that way for generations. What we need right now is to know that he is the one who has been foretold in the scriptures and not another false prophet. I am beginning to wonder if we have him all wrong."

Zealotes replies, "I see him differently. I believe that he is a shrewd leader. He may very well be teaching us how to lull our enemies into a false sense of security until the very moment he chooses to rise and defeat them. He has only revealed himself to us so far, so I believe he is biding His time. His precepts also will save lives by lowering the chances of confrontations with our enemies. Call it passive resistance, maybe. In any case, you cannot deny the fact that he has powers that can only have come from God. You yourself have seen too much to disagree. I can't see him going down

The Cyrenian

in defeat, especially when you measure him by the prophecies. I say that we should trust, wait, and keep an open mind. I personally trust him, and I believe that he is who we believe he is. Give him time."

Zeoletes' positive views win the moment. "Maybe you are right. At least, I pray you are. We shall see," Judas concedes.

Moments later, their fellow disciple Andrew walks up and changes the subject.

He says to his colleagues, "It's late. The people are hungry, and we have nothing to feed them with. I think we should approach the Master and ask his advice."

The men agree and make their way through the crowd to where Yeshua is sitting and talking. Andrew approaches him and explains their concern about feeding the mass.

Yeshua smiles and says without hesitation, "You give them something to eat."

Puzzled, Andrew replies, "But we have only five loaves of bread and two cooked fish left with us. We will have to find somewhere to buy food for all these people. There are more than 5,000 men alone, and we must also consider the women and children."

Yeshua calmly says, "Bring what you have to me. Then make the people to sit in groups of fifty."

The men do as they are told and then take their places at Yeshua's side. Yeshua takes the basket containing the food, and then, looking up to heaven, he blesses it and breaks it into pieces. When he is finished, he hands the basket to the disciples and tells them to set the food before the people. Then, he instructs them to call the people to serve themselves group by group. In an orderly fashion, each group takes food from the basket and sits back down to eat their fill. Yeshua's group watches in amazement as the seemingly endless line of people keeps coming to the basket and leaving with food. While it should be the norm by now for them to see and even expect such supernatural manifestations at Yeshua's hand, the state of sheer astonishment that comes with each occurrence affects them just as powerfully as it did the very first time they experienced it.

Closely watching this latest miracle unfold, Zeoletes whispers to Judas Iscariot, "Do you see? Imagine how he will be able to supply his armies and sustain his people!"

Judas smiles for the first time in a while. "Yes…I see!" his previous doubts assuaged, at least for now. Little do any of the men realize that the climax of this miracle is just about to unfold.

After some time, it is apparent that the hunger of the multitude is satisfied and that they are most contented. Yeshua says to his disciples, "Take baskets and collect the fragments left by the people." They do so immediately and eventually return with twelve full baskets of leftovers. They place the baskets before their rabbi, and without another word exchanged, they erupt in a chorus of joyous laughter.

"Blessed be the name of the Lord!" they exclaim.

A jubilant Yeshua answers, "To God be the glory!"

The cool of the evening is a welcome relief from the heat of what has been a most eventful day. The breeze from the lake finds Simon and Chana sharing a quiet moment alone—which is a rarity these days. Chana holds onto Simon's arms, which he has wrapped around her, as they sit on the cool grass.

"This feels so good. I could stay just like this forever!" she coos.

"Me too, my love. At a moment like this, it is hard to imagine that there is anything wrong anywhere in the world," Simon replies, his chin gently resting atop her head.

"Someday it will be that way, Yeshua says. I pray that we live to see it."

Chana says, "After what we've witnessed in the past few days, I believe him."

Simon leans back on his elbows and shares his thoughts. "I am in awe of all I have seen and heard. I am finding it harder and harder to deny his being the Messiah. Don't get me wrong, though. I am

The Cyrenian

afraid to believe it at the same time. First, what if we're wrong and he is a fake, using tricks to fool us? In any case, no matter what happens, there will no doubt be big trouble with the Pharisees, the Sadducees, and the Sanhedrin over him. He will be the biggest threat to their power they've ever known. They will not take that lying down, to be sure. The first thing they'll do is brand him an agent of the devil and a blasphemous heretic. They'll kill him. Then, they'll go after his followers. They will see to it that his ministry dies. Literally."

Chana abruptly sits up. "How can they do that when all he does is miraculous good works? How can they deny or discount what we have witnessed and know firsthand? Besides, why wouldn't they want the same things? Isn't this the prophecy fulfillment that they have been waiting for as well?"

Simon replies, "Sadly, ambition and absolute power are the gods they worship. I've seen too much to doubt that. On the other hand, however, I can't imagine that Yeshua doesn't already know all of this and see it coming. I tell you, he knows what you are thinking before you do. It is as amazing as it is unnerving. He must have a plan."

Chana agrees. "I am sure he does." She pauses for a moment. "Do you trust him?" she asks with great anticipation of the answer in her voice.

Simon looks deeply into her eyes. "With all I am and all I have. I believe in him. I don't fully understand it, but I can't help it."

Chana's face lights up. "I feel the same way, and so do the boys."
Simon chuckles.
Chana queries, "What's so funny?"
He says, "You've always wished for the boys to study under a rabbi. Not only did you get your wish, but you've got your husband doing the same also as a bonus!"

Chana is chuckling now and throws her arms around his neck. She says softly, "It is more than the answer to a wish. It is the answer to a prayer."

The next many months pass quickly as Yeshua and his disciples travel from town to town, village to village throughout Judea and across Palestine. The days are filled with new wonders and an ever-increasing faith in God. More lessons are taught. More sick and infirmed people are healed. More blind people are made to see, and more hungry people are fed. More demons are exorcised. More hearts are lifted. Most importantly of all, hope is growing. The House of Simon has, at this point, dedicated itself fully to this Ministry of Love. The joy and the growth it has brought them all in return are immeasurable. Also growing exponentially is the name and fame of Yeshua. His teachings and his works are the talk of all the regions from Galilee to Judea. The number of his followers grows with each passing day. One hardly knows how to gauge the promise of this ever-expanding movement—or the danger. Especially now that they are on the road and close to the epicenter of their mission, Jerusalem, for the first time.

There are many mixed feelings among the group as they make camp for the night on the Mount of Olives near Bethany, a town just about two miles outside of the city of Jerusalem. Simon lies awake, weighing his thoughts and observations, gleaning from what he has seen and heard on this journey.

First, there is the senior of the twelve, Peter. A man of deep but conflicted emotions and passions, he is now most concerned about how to protect Yeshua from what he knows will be a dangerous, if not deadly, confrontation with the Jewish establishment. While on the surface, he is boisterous and almost arrogant in his confidence to stand up to anyone, in his heart, he fears for his own safety as well as that of the others in what he sees as an inevitable clash of powers on the horizon. He is also concerned for his own, now distant family should anything happen to him, as he is the only married disciple.

Judas and Zeoletes are counting down to what they believe will be the greatest overthrowing of established powers of all time. Their internalized excitement is reaching a fever pitch as they contemplate what it will be like to witness the Messiah in his moment of absolute victory, as the ancient prophecies have foretold. They picture in their hearts the Empire of Rome as well as all of their generational enemies vanquished forever and a new *king* and kingdom enthroned. Best of all, they picture themselves seated at the right hand of the throne of eternal power.

As for Andrew, James, and John, they are on fire with an intense enthusiasm for the gospel "good news" that they are bringing to the people. They are looking forward to reaching the center of the religious universe as they know it, unleashing the power of the words and the works that are Yeshua to a spiritually starving multitude in Jerusalem. They can't wait to see the resulting expanding growth of new followers of Yeshua's message, as word of mouth carries it to every kindred. They are the most excited at the prospect of meeting and shaping new disciples.

Conversely, others in the group, like Matthew and Thomas, are much more pragmatic. Matthew is especially concerned. His former position as a most reviled tax collector has given him much firsthand knowledge about the politics and power struggles at play in Jerusalem. He knows that the Jewish religious and social powers are not going to take kindly to a ministry that operates outside of their direct control, especially one that claims that its leader is the Messiah, as described in their scriptures. Blasphemy warrants the death penalty for all involved, and the Pharisees will not hesitate to use it if they feel that their power is being threatened. Then there are the Romans, who will no doubt crush anyone that disrupts the status quo as they have ordered it. They will jump at the chance to make examples of perceived transgressors just to drive the point home. In addition, they know that there are many of the people who are going to reject any form of change, regardless of their desire to see their oppression cease. As far as these disciples can see, there can be only trouble ahead. However, they also have strong faith in Yeshua and trust in him to triumph despite their fears. They've seen and heard too much to believe otherwise. They will press on without wavering. This is also where Simon and his house now stand, bolstered by the same spirit being displayed by Joanna and Susanna, as well as the other women and followers.

The group enjoys a quiet meal together to end the day. Afterward, the men sit around the fire in fellowship, as is the norm. It is usually a time for listening to profound parables and lessons from Yeshua and a time to reflect on the wonders of the day. However, tonight is different. Yeshua seems somber—sad even. It is something that everyone notices, given their closeness and devotion to their rabbi. After dinner, as is their custom, the disciples open a discussion with their teacher.

One of the disciples asks a question. "Yeshua, in the end, are there but a few who are saved?"

Yeshua answers in a subdued voice, "Strive to enter the kingdom through the narrow gate. The truth is, many will try to enter and will not be able to. Once the Master of the house has arisen and locked the door, they will stand knocking on the outside and will cry out, 'Lord, Lord, open the door for us,' and he will say, 'I don't know you...Where are you from?' They will explain, saying, 'We ate and drank with you. You taught in our streets. We even preached and cast out demons in your name.' But He will say to them, 'Depart from me, all of you, doers of iniquity. You will weep and wail when you see Abraham, Isaac, and Jacob and all the prophets seated in the kingdom of God, and you yourselves are thrust out. Those who are there last will be first, and those who are there first shall be last.'"

Knowing that what he has just said will surely do nothing but confuse and confound his listeners, Yeshua continues, "I say this to you so that you may realize that just being Jewish does not guarantee you a seat at the feast. You must be first and foremost concerned

The Cyrenian

about your own individual salvation and not everybody else's. The saved don't come in groups but rather one soul at a time. Concern yourself first with getting yourself through the door. I am the door. There is no other way inside, and to that end, religious activity is of no help. That will not bring you salvation. It's all about having a personal relationship with me. There is more going on around you that you do not know or can be explained to you for you to understand. You must call upon my name, and you will be saved. The religious elites of the day think that they will be first in line into the kingdom because of who they are and the works they do, but they will find themselves excluded. Instead, it is the Gentiles that will find themselves welcomed by God himself first."

Simon is stopped cold in his mental tracks by what he has just heard. Since the time of Moses and the Commandments, all Jews have looked to their priests and religious leaders to be saved. Therefore, the burnt sacrifices and offerings in the Temple count for so much. Each year, on the Day of Atonement, the Jewish believers count on the blood of the sacrificial lamb and the intercession and subsequent blessing of the High Priest for the forgiveness of their sins. This is always done as a people and has always been so. Individuality has never been a condition or a requirement for salvation before. Moreover, the Gentiles have never been privy to salvation at all. It has always been something reserved strictly for God's chosen. Now, Yeshua says that they've been doing it wrong all this time? While the thought of an open invitation to all to join the kingdom of God intrigues Simon and somehow even feels right, he is now more nervous than ever about the retribution they will all surely face once the Pharisees hear this doctrine. He fears most for Yeshua. Simon asks him, "How will this message be received in Jerusalem?"

Instead of answering Simon, Yeshua turns to his disciples and asks them, "Who do the crowds say that I am?"

They respond with various answers. "Some say you are John the Baptist," says one.

"Some say that you are Elijah," says another.

Yet another says, "Some say that you are one of the old prophets who has risen again."

Yeshua turns to Peter and asks him, "But who do you think I am?"

Peter responds without hesitation, "You are the Christ of God."

Yeshua smiles and says to him, "That has been revealed to you from above. That didn't come from your own mind."

Yeshua then turns to them all and says most strictly, "Say nothing of this fact to anyone! The Son of Man must first suffer many things. He must be rejected by the elders, chief priests, and the scribes. He must be killed and then raised on the third day. Looking at them all most intensely, he says to them, "If anyone seeks to carry on after me, he must deny himself, take up his cross, and then follow me. For he who seeks to save his worldly life will lose it, but he who loses his worldly life for my sake will save it. For what does a man profit if he gains the whole world but is himself destroyed or lost? For whoever is ashamed of me, and my words will find the Son of Man to be ashamed of him when he comes in his own glory, his Father's glory, and that of the holy angels. But I will tell you the truth; some of you will not taste death until you see the kingdom of God."

The disciples are most confused by Yeshua's words, as is often the case. Simon himself is deeply convicted. He desperately needs to understand this message completely. He knows instinctively, just by its tone, that this message, above all others, holds the key to Yeshua's entire ministry. He must find a way to approach the rabbi on this subject, but he knows also that now is not the time.

For the first time, Simon and the disciples see Yeshua's normally smiling eyes fill with tears. He bows head and cries aloud, "Oh Jerusalem, Jerusalem! You are the one who kills the prophets and stones those who are sent to her! How often I wanted to gather your children as a hen gathers her brood under her wings, but you were not willing!" While Simon does not fully understand what Yeshua is saying, he understands enough to know that his deep lament is somehow a harbinger of things to come. Some of the others are on the same page. Their silence is a testament to that fact. It is the kind of silence that one can feel.

After a time, Yeshua lifts his head and speaks to his disciples once more. "We are going up to Jerusalem, and all things that the prophets have written concerning the Son of Man will be accomplished. For he will be delivered to the Gentiles and will be mocked and insulted and spit upon. They will scourge him and kill him. And on the third day, he will rise again."

Again, no one present fully understands what Yeshua has just told them. He has said this very thing to them before on other occasions, and it is not any clearer to them now as it was then. Peter stands and speaks up, "Nobody shall do any such thing to you, Master. Not while I live!" Yeshua looks up at Peter and smiles for the first time all evening. A moment later, Yeshua leaves the group to go and pray. Though he does not yet know the sequence of events to come, Simon is sure of one thing—the game is about to change.

CHAPTER 27. "...AND AGAINST SPIRITUAL WICKEDNESS IN HIGH PLACES" (EPHESIANS 6:12, NKJV).

King Herod Antipas is most definitely uneasy as he paces the terrace of his ornate and sprawling Jerusalem palace. He would so much rather be in his palace-on-the-sea in Caesarea Maritima, where the sea breezes and the waves of the Mediterranean could help serve to calm his frayed nerves. However, since the Passover season is upon him, he is required to be in Jerusalem for the celebration. It is always a trying time for him. Firstly, he is much maligned and hated by the Jewish people. Now, he must make regular public and Temple appearances, making himself both accessible and vulnerable to these same people and the powers that be. Then there are the delicate politics that are constantly at play between the Romans, the Pharisees, and the Sanhedrin, the balancing of which is always a stressful affair.

Today, however, something even more troubling is on his mind. The growing news and the fame of Yeshua of Nazareth have followed him relentlessly from his jurisdiction in Galilee to his palace in Jerusalem. This is not the first time that he or his royal lineage has had to deal with the threat of a purported new "King of the Jews," but this time, the situation is vastly different. The stories of this Messiah are hot on the lips of every Jew in Jerusalem at the height of the most religious season on the calendar. And not just some run-of-the-mill stories of inspiring oratory and promises either. Among the rumors and accounts being circulated by the people, it is said by some that the holy prophet Elijah has appeared from heaven and by others that one of the old prophets from the Torah has risen again.

Then there are the stories of the miracles. Many miracles. Mighty miracles. More troubling still is the fact that the miracle stories are consistent in their details from telling to telling, something that rarely, if ever, occurs. This Yeshua is fast becoming the people's greatest folk hero. He is daily breeding a new hope among the desperate and oppressed. This kind of hope is dangerous. It is how revolutions start and how blood gets shed.

However, as upsetting as all of this is to Herod, there is something else about this Yeshua situation that has him rattled to his core. It is being said by many that this Yeshua is John the Baptist, who Herod had beheaded, returned from the grave. This belief has spread even into his own royal court. It is this possibility, most of all, that has Herod pacing the floor. John the Baptist had openly been highly critical of Herod and his adulterous marriage to his half-brother's wife, Herodias. So much so that he had John arrested and thrown into prison. At his wife's constant insistence and plotting, Herod was forced to execute John to maintain his credibility and standing as king. Herod is tortured by his act and feels that he will be so for the rest of his life. Deep inside, he saw John as a holy man and is constantly afraid that one day, he will be punished for killing him. Now, he wonders if this Yeshua is the way his punishment will come.

Herod decides to summon Chuza, his chief steward and Joanna's ex-husband, to his presence. Chuza responds quickly and enters the room.

Bowing, Chuza says, "My lord, what would you ask of me?"

Herod puts his hand on Chuza's shoulder. "Chuza, you are my most trusted servant. I am sure that you have heard the tales about the man that they call Yeshua of Nazareth.

"Yes, my lord. Some hail him as the Messiah come at last. The rumors are that he is due to arrive in Jerusalem in time for Passover," Chuza answers with a concerned tone.

Herod shudders at the thought. "I am afraid of what may happen when he does. I see nothing but trouble. There is also…" Herod halts his speech abruptly, suddenly looking very shaken. He lowers his voice almost to a whisper and asks Chuza, "Do you think that this man could be John the Baptist come back from the dead to take his revenge on me?"

Noticing the king's distress, he answers, "No, my lord. I do not believe in such things, and if I may say, my lord, it would be better for you all around if you didn't as well. You might be viewed as being weak and unstable in the eyes of Rome and the Temple. We have enough issues with them both as it is already."

Herod nods his head in agreement. "You are right, Chuza. Once again, your council is wise. Nonetheless, I want to see this man. I want to question him. I want to see him do the things I have heard about with my own eyes."

Chuza knows that Herod will be seeking a way to kill Yeshua once he has him in the palace. He also has another reason for concern, albeit a sentimental one. Chuza knows that his former wife Joanna is a devout follower of Yeshua. He also knows that whether he believes in miracles or not, Joanna testifies and swears that she was healed of her insanity because of her encounter with Yeshua. Chuza suspects that when the rabbi arrives in Jerusalem, she will be among his entourage. That could mean that she could be caught up

The Cyrenian

in whatever consequences stem from her association with him. After all of this time, his past love for his former wife is at the forefront of his mind at the moment. He fears for her safety.

At that same moment, he has a thought. "My lord, if Yeshua is coming to Jerusalem from Nazareth, he will likely come by way of the Jericho Road along the Jordan. It would be safer for him to do that than to travel through Samaria. I could go and try to intercept him and bring him directly here."

Herod turns to Chuza and strokes his beard. "Hmmm, I do like the idea. However, I need you here. I have another thought. Go to the Pharisees and tell them that I wish to have them send a party to intercept Yeshua of Nazareth and bring him here. I am sure that they will be just as interested to meet him as I am."

"Your wish is my will," Chuza says to the now calmed king and immediately goes to carry out his orders. Though he would have preferred to go himself, he will send the Pharisees to seek Yeshua, but with a different message for him than the one that Herod had given for them to deliver. He will present the case to several of his trusted Pharisee contacts that Yeshua of Nazareth must be warned and convinced to stay away from Jerusalem during Passover while Herod is there, as Herod is plotting to kill him. This way, Joanna will be safe, and the confrontation and threat can be avoided, at least for now. These Pharisees share Chuza's same interests and concerns, so Chuza has no doubt that they will carry out his request. Most importantly, Joanna will be safe.

Chuza reaches the Temple and immediately meets with his Pharisee messengers. He gives one of them a gold medallion of his office to give to Joanna to demonstrate the credibility of the message. Chuza's position as King Herod's chief steward affords him immediate and unquestioned cooperation.

As he leaves them, he sternly orders, "Report back to me and only me upon your return."

They answer, "So shall it be."

The Pharisees make ready to set off on their quest, and Chuza returns to the palace. He can only hope that Yeshua and his followers heed the warning.

The following day, the Pharisees arrive, where Yeshua and the disciples are camped along Jericho Road, not far from the Garden of Gethsemane. The crowd of followers present is a dead giveaway. Yeshua is amid teaching his disciples in parables and notices the men. He invites them to join them in the lesson and take a seat with the group. They do so quietly even though they are temporarily the center of attention. Yeshua smiles and continues, "What is the kingdom of God like? What shall I compare it to? It is like a mustard seed, which a man took and put in his garden. It grew, and it grew, and the tiny seed became a large tree, and the birds of the air nested in its branches."

The message in the parable is one that lifts the hearts of the disciples because they understand that they are the "mustard seeds" and that they are a part of something that is going to grow into something large, wonderful, and beneficial to many. The same message is understood by the Pharisees, but instead of lifting them up, it only serves to confirm their fears.

They stand up to approach the rabbi and say, "We have been sent to warn you. You must get out and leave Judea. Depart now because Herod wants to kill you!"

With that said, one of the Pharisees asks, "Who is Joanna?"

"I am!" comes her fearless yet caring voice.

He walks up to her and takes her hand. In it, he places the gold medallion that Chuza sent for her. He says, "This is sent to you from King Herod's chief steward so that you will know that we speak the truth."

For the first time in years, Joanna finds herself rendered speechless by this act of concern from her ex-husband. She is instantly transported back in time to the days of a long-lost love. She had resigned herself to the fact that he had forgotten her a long time ago.

The Cyrenian

She had finally come to terms with that fact and was at peace with it. Now, it seems that he hasn't forgotten her or stopped caring. Not being sure what to do, say, or think, she can only manage to utter, "Thank you." She walks away to be alone with her thoughts.

The Pharisee who spoke the warning now stands face to face with Yeshua and asks him, "What message shall I bring back?"

Yeshua stands back and says in a cryptic response, "Go and tell that fox that I say, 'Behold, I cast out demons and perform cures today and tomorrow, and on the third day, I shall be perfected. Nevertheless, I must journey today, tomorrow, and the day following; for it cannot be that a prophet can perish outside of Jerusalem.' Go now."

The Pharisees instantly recognize that Yeshua is speaking prophetically, although they cannot comprehend all that Yeshua is saying. However, it's also clear to them that Yeshua has no intentions of staying away. They obey, however, and begin back down the road to Jerusalem. Yeshua knows that they will speak of this meeting to many more persons than just Chuza. In fact, those conversations are crucial to his grand plan.

Later that day, a young man can be seen breathlessly running down the road toward the camp. He pauses upon his coming up on Yeshua's entourage. After scanning the faces of all present, his eyes open wide after he recognizes Yeshua's face.

"Master!" he cries while falling to his knees, "I have been searching for you. I thank God that I have found you!"

Yeshua kneels and says softly to the young man, "Arise. Tell me why you seek me."

The man catches his breath and begins. "Your beloved friends, Mary and Martha, have sent me to find you. They were in the midst of preparing for your promised visit to their house in Bethany before you go into Jerusalem, but now something has happened. Their brother Lazarus, who we know you love dearly, is gravely ill. They are begging you to come quickly to heal him. There is not much time."

All eyes are now fixed on Yeshua as they await his response. Simon, especially, is listening intently, expecting another supernatural manifestation, as are the others. He has seen Yeshua heal people without even being where they are. Maybe he will do the same here. Instead, the rabbi says to the young man, "This sickness is not about death, but instead a chance for God to be glorified through His Son. Go and tell them I will come."

The young man smiles and immediately leaves to bring word back to Mary and Martha in Bethany.

Dusk is falling over Judea and Palestine as the party of Pharisees makes their way back to Chuza in Jerusalem. They are nervous about the time of day because the Jericho Road is notorious for bandits and highwaymen who lay in wait to plunder and rob innocent and unknowing travelers. Darkness only increases the odds that one will be a target. Generally, Pharisees and other official types are left alone, as the penalty for victimizing them is death. However, these are desperate times, and given the increased traveler traffic for Passover, the temptation is too great. Today is no exception.

High above the road on a cliff, a band of cut-throats gazes down the approaching road on their possible quarry.

One whispers, "Look, Barabbas! Pharisees are approaching. You know that where there are Pharisees, there is silver and gold!"

Barabbas groans, "And sure death for the captured thieves."

Another of the group chimes in, "This strike would be easy, though. They must make a blind bend in the road just ahead. We can easily surprise them and cut off any chance of escape. They are on donkeys, and we are on horses. We can be off and out of sight in no time with our pockets full!"

Barabbas pauses for a moment and says, "We are in desperate need of meat and bread. I could do with some wine as well. All right, a quick strike and gone then!"

The bandits ride ahead and down the slopes to take up their positions.

Barabbas calls out, "Remember, we will only take their gold and silver. There will be no killing of priests, understood?"

The men acknowledge and wait for the signal to attack.

Shortly thereafter, the priests reach the designated spot. By the time they hear the thundering of the hooves of the horses, it is too late. They are quickly overtaken and surrounded on the dusty road.

It is but a quick scuffle, and Barabbas calls out, "Give us the moneybags if you want to see another sunrise!" their long knives drawn.

The Pharisees realize that they have no choice. As they grudgingly hand over their coin-laden moneybags, one of the Pharisees says angrily, "You will die for this! You will be caught, and you will be punished, I promise you! You will not find mercy!"

Barabbas rides closer to his taunting victim. He laughs as he says, "Fortunately, it is you who have found mercy this day. Rather than kill you, in the spirit of Passover, we release you to go on your way. If any should ask you how you managed to escape your ordeal alive, tell them that Barabbas is merciful!"

The eyes of the priests widen almost in unison. They cannot believe that the man Barabbas of myth and legend really exists and, moreover, that he let them live to talk about it.

The thieves spin around to make their escape when suddenly, one of the lead riders is fatally struck in the chest by an arrow. More arrows cascade down on the marauders, many finding their mark. Within seconds the confused and shocked bandits now find themselves the ones surrounded by a detachment of the Temple Guard. Wounded and outnumbered, the remaining bandits surrender. While the soldiers take the prisoners into custody, their commander checks on the priests.

"Are you alright?" he asks the relieved and grateful Pharisees.

"We are, but how did you come to be here, especially at this moment?" says one in obvious amazement.

"Chuza sent us ahead to meet you as he was concerned for your safety on this road. It seems that his concerns were well founded, and his instincts correct...lucky for you!"

"We cannot thank you enough. And not only have you saved our lives, but you have also captured the notorious Barabbas and his henchmen!" says another of the priests.

"Barabbas, you say!" the Commander shouts in disbelief.

"I thought that he was a ghost story made up by drunken storytellers. Which is he?"

The priests point him out, and the soldier rides over to meet him face to face. He stares at the grimy, scowling face of his captive and savors the moment.

"I suppose I should thank you, Barabbas. Capturing you should get me a promotion, some gold pieces, and some time off. As for you, well, if you're lucky, Pontius Pilate will kill you quickly. But don't count on it!" he jeers, followed by an all-out belly laugh.

News of Barabbas' capture spreads quickly. Before the changing of the guard that night, the story has already reached the garrison at Antonia Fortress in Jerusalem and Centurion Drusus' ears. He is not happy. Barabbas is, after all, supposed to be one of *HIS* trophies. Now, not only is he caught, but he is imprisoned within these very walls as if to taunt Drusus. The soldiers who are aware of Drusus' personal vendetta certainly are now taunting him, which only infuriates him even more. One of the senior Centurions pokes his head in Drusus' quarters and jeers, "It looks like the Jewish Temple Guard has accomplished in one outing what you couldn't in all these months! Oh well, better luck next time, rookie!"

That is the last straw. Not wanting to start a scuffle with a fellow soldier within the garrison, he ignores the comment, grabs his sword, and asks curtly, "Where is Barabbas being held?"

"You'll find him on the lower level of the dungeon," answers the Centurion as he walks away with a smug look on his face.

A now seething Drusus storms down the dim halls of stone towards the dungeons. After descending many flights of stairs, he finds himself on the lowest level, in all of its dark, dank mustiness. He spots the jailer making his rounds and goes to confront him. "Where is Barabbas?" he asks in a most commanding tone.

"I'll lead you to him, but I must take your sword as per the General's orders. It seems that there are many soldiers who would love to dispatch him before he comes to trial, and the General wants him alive to be made a public example of."

Drusus grudgingly complies while also admiring the General's wisdom, as he knows that he is most definitely one of the soldiers that the General is concerned about. He is perhaps even the only one. The two men follow the corridor to the cell, where Drusus finally lays eyes on the man who has tormented his mind since hearing of his friend Rooster's death. Barabbas is chained to a wall, but he can walk to the cell door and confront them. He is as defiant and as arrogant as ever.

"What do you Roman pigs want now?" he bellows.

Drusus faces down his sworn enemy with smoldering eyes and answers, "I just want to look deeply into the face of the man I vowed I would kill at my first chance. You and your Zealot cut-throats brutally murdered a brother of mine in an ambush in Cyrene, and you don't know how lucky you are that you were captured before I could find you.

Barabbas chuckles and says obstinately, "So sorry to disappoint you, but know this...you are just one of many with the same mission. It's become the story of my life!"

Drusus can feel every muscle in his body tightening up, his jaw clenched to its maximum in silent rage. He retorts, "Rome will only crucify you. I promise you, that will be more merciful than if your fate was in my hands. But rest assured, I will be in the front row to watch you suffer! In the meantime, I will still pray to the gods that, by some miracle, you end up on the outside again so that I might get a second chance at avenging the death of my brother!"

The smirk on Barabbas' face starts to fade as he is sobered by the reality of the words that Drusus speaks. He decides to make the moment a patriotic one. "My only crime is avenging the deaths of the countless brothers, sisters, and children that have been murdered at the hands of Rome. You are no different than I am! The only difference is that you stand where you are, and I am in this cell. When I die, many others will rise in my place, so you are not accomplishing anything by killing me. And so it shall be until Rome falls and Israel is free!" shouts Barabbas, who concludes his rant by spitting at the men.

Drusus reaches for his empty scabbard, forgetting that his sword is not there. He screams at the jailer, "GIVE ME MY SWORD AND OPEN THIS DOOR! Let me end this fool here and now!"

The jailer responds, "If I could, I would! But he will suffer and die soon enough. In the meantime, I must go back to my rounds."

Drusus stares long and hard at the grungy rebel before him and then reluctantly follows the jailer. As he walks, still ablaze inside from the encounter, he thinks to himself, *I have one quarry left to find. I will find this Simon and make him pay the price for all that has happened. I swear it by the gods!* His steps quicken as he sets off to grab Saccius and force him to deliver or die.

In no time at all, Saccius is rudely awakened by the bursting open of the door to his holding cell.

"ON YOUR FEET!" Drusus yells at his startled prisoner. "We are going into the city, and we will not return until we have found this Simon. If we do not find him tonight, then I promise you that I will be returning here alone!"

Drusus grabs Saccius by the sleeve and pushes him out of the door. After navigating all the fortress' gates and maze-like halls, the two men arrive on the streets of Jerusalem, busy with throngs of people moving about. Drusus decides that he will start with the taverns and eating establishments. After all, a man must eat, he thinks. Whatever the case tonight, Drusus is intent on completing his mission once and for all.

CHAPTER 28. OUT OF MOURNING COMES MORNING

Yeshua and his followers have been camped on the Jericho Road now for three days. In that time, the disciples and followers have had time to rest and learn. Yeshua has shared many a parable and teaching, leaving the group both enlightened and, at the same time, bewildered. There is such depth in his stories, yet the true meaning of the lessons often escapes them. Truth be told, many also wonder about the path that they are on. Everyone knows that they are being targeted, and yet, there seems to be no effort on the part of Yeshua to go underground or flee the impending danger. Today will be another example of that fact.

Yeshua, along with Peter, James, and John, are returning to camp from Gethsemane, Yeshua's favorite place to pray. Everyone in the camp greets them and awaits Yeshua's word with keen anticipation. He sits down in the grass and says calmly, "Let us again return to Judea. We will first go to Bethany."

The command stirs up immediate anxiety among the group. "But rabbi," Thomas pipes up, "Judea is where the Jews sought to stone you, and we have just been warned by the Pharisees that King Herod himself is plotting to kill you! Why would you choose to go back there?"

Yeshua responds, again most calmly, "Our friend Lazarus is asleep, but I go to wake him up."

Not understanding what Yeshua is really saying, another disciple, Nathaniel, speaks out, "Lord, if Lazarus is sleeping, he will surely get well. Why take this dangerous chance?"

"I know that you do not understand, so I will speak plainly. Lazarus is dead. I am also glad for your sakes that I was not there so that you will have this chance to believe. Nevertheless, let us go to him."

There is a long silence until Thomas finally breaks it. Looking at his fellow disciples, he says, "Let us also go. If he is going to die, then let us die with him."

Loyalty at that moment trumps their fears, and all prepare to break camp and leave.

The one-day journey from Bethabara to Bethany is one filled with nervous chatter and prayers. At the top of the list of topics is the "waking" of Lazarus. While everyone has seen unimaginable marvels from Yeshua on this journey, this proposed miracle is one that is hard to fathom. Simon, Chana, and the family, along with Menachem and Gideon, are walking and talking together. Simon makes his ponderings known.

"I don't know what to make of this. Aside from the fact that we are returning to the hostile environment that we just escaped from with our lives, we are doing so for Yeshua to bring back to life a man already three days dead. I know that we have seen miraculous events at his hands, but this man is surely in a decaying state by now. I'm not sure if there is anything that can be done there."

Chana says soberly, "He said that this would be our chance to believe. I don't think he would have said that if there was any doubt of the outcome in his mind."

Alexander joins in, "I am with Mother on this. I don't think that there is anything he cannot do!"

Now it's Rufus' turn. "Like father said, he's got to be rotting by now. How can he possibly reverse that?"

Gideon nods in agreement. Menachem broaches the subject from another angle. True to his strategic and calculating nature, he says, "Where do we go to remain out of sight? You know that if, by chance, this miracle occurs, there will be nowhere to hide and no way to keep the story from spreading. It's not a matter of if we'll be caught, but when. I think when we arrive in Bethany, I'll continue into Jerusalem to look for some former colleagues who I know will have safe havens that they can arrange to shelter us in."

"You mean Zealots, don't you? Wouldn't that be like throwing oil on the fire? Now we would become fugitives from justice in the eyes of the Romans, who I fear more than the Pharisees and Sadducees," Simon states in a very matter-of-fact tone."

Menachem replies, "While I understand your point, I believe that getting aid from the Zealots in terms of hiding us puts us at better odds."

Simon mulls the point for a few moments and capitulates. "This is a paradox in every sense of the word. However, if you are going to go into Jerusalem, I will not let you go by yourself. You've always watched my back, and so now it's time for me to watch yours."

Alexander voices his willingness to be of service. "Father, I want to go too. Someone must watch your back!"

Chana, obviously nervous about the prospect of her son putting himself in danger, interjects. "I need you here with me and Rufus. I need to know that I have my men near me to protect me."

As usual, Chana has skillfully found a way to diffuse the situation. By making herself sound needy, she leads Alexander to a decision that she has already made for him. "Of course, I'll protect you, Mother!" he says, both boys suddenly feeling masculine and important. Simon also realizes what has just transpired and smiles at her in a way that lets her know that he knows. It is also a smile of gratitude in that she saved him from having to disappoint his son by relegating him to staying home.

The entourage arrives at the town of Mary, Martha, and Lazarus and is greeted by the sounds of wailing and crying of friends, servants, and family alike. There are a great many people outside of the home, and word gets through to Martha and Mary quickly that Yeshua has arrived. Martha, hearing this, quickly runs outside to meet him, leaving Mary inside the house. Crying and trembling, Martha pours out her grief.

"Oh, Lord! If only you had been here! My brother would still be alive if you had come sooner!"

Yeshua dries her tears and gently says, "Do not be troubled. Your brother will rise again."

The words do not seem to bring Martha any comfort. "I know that he will rise again at the resurrection, on that last day. What I am saying is that had you been here sooner, he would not have died."

Yeshua lifts her head so that he can gaze into her eyes. Lovingly, he says to her, "I am the resurrection and the life. He who believes in me, even though he may die, shall live. Do you believe me?"

Martha says to him, "Yes, Lord. I believe that you are the Messiah, the Son of God, who has come into this world. I know in my heart that whatever you ask God for, God will give you."

After embracing the rabbi, Martha returns to the house and secretly tells Mary, "Yeshua has come and is asking for you."

She quickly runs out of the house to the place where Martha has left them, as he is not arrived at the house yet. She makes excuse that she is going to the tomb to weep privately so that the mourners would not follow her. She wants to be alone with Yeshua.

When she reaches him, she falls at his feet, sobbing uncontrollably. "Lord, had you been here, you could've healed him. He would not have died, I know it! You loved him so much, and he loved you so much. Why did you not come?"

At that moment, the mourners caught up with her. They, too, are weeping. The scene was almost too much for Yeshua to bear. Deep down inside, their pain is what's affecting him. After a moment, Yeshua asks Mary, "Where have you laid him?" The mourners look at him and ask him to follow them. Yeshua begins to walk with them, with both Mary and Martha in tow. When the moments allow, one can hear strains of the same conversation repeatedly. "This man loved Lazarus so much. He has made the blind to see and healed so many infirm people. Couldn't he also have kept this man from dying?"

When they arrive at the tomb, Mary and Martha accompany Yeshua to its entrance. It is a cave with a stone rolled in the front of it to secure it. Yeshua turns to some men in the crowd and tells them to remove the stone. It is at this moment that all the faith that Martha has been holding onto suddenly takes its flight.

She exclaims, "Lord, he has been dead four days! His body is rotting, and there is sure to be a terrible stench!"

He answers her firmly, saying, "Did I not tell you that if you believe, you will see the glory of God?"

Martha bows her head in the realization of the meaning of his words. The men move the stone, and, as expected, the putrid smell instantly blankets the entire crowd. There is a collective and simultaneous gasp from everyone there. There is no doubt in anyone's mind that Lazarus' body is already in a deep state of decay. Yeshua stands in front of the opening to the tomb. He then lifts his eyes towards heaven and begins to pray.

"Father, I thank you that you have heard me. I know that you always hear me, but I am saying this aloud for the benefit of all those standing here today. In this way, they will know that you have sent me.

Yeshua pauses and takes a deep breath. Then he cries out in a loud voice, "Lazarus, come out!"

The deafening silence is only broken by another and more intense gasp of the audience as the fully death-dressed and bandaged form of Lazarus emerges from the tomb. Panning the audience, there are faces displaying every possible emotion. Most common is that of disbelief at what they have just seen. Yeshua then commands that Lazarus' death clothes be taken off him. As they remove the shrouds and bandages, disbelief gives way to jubilation at what is undoubtedly the greatest miracle ever witnessed by human eyes. Shrieks and screams of joy fill the air in a way that the previous putrid odor never achieved. There is dancing, hugging, and singing as the people give thanks to God for what they have just seen. Even more are the chants and shouts in adoration for Yeshua. There are no doubt new believers and converts who will be telling this story far and wide.

However, amid all the celebration, there are other faces also. These faces are painted over with fear. Fear that maybe what they have seen may not be the work of God but of evil spirits. Fear of the unknown is perhaps the greatest fear of all of them. Some of the people make haste to Jerusalem, only a mere two miles away, to inform the Pharisees of what they've witnessed. Their testimonies more than shake the halls of the Temple. The Pharisees quickly assemble a meeting of the council to discuss what they believe to be the greatest threat to the status quo of all time. The tone of the meeting reflects the overall panic of the parties involved.

"What shall we do with this man?" comes the lament of one of the priests, who is undoubtedly speaking for everyone in the room. "If we leave him to his own devices, working his signs and wonders, sooner or later, everyone will believe in him. Besides the trouble that that would be for us, Rome will view the situation as an uprising or even an insurrection. They will not only crush us, but we will be eliminated also. Worse yet, our nation will be eliminated forever!"

Amidst the chatter of the priests, the ears of the High Priest, Caiaphas, are burning most intensely. He stands up and commands the attention of the other subordinate priests.

"All of you are so consumed with your emotions that you were missing the point of the solution. Why would we risk the destruction of our entire nation and the shedding of blood over the works in words of one man? The solution is simple. This man must die. He must be made an example of. He must be sacrificed for the greater good of the nation."

The volume of the chamber increases almost exponentially.

"Caiaphas is right!" shouts another priest. "Why should all die because of one man? And is it not our duty to protect the people in the nation in this way? As far as I am concerned, we will be doing the work that God has ordained us to do!"

Another priest chimes in, "And not just this Yeshua, but this Lazarus too. For the more he tells his story, and the more he is seen, it will be impossible to stop the flow of Jews leaving the side of Temple and joining this man."

Again, the voices reach a fever pitch. Caiaphas once again interjects. "Priests, there is something of a blessing in this. It is only six days until Passover. Being that he is a rabbi, he will most definitely come to Jerusalem to participate in the Passover feast. This will make him easier to find. In addition, let it be decreed that anyone who knows where he is to report to us immediately. In fact, let it be known that they will be rewarded. In this way, we are sure to seize him."

The plan is ratified by the priests and set in motion.

In Bethany, a different meeting is taking place. It is one of celebration. Jesus and his core twelve disciples are in the house of Mary, Martha, and Lazarus, enjoying a restful and relaxing supper. This gathering is special beyond words because Lazarus, a man once dead, is seated beside Yeshua at the table. Martha, being the consummate hostess, is busy seeing to the success of the supper. Mary, on the other hand, is moved to serve a different way. She leaves the room and returns with a pound of a very costly perfume oil. It is sealed in an alabaster case, which, once opened, cannot be closed again. The contents must be used there and then. The value of this precious commodity is a hundred denarii (about 5800 dollars in current money). Mary proceeds to open the container by smashing it on the floor at Yeshua's feet. The fragrance of the precious oil fills the house to the point where no one doubts why it is so expensive. What she does next is even more captivating, if not curious. Mary kneels and mops the oil up with her hair. She then takes down her hair and uses it to wash and anoint Yeshua's feet. No one has ever seen such an act of pure devotion, especially at such a cost. However, of all the disciples, one is viewing this act not as one of love but one of selfish impracticality.

Judas Iscariot speaks out, "Woman, why did you do this? Don't you know that we could've sold this oil for 300 denarii and then given the money to the poor, where it could have done some real good? How wasteful you are!"

However, as always, Yeshua knows what is underneath the surface. Unbeknownst to everyone else in the room, this same Judas used to steal from the moneybox that was designated for the poor and use the proceeds for his own benefit. He has no real care for the poor. He is just trying to make himself look noble.

At this moment, Yeshua speaks up. Staring intensely at Judas, he rebukes him, saying, "Let her alone. She has kept this oil aside for the day of my burial. Understand this... the poor will always be with you, but as for me, such is not the case."

No one dares to speak after his stern rebuking of Judas. At the same time, it is also clear that no one understands what he is alluding to. With each passing day, they are unaware just how close they are to understanding these things on a level they've never imagined.

The stage is set. And so, it begins.

CHAPTER 29. MAYBE FATE WILL LEND A HAND

While the core group is still visiting in Bethany, true to his word, Simon has accompanied Menachem into Jerusalem to help seek out his Zealot contacts. Hopefully, they will also find safe-haven through them as well because, for all intents and purposes, they and their band are outlaws.

The streets of Jerusalem are packed with people. Most are from regions outside of the city who have come to celebrate the Passover. There are the sounds of various languages being spoken, and the beckoning of the merchants selling their wares sound almost like a giant chorus singing in the background. The evening is beginning to creep in, and Simon starts to wonder about their plans for the night. Even though Bethany is only two miles away, it is two miles that he would rather not walk at night. Where there are crowds, there is money and those who would gladly deprive one of it, if given the chance. Passover is also a most welcome season for thieves.

"Do you think we might find your friends by nightfall?" Simon asks his intimidating-looking friend.

"Hopefully. We are going to a place where we used to meet. Naturally, it has been a long time since I've been here, so I am hoping that things have not changed too much," Menachem answers.

Simon continues to take in sights and sounds as they continue to walk more deeply into the expanse of the great walled city. He

The Cyrenian

can't help but notice the hulking and austere Roman garrison, the Antonia Fortress. To look at it is to know that whoever is unfortunate enough to wind up behind those impenetrable walls will either die or wish they had. In Simon's mind, its very presence is enough to make one want to keep the peace and walk the line. At least it is for him. With this thought in mind, his concerns about this current mission jump tenfold.

In an effort to break his internal tensions, he says to Menachem, "Well, if I must be here, I'm glad that it's next to you, my friend!"

"Don't worry. We'll be fine. Turn here," he says as they enter an alley. Almost at its end, there is a small tavern with a man seated outside.

Menachem approaches him and says, "I've been told that you have the best cuts of meat in the city. Is it still true?"

The man eyes Menachem up and down and responds, "What cuts of meat do you need?"

Menachem answers, "I have a long list. I need many cuts."

After a long pause, the man stands up and allows the men to enter.

"See the man cooking in the back, my brother," says the man, smiling slightly as they walk in.

Menachem says to Simon, "Sit and order some wine. This may take a while," as he exits the back of the room. Simon finds a table towards the back and complies.

There are two other men taking in a walk through the city this evening, equally intent on completing their mission. Drusus, covertly dressed in street clothes, is working his prisoner Saccius to a pulp. There is not a doorway, inn, eatery, or brothel that they haven't searched for their target. And with every failure, Saccius can feel the noose tightening around his neck. He has been on borrowed time for a long time, and the sands are most definitely draining out of his hourglass. He has run out of ideas, and the odds of his success are none that even the boldest of gamblers would take. On the other hand, Drusus' thoughts on the subject are changing as well. This has been a long and fruitless journey. Each day of failure only infuriates him, and he has no outlet to relieve his tensions. His fellow soldiers find his quest a daily source of entertainment, and he is tired of being ridiculed. He is starting to think in terms of giving up the hunt and taking his lumps. At least he'll have Saccius to help him satisfy his bloodlust and enough anger left over to help him shorten the lives of any and every adversary. The idea is starting to sound better and better to him. He's also done everything he can think of to increase his chances, including putting out paid informants to help steer him to any Zealot hangouts. All to no avail.

"You have been a mistake, Saccius. I intend to correct that mistake shortly!" he growls in a low tone. Now that he has voiced his current thoughts, he has decided to carry out what he has said immediately. He has had enough. He grabs Saccius by the throat but decides that the spot they are standing in is too public for the act. Saccius begins to whimper loudly, begging for his life.

"Please! Please, Centurion! Spare me! Spare me! I will find him! I will find the Zealot, I swear!"

The pitiful cries of Saccius have reached a small group of men standing almost directly in front of them.

One hooded man steps towards the two men and says, "If it's Zealots you are looking for, I can tell you where to look. I can see from your cleanly shaved face that you are a Roman…a soldier, no doubt. For ten denarii, I'll tell you what you need to know."

"Why should I believe you, and why would you give up your own people to a Roman when I know that there is no love here for us? Besides, how do I know that this is not a trap?" Drusus retorts.

"Because the Zealots don't speak for us! They have made our lives even more difficult and have cost my people many lives because of their radical beliefs and actions. Dispatching them would be to do us a favor. As for this being a trap, how long would we live or our people live if we assassinated a Roman soldier, especially with the garrison right there?" he says, pointing at the fortress.

"As for the money, well...anything worth doing is worth doing for money, isn't it?" the man says laughingly.

Saccius then falls to the ground, sobbing like a child. He is not sure if he has been saved or condemned. Drusus pulls out his money purse and pulls out twenty denarii.

"I will make this bargain with you. You will accompany me to this place you speak of. If your information holds true, I will pay double your price. If it does not, you will die along with him. Agreed?"

The man's face lights up. He looks at his comrades, who nod emphatically in agreement.

"However, first, you will come with me to the garrison, where I will have some soldiers join me for this raid," Drusus commands. The party then sets off for the fortress.

After a painfully long time, Menachem re-emerges from the back. Simon has been frantic on the inside while trying to remain calm on the outside. Many an inspecting glance has let him know that he is being sized up for whatever reason, likely none of them good.

"Well?" is all he can muster as Menachem sits down.

"All is being arranged. It will cost us, but we will be safe. In the meantime, order something to eat. We will wait here until they return."

The men do so, and after some more wine, Simon starts to relax a little.

Drusus commandeers four uniformed soldiers and now follows the men to the place that they promised. They stop within sight of the building, where the man leading the group says, "It is that place there," pointing to where a man is sitting outside.

Drusus says to them, "You will wait here." He turns to the soldiers and says, "Two of you, come with me. The other two, give us time to work our way around to the back. When you enter, no outlaw will look to leave through the front door. As for you, if this is successful, you just may live to tell the tale!" he says tepidly to the still-trembling Saccius. The group splits up and stations themselves as instructed.

Simon and Menachem sit in repose after a good meal and raise their cups. "Here's to being friends and brothers!" toasts Simon.

Menachem counters, "No, here's to being brothers and friends!"

The warmth and bond between the two men has never been greater. There is a special moment of quiet and deep brotherly love in the exchange as they sip from their cups. In a flash, Simon replays every memory of his beloved brother and feels his eyes moistening with every pane of the picture passing in his mind. He thinks to himself how lucky he is to have such a true friend.

The calm is shattered by the man from the front door running inside with widened eyes.

"Roman soldiers are coming here with drawn swords!" he shrieks as he heads for the back door. Not a second behind him, the soldiers are on his heels. Menachem instinctively jumps up, throws his stool, and knocks over a table, which buys him a little distance between him and the charging soldier.

"Simon! Get out! Get out now!!" he yells at the top of his lungs. The flying stool finds its mark, hitting the first soldier squarely in the face, causing him to drop his sword. With unexpected cat-like reflexes, Menachem picks up the sword, and the fight is on. By this time, the second soldier engages Menachem, and the sound of iron meeting iron fills the air. Saccius manages to get to the back door on his hands and knees when he recognizes Simon scuffling with the first soldier.

"Simon of Cyrene!" he screams. "It is you!"

The man from the front door draws his long knife and mounts his own assault on Drusus and the other two soldiers. While his attack is a futile one, he manages to hold them off long enough for

The Cyrenian

Simon to make it outside. He finds a wooden walking staff on the ground, sadly, next to the body of the fallen cook. However, this is good fortune, as Simon is an expert at using the staff as a formidable weapon. Instead of fleeing, he returns to the fray to come to the aid of his dear friend. Simon handily dispatches one of the soldiers and now re-enters the room to rescue Menachem. The two men line up back-to-back, fighting with the desperate ferocity of men that must either do or die.

Saccius, standing in the back door, yells out, "Drusus! The man with the staff is Simon of Cyrene!"

With that, he turns tail and runs into the growing darkness with all his might.

Drusus now feels every ounce of the anger, the unmitigated fury he has been carrying since the killing of his blood brother, Rooster.

"Simon of Cyrene!" he bellows with a hate in his eyes that could kindle a fire, "Tonight, my brother, who you murdered in Cyrene, will be avenged! I swear it!!"

Menachem turns and sees the opening for Simon to flee through the back door. He looks at Simon and yells, "GO! GO NOW!!"

These are the last words that Simon hears him say. At that very moment, Drusus thrusts his sword. Simon's last view of his beloved steward is his grimace as the sword impales him and bursts through his chest. Stopping only long enough to remove his sword, Drusus takes off after the now-fleeing Simon.

Simon is running in a way that he hasn't since he was a youth. But all the while, he hears the breathing, the steps, and the cursing of his pursuer. Simon knows that he cannot maintain this pace much longer, and the Roman is younger and better conditioned than he is. He must think strategically because if he stays in this all-out footrace, he loses. There is an archway ahead with stairs that lead to a ledge that runs above the houses but below the wall. He makes for it and begins his ascent. Drusus sees him and follows suit, seemingly never losing a step. Simon continues at the pace now of a cross-country runner, something that he also excelled at in younger days.

"Cyrenian! You will die tonight! You cannot run forever!" shouts Drusus, sparking one more burst of adrenaline that Simon churns into speed. Drusus is still closing in on him, however, sword still in hand. Simon sees the door to a staircase that will take him up to the top of a watchtower. He can only hope the climb will drain Drusus enough so that he can escape if it is not locked. He prays with all his heart. "Lord, please don't let it end this way. Please don't take me from my family…not like this. Please have mercy on me!" He reaches the door and finds it open. He prays that this is a sign from God of answered prayer. The climb is brutal. There isn't a muscle, joint, or lung that isn't burning with searing pain. But he knows that to stop will mean the end of him. However, he notices that Drusus' pace has also slowed.

Simon reaches the top of the tower. He is gasping and wheezing for all he is worth. He can also hear the same from his counterpart below him. Drusus is still coming. *Now what?* he thinks to himself. He could throw himself off the tower and at least spare himself any torture the soldier might have in mind. The fall would be at least forty feet, not to mention the rocks and the ravine below. His death would be quick, at least. Then, he stops himself from thinking like a coward. After all, he is innocent of the charges against him. God knows that. This was all a set-up from the beginning, at the hands of some evil men. Then, his need for personal justice takes a turn toward vengeance. Menachem is dead. Dead at the hands of this crazed soldier. He was also innocent. This Roman should be made to pay for that. It should be him falling from this tower. Simon feels his anger welling up inside. After all, if these are his last moments on earth, he is going to go out fighting. Otherwise, all of this has been for nothing. Simon stands up straight and steels himself for what will be his last confrontation with this Roman, or perhaps in life.

The Cyrenian

One last time, he lifts his eyes toward heaven. "I am once again in Your hands. As You will, so let it be," he whispers in prayer.

His thoughts are interrupted by the clank of Drusus' sword, announcing that he is approaching the top. Simon's heart is pounding, and every sinew stiffens to brace him for whatever is about to transpire. It is at that moment a stiff breeze passes, and Simon hears a voice in his mind clearly and distinctly say, "Listen well, all who hear me. I tell you today, love your enemies. Do good to them that hate you. Bless those who curse you and pray for those that spitefully use you. If someone should strike you on one cheek, offer the other one also. If someone takes your cloak from you, be willing to give him your tunic as well. If someone steals your possessions from you, do not ask for them back. As you want men to do to you, you do likewise to them. It is no credit to you if you only love those who love you or those who do good to you. Even a sinful man can do that. When you do as I have told you here, you will become sons of the Highest because He does these things. He is kind to the thankless and the evil. Therefore, be merciful, as He is. Love your enemies, as He does. Do good and lend, expecting nothing in return, as He does. Do this, and your rewards will be great."

He sees Yeshua's face and hears his voice as clearly as he did that day on the Mount of Olives. He pondered that message then, and now he finds himself once again pondering Yeshua's words.

Drusus' form emerges from the darkened stairwell. He is still breathing heavily and dragging his sword. His chest heaves as he says, "Prepare to die, swine."

Simon says with newfound strength of conviction, "Would you hear the testimony of an innocent man before you kill him?"

Drusus says coldly, "I no longer care about anything except sending you to the grave as you did, my brother."

Simon starts, "I did not kill your brother or any other man in my life, for that matter. I was plotted against and betrayed by that snake Saccius who was with you, along with his crooked partner

Aemilius. I owned the most expansive and productive Silphium fields in all of Cyrene. I was a wealthy and highly respected member of society, as well as a City Elder. I unwisely took on those crooks in a pact to open an exclusive trade agreement with Rome, which they had the connections for. However, in the end, their plan was to eliminate me and take my estate. When Zealots killed your friend, they convinced the Romans that it was I and some Zealots that did it. I have been a fugitive ever since, along with my family. We lost everything and have come here to try to start a new life. Your quest for me is based on a lie. I swear this before the God of Abraham. Now, I, too, feel your pain. My friend Menachem was the brother I never had. I loved him unto death. But know this, Centurion, I did not have anything to do with the death of your friend. I would as soon that you do not kill me for something I didn't do. Most of all, my God has told me to love my enemies and show kindness in the face of hate. I seek to live that way."

Simon then goes silent as a man awaiting a verdict.

For a moment, it seems that Simon's speech is getting through to Drusus. There is a momentary calm and the look on his face of a man who is weighing things. But then the furrows in his forehead reappear, morphing into a full-blown frown.

"You talk a good game, Cyrenian, but your God is weak. No doubt you've had a lot of time to rehearse this little speech of yours," Drusus fires back.

"I believe that you are in with that rat Saccius, only unlike you, he escaped. I have chased you across the Mediterranean and all the way to Judea. I have been scorned and even ridiculed over you, and now I will have my revenge. Moreover, I will avenge my brother's death!!"

With that, Drusus swings his sword, barely missing Simon's head. Simon takes a defensive posture, knowing that his only chance is to avoid the blade until Drusus tires again. Another lunge from him misses its mark. Now fully frustrated, Drusus raises his sword and launches himself full force at his target. Simon slips aside just in time to let Drusus' momentum carry him, tumbling over the edge of the tower to a sure death, his sword falling into space. With almost superhuman speed and strength, Simon grabs the arm of the airborne soldier, almost being pulled over himself.

"Let me go, Cyrenian!" a perilously dangling Drusus yells out. "It is over, and you have won. Let me die with honor!"

Simon yells back, "There is no honor in dying unnecessarily! Let me help you. My God loves you every bit as much as he does me! He is not done with either of us yet!"

Simon feels as if his shoulder will dislocate at any moment when he is reminded of his encounter on the ship during the storm. Only this time, he knows who the rescuer is. "HELP ME, LORD!" he cries. In an instant, that same amazing supernatural presence helps him lift the flailing soldier with ease.

The two men fall to the floor, exhausted. After a time, Simon looks at Drusus, a man whose eyes betray his confusion.

"I don't understand you, Cyrenian. Letting me die would have been your best move...the perfect solution. You would be forever free. You and your family."

Simon looks intently at him and tells him, "How could I possibly be free knowing that I let you die for my own selfish gain when I could have saved you? That's how my God lives and has taught me to live. This is how I choose to live. I know that in the dark of slumber, you still see the faces and hear the voices of your victims. It is you who is not free. However, my God will free you forever. You only need ask Him to. Now, I must ask you, do you still plan to kill me?"

Drusus has been rendered speechless by Simon's testament, but his ego requires that he say something.

"Not today, Cyrenian. But I warn you, do not let our paths cross again. I am making you no promises. Now go. I'll give you a head start. I owe you that."

Simon gets up and says, "I'll take it." As he reaches the steps, he turns around to see Drusus still lying there. Simon says to him softly, "God bless you, Roman."

Drusus maintains his skyward stare and says without any emotion, "Be on your way, Cyrenian."

The walk back to Bethany for Simon is much more difficult than it was coming to Jerusalem, both physically and mentally. His limbs feel as if they are many times their normal mass, not to mention the indescribable pain he feels everywhere in his body. It is all that he can do to stay on his feet, his leg muscles trembling uncontrollably. The pounding in his head rivals the loudest drum he has ever heard. Add to that the fact that his mind feels like it might explode at any moment from all the information that is coursing through it like a giant ocean wave. It is just now settling in how close he has come to dying yet again tonight. Cheating death has almost become a full-time occupation. The Roman could have killed him. The Roman should have killed him if revenge was his mission. Why did he change his mind? Is this the power of "loving your enemies," as Yeshua teaches? Yet, there is something even heavier about these facts in his mind. Each time he replays his close encounters, he can't help but acknowledge this ever-present supernatural presence that manifests itself at the most crucial of moments…the impossible moments. But why has he been spared when Menachem, such a good man, was not? The unselfishness of his act alone should have, at the very least, earned him another chance at life, shouldn't it? Where was God for Menachem? That thought starts to rile Simon a bit. In the middle of his questioning, the grim reality of Menachem's death suddenly settles in, breaking Simon down completely. He begins writhing on the ground, wailing at the top of his lungs, calling the name of his fallen friend and brother repeatedly. As dangerous as it is to be on the road at night, Simon, at this moment, has no thoughts for his own well-being. He grieves aloud for a considerable time until the faces of his beautiful wife and his sons interrupt his thinking. He must get home. There will be time to grieve later.

He brushes the dust from his hair and his body as best he can and then continues his trek with a heightened sense of purpose. Simon breathes out loud, "I'm still here. I don't know why, but I'm still here."

CHAPTER 30. POINTS OF NO RETURN

Yeshua and his followers are on the last leg of the Jericho Road before Jerusalem. For Simon, it has been an exhausting few days, and he is apprehensive about going back to the city. Chana has been extremely attentive to him, not only because of his latest experience but because she also realizes how close she came to losing her husband yet again.

She squeezes his hand, asking, "Are you alright, my love?"

Simon answers, "No, but I will be."

Chana responds, "Well, that is good enough for now," trying her best to put a smile on. She glances at the boys who are walking together with Gideon. As one would expect, Gideon is deeply affected by the loss of his father. He has been silent for most of the walk; in fact, strangely, he has shown no emotion at all up to now. Simon, too, is concerned for him. He also wishes to deepen his relationship with Gideon and care for him as a father would.

He rests his hand on Gideon's shoulder and tells him, "It is alright to mourn. No one expects you to hold your feelings in."

Gideon looks at Simon, anger in his eyes. "He did not deserve to die! It wasn't even his fight; it was yours! But when we get to Jerusalem, I am going to join the Zealots and kill Romans!"

The Cyrenian

As Simon desperately searches his mind for just the right response, Yeshua comes up from behind them and throws his arms around the troubled youth.

"Killing only breeds more killing, my son," he begins. "Your death or death by your hand will not bring your father back. In fact, all that will come of it is more death. Death to you and likely death to everyone close to you. Listen to what I tell you now. There is no greater level of love than the kind where one will lay down his own life for that of a friend or loved one. Let your heart be at peace, for I promise you that your father will live again."

Gideon allows tears to fall for the first time since hearing of his father's demise.

"How? How can that even be possible?" he cries.

Yeshua tightens his embrace. "I am the Resurrection and the Life. Just believe in me. Will you do that?" he asks.

Gideon chokes back his sobs and says to him, "I do not understand, but I will believe in you. I do believe in you. I have seen too much for me to not believe in you."

Yeshua squeezes Gideon one more time and whispers in his ear, "You are a good son. Your father will be proud!" With that, Yeshua goes ahead to meet the twelve, who are walking in front. Simon can feel the peace that has come over both him and Gideon from the encounter. He takes comfort in the thought that all will be well somehow.

Yeshua says to James and John, "We are nearing the village of Bethpage in our descent from the Mount of Olives. Go ahead of us, and when you get there, you will find a white colt tied up. It has never been ridden. Untie it and bring it here. If anyone asks you what you are doing, tell them that the Lord has need of it."

The two obey without question or pause. They arrive at the entrance of the village and find the colt, just as Yeshua had said. As they untie it, the owners approach them and ask what they are doing.

James answers, "The Lord has need of him."

The word has spread about Yeshua coming to Jerusalem, and the owners think that it may be him needing the colt.

"We will accompany you and bring the colt with us," they say as they finish untying the young donkey. Soon, they all return to the group and put Yeshua on the donkey so that he can ride him into Jerusalem. Upon seeing him this way, everything suddenly makes sense to anyone who knows the scriptures.

It is written, "Fear not, daughter of Zion. Behold, your King is coming, sitting on a donkey colt!"

The riding of a white yet unridden donkey colt is written as a sign of the triumphant arrival of the King of Israel. Realizing this, the disciples cut down palm fronds and begin to wave them in honor of Yeshua while also laying down their clothing before him. All of them begin to shout and praise God for all the works that they have seen, for Yeshua absolutely must be the promised Messiah.

Jubilantly, the disciples cry out, "Hosanna! Hosanna! Blessed is he who comes in the name of the Lord! The King of Israel! Peace in heaven and glory in the highest!"

Many of the people that are walking with the group were present at the raising of Lazarus from the dead and have given eyewitness accounts to many others. They needed no convincing as to the identity of the King. They, too, get palm fronds and lay them down before Yeshua, along with clothing. They join in along with the disciples in shouting the words of praise. And so, the overjoyed throng enters the gates of Jerusalem, picking up more and more worshippers every step of the way. They are in no way unnoticeable. They have caught the eyes of the Pharisees especially. They are more than displeased.

They call out to Yeshua from the crowd, "Rabbi! Rebuke your disciples!"

Yeshua replies, "Believe me when I tell you, if I were to silence them, the very rocks and stones themselves would continue the cries!"

The Cyrenian

Yeshua's followers are in complete awe of what is happening before their eyes. After all the days they have spent trying to stay safe by keeping a low profile, this open outpouring of adoration is the last thing that any of them expected. It has all the trappings, sights, and sounds of an actual royal coronation procession, except that this time, they are not the spectators. Instead, they are part of the royal court. The change, while surreal, is most welcome. The disciples are buzzing among themselves with glee, but Simon notices that Yeshua's face reflects the opposite emotion. As Simon draws closer, he can hear the Master talking and weeping as if to another person.

"If you only knew, especially today," he cries, "the things that make for your peace. It is so hidden from your eyes. How I wish I could gather you in my arms. But you, who stone and kill the prophets sent to you, will see the day that your enemies will surround you and your children and close in from every side. They will level you and not leave one stone upon another, all because you did not recognize the truth when it was sent to you."

Simon realizes that Yeshua is referring to Jerusalem itself and a time to come. He doesn't ask the rabbi about his lament, not wanting to disturb his thoughts. He is uneasy, though, not knowing the answers to the new questions in his mind, especially as to when this dark time will take place.

Finally, the group arrives at the most revered spot in all Hebrewdom, the Temple, built by Herod the Great. It is a massive structure, complete with its huge, soaring marble columns and its wide courtyards. Gilded in gold, along with its polished marble steps and floors, it shines almost as bright as the sun itself. The gigantic foundation stones on which it rests cause one to marvel at how they could have ever been put in place. Here is where the Passover will culminate, with the altar for the sacrificial lamb in the forefront.

As they arrive at the entrance, they are met by long lines of people trying to exchange their currency for the official temple currency. It is mandatory to do so per Temple law in order to purchase the priest-blessed animals that will be used for sacrifice. The practice is also big business for the Temple high priests. The money changers work for them, and the exchange rates from person to person vary according to their place of origin. No matter where they are from, however, one can be sure that there is plenty of profit built into the transactions for the Temple and the changers themselves, to the point of blatant usury. And since the sacrificial animals can only be purchased from the Temple, their brisk business is guaranteed. Unlike his disciples, Yeshua is totally aware of what is going on. What happens next shocks everyone in the Temple compound to their core.

Yeshua, in a loud voice, cries out, "It is written, 'This house is a house of prayer!' But you have made it a den of thieves!" With that, the normally calm, docile, cheerful, and forgiving rabbi flies into a rage never witnessed before by any of his followers. He grabs a bunch of stout cords that he turns into a flail, which he uses to disperse the crooked moneymen. He storms through the outer courtyard, kicking over and otherwise destroying their lending stations. His attack sends the piles of various currencies, as well as the sacrificial animals, flying everywhere. Some spectators seize the opportunity to grab as much of the unexpected windfall as they can before the Temple guards intervene. In the meantime, total chaos ensues. Yeshua leaves the scene undaunted and commences a daily teaching, as unruffled as he was before the previous encounter.

While Yeshua is completely composed once again, the same cannot be said for others in the same orbit. The chief priests, the scribes, and the Temple leaders, all of which want to destroy this man, are confounded by the fact that the people are assembled and listening intently to the teachings, all of which are indisputable. This makes creating another scene most undesirable, as it would make them look like the authoritarian heavies that they are. They will have to retreat for now, but this Yeshua has now most definitely incurred the wrath of the religious elites. This act will not and cannot go unpunished. They waste no time in going to seek out the High Priest, Caiaphas, to give him a full account of the days' events.

Someone else is also deeply upset. Pulling his confidant Simon Zeoletes to the side, Judas begins an only slightly muted rant.

"He is doing us in!" he starts. "He has sealed our fate! Bad enough that he has the entire city hailing him as king, which is sure to incur the wrath of the Sadducees and Pharisees, but he has put us on a direct collision course with the Sanhedrin as well with his antics at the Temple today! More concerning to me as well is that this talk of him being 'King of the Jews' is surely going to kindle the ire of both Herod Antipas and the Romans. I tell you, we have just become enemies of the State in every possible way!"

Zeoletes is trying desperately to find a positive to counter with, but the sober look on his face is giving away his own concern. He cannot deny the facts that Judas is espousing.

He responds, "Look, I cannot argue the logic of your statements. But if we see all of this, you must be sure that Yeshua sees all of this and more. We've witnessed too much for me to write everything off the way you are. This is where the faith that he has taught us so much about has to kick in. He must have a plan."

Judas looks scornfully at his comrade and says, "I never would have counted you as being so naive or gullible. Everything is crumbling all around us. I cannot explain all his magic tricks, but I am no fool. He must be working with a demon. He is not the Messiah but just another imposter, like so many before him. There is no good ending to this story, and I, for one, am not going to allow us to die this way. I will find a way to stop this madness before it costs us our lives!"

Judas feels a powerful presence growing inside him and controlling him with every word he utters, and it compels and steers him to leave and seek out the religious leaders to confer with them. Before Zeoletes can say another word, Judas bolts out of his sight.

Simon overhears just enough to piece together the upcoming conflict. He has decisions to make, and he must make them quickly. Now more than ever, he needs to talk with the rabbi. For now, however, he first needs to get back to the solace of his family. There hasn't been much time for bonding lately, and family time is what Simon needs most right now. He heads in the direction of their encampment near the Mount of Olives, towards the Garden of Gethsemane, where he knows Yeshua loves to go to pray. His heart is heavy with the anxiety of all that he has seen and heard this day. He is hoping that Yeshua will provide him with some answers or at least some direction as to what to do next. The lives of his family, as well as himself, are riding on it.

As Simon approaches a bend in the road, a breeze carries the offensive odor of rotting flesh into his nostrils. He covers his nose and quickens his pace so that he can put the smell of carrion behind him. He can see the presence of vultures ahead, confirming his thoughts that some animal carcass is being scavenged. Simon reaches the spot where the smell is emanating from. Whatever it is, it is just past the edge of the road in some low brush. He keeps walking, not at all interested in finding out what lies there. That is until he sees a sandal just ahead of him. Now, he knows that it is a human body that is the source of the odor. He stops walking. He thinks to himself, what if it is one of the disciples or perhaps another member of his group? Worse yet, what if it is Yeshua? He knows now that he must investigate. He draws near and startles the feasting birds, who temporarily leave with loud commotion. They, at the same time, reveal the identity of the corpse. Simon freezes as he recognizes what is left of Saccius' face. By all indications, he died violently at the hands of robbers on the Jericho Road. Simon breaks away from the scene at full speed until the need to empty his stomach overwhelms him. After he recoups, he hears words from Yeshua in his head, "Whatever a man sows, that he shall also reap." He says out loud, "So the thief has now become the victim of thieves. The murderer has now become a victim of murderers. What he intended for me became his own death sentence. It ends here."

A new wave of emotions comes over Simon. It is the realization that his life as a fugitive is all but over. His encounter with Drusus has passed without fatal consequences. His betrayer, Saccius, is now dead, and Aemilius is nowhere to be found. The fact that Saccius was alone means either his partner is also dead or otherwise missing or perhaps has fled. Slowly, a feeling of relief comes over Simon as he comes to realize the magnitude of this miraculous change in his circumstances. He also realizes that God's divine intervention is now undeniable. He has been spared too many times against all odds in ways that defy all logic. Surely, God has a reason and a plan.

Falling to his knees, Simon prays aloud, "I thank you, my God. You have saved me again and again. You have saved my family. You have vanquished my enemies. Forgive me for ever doubting You and for my unbelief. Forgive me my sins and failings in the flesh. I know not why You have spared me or what You will require of me, but whatever Your will is for me, I am forever Yours. Amen."

CHAPTER 31. THE BEGINNING OF THE END BEFORE THE BEGINNING

Yeshua's followers, including Simon's family, are celebrating the Passover supper together. Yeshua and his chosen twelve are not with them, as they have gone to an undisclosed location. Simon is enjoying this particularly special time with his family, as he always does. Menachem's son, Gideon, is now like another son and has been adopted as such by Simon and Chana. As they prepare to eat, their conversations are filled with memories of home in Cyrene. The mood is both jovial and melancholy. They are thankful for their lives, but there is no mistaking the tones of homesickness in their voices. This is especially true for Gideon, as he is missing his slain father especially this day. The moistness in his eyes betrays his feelings. Susanna is serving as the group comes up to fill their plates. She looks at Gideon's face and instinctively stops what she is doing. She had become quite attached to Menachem, even romantically. It was also very apparent that the feelings were mutual. She immediately stops what she is doing and tightly hugs Gideon.

"I know my child…I know," she says, as a tear begins to roll down her cheek. "I grew so attached to him. More than I realized."

Gideon says back to her, "He felt that way about you, too. I could tell. I hadn't seen him so happy since the days with my mother. I was happy to see him that way. I was happy for you too."

Not expecting such words of revelation or confirmation, Susanna smiles and says, "Thank you for that," hugging Gideon one more time.

Simon's heart is touched by the scene, and he says to them, "Remember Yeshua's words. Your father will live again. Just believe."

Gideon says, "I am trying to. I just miss him being here right now."

Simon responds, "I understand."

Just then, Peter stumbles into the camp, breathless and weeping bitterly. "They've arrested him! Yeshua is as good as dead! They are going to kill him, I am sure of it, and I have failed him! I have failed him!" the distraught disciple wails over and over. The words Peter speaks have the effect of a lightning strike. The shock has initially rendered everyone virtually speechless. Then, almost all at once everyone's attention falls upon Peter. "What happened? Who has him?" are the words on everyone's lips. Simon goes even further. He grabs Peter by the shoulders and shouts, "Speak up, man! What has happened?" Peter starts to slowly compose himself and begins the tale.

"Earlier tonight, we celebrated the Passover supper together. As you know, we did so in a private and undisclosed place so as not to be found out in any way, for we know that the Pharisees are searching for us. Then Yeshua said that someone was going to betray him tonight. None of us could believe it. At that point, he looked directly at Judas and told him to do what he must do, but quickly. Judas just stared, then he left us in a hurry. Yeshua went into the garden to pray, with James, John, and I left behind to keep watch. Unfortunately, we fell asleep. When he woke us later, we started to head back, when suddenly a squad of Temple Guards confronted us with Judas at the lead. He kissed Yeshua, surely a signal to the Guards as to who Yeshua was. We tried to fight; in fact, I cut off the ear of one of the enemies. Yeshua stopped us, healed the man's ear, and had us stand down. They took him away, but I trailed them at a distance to see where they were going. They were beating him savagely and mocking him the entire way. I feared that if I intervened, they would arrest me too. They eventually led him to the High Priest Caiaphas' house and took him inside. I know he is in desperate trouble. That's where I failed him."

All of those present are aghast at what they have just heard. None of them can believe that this is happening.

Simon speaks up, "Wait, you said that you tried to defend him, and he made you stand down?"

Peter confirms, "That's right. He said that he must drink the cup that his Father has given him, whatever that means."

Simon continues his inquiry, trying to make sense of this event. "So that I understand, if you tried to defend him and he stopped you, how then did you fail him?"

Peter hangs his head, and there is a noticeable quiver in his voice as he explains further.

"At supper, when he revealed that one of us would betray him and that he would be arrested, I told him that will never happen for as long as I live, as I will lay down my life for him. That's when he said the most curious thing. He told me that before the cock would crow in the morning, I would deny knowing him three times. I meant every word I said with all my heart. But when they took him into Caiaphas's house, I got scared. I knew that if they caught me, I could be sealing my own fate. So, I decided to wait outside at the bonfire to see what would happen. It was then that people began to recognize me as a disciple. I then did exactly what he said I would do. I denied him. THREE TIMES I denied him. And just as he foretold, upon the end of the third denial, I heard a cock crow as if by command. I failed him so shamefully!" Peter finished while sobbing openly once again.

The Cyrenian

What was silence in the group is now replaced by the vocalizing of every emotion by everyone.

Simon then says to some of the male followers, "We must follow him and see what becomes of him."

One speaks up and says, "But how do we keep ourselves safe?"

Simon replies, "There is safety in numbers. There will always be a crowd following from now on. We need to stay covered and just blend in. Fortunately, we aren't known to anyone there."

They all agree and set out to wait at the bonfire for any news. Peter straightens up and says to the others," Should any trouble arise, you know the safehouse to go to. In the meantime, I will take the other disciples with me, and we'll all meet there."

Everybody agrees, and Simon and his group head back to the bonfire near Caiaphas' house to watch for any movement of their beloved rabbi. It will be a long night, no doubt.

As morning breaks, a member of the entourage keeping the vigil comes running up to the others at the bonfire.

"They are taking Yeshua to the governor of Judea, Pontius Pilate!" he announces. "By Roman law, the Sanhedrin cannot condemn him to death, so they are trying to get Pilate to do it. The word is that he has acknowledged to them that he is the Christ, Son of the true and living God. They have charged him with blasphemy, which you know carries a sentence of death. There is a crowd already following him!"

Simon knows that if the Sanhedrin succeeds in persuading Pilate, Yeshua is dead for sure. Yet, he can't help but ponder the situation. It just doesn't make sense. Yeshua has *got* to know all of this ahead of time, yet he is willfully walking into a trap. A trap with fatal consequences. Why? Is he TRYING to get himself killed? In that very instant, the question starts Simon looking at everything from a different angle. Everything is moving so swiftly. If he is truly the Messiah, who is come into the world to save it and free all of mankind, how can he accomplish the task by dying? This all must be a ruse or some sort of diversion. If that's true, then Yeshua's moment of victory is surely at hand. If the prophecy is to be fulfilled, the moment of truth is fast approaching. A new spark is kindled in Simon's spirit. He covers his head and follows the crowd moving towards the residence of Pontius Pilate.

Pilate has already received word that the priests are coming with Yeshua in tow, the man whose name has been the topic of almost every discussion in his circle of late. Pilate, in fact, was hoping against hope that all of this "Yeshua business" would blow over and dissipate on its own long before he would ever have to deal with it. However, Pilate realizes, too, that such is generally never the case. As far as he is concerned, this overall situation is a nuisance and more trouble than it is worth. This province of Judea has been a pain to govern, and all he wants is for it to remain orderly without the need for him to exercise too much in the way of brute authority. Matters are becoming even more prickly now because of the Passover season. Despite that fact, however, his mindset is to diffuse and dispatch the situation as quickly and as painlessly as possible.

Before long, the priests and their prisoner arrive, and they waste no time in passionately presenting their case.

Caiaphas begins the rant, "Prefect! This man has been perverting our nation!"

Pilate begins to pour what he feels is some much-needed wine and responds, "What has this to do with the people of Rome?"

Caiaphas, realizing that this is going to be a match of wits, lyingly answers, "He forbids the people to pay taxes to Caesar and proclaims himself to be the Christ, the King of the Jews!"

Pilate takes a long sip from his cup and says, "The responsibility for the paying of Roman taxes lies with you and not him. As for proclaiming yourself King of the Jews, well, are you?" he asks Yeshua directly.

Without the slightest raising of his head or eye contact, Yeshua answers, "Is it you who says so, or did others tell you this concern-

The Cyrenian

ing me? My kingdom is not of this world. If it were my kingdom, my servants would fight to make sure I was not turned over to these Jews. But my kingdom is not from here."

The priests begin their protests once again, saying, "You see, he admits it! He claims to be King, which is insurrection by Roman law! He has spread his lies from his home in Galilee to the very Temple of Jerusalem. You must crucify him!"

Pilate hears the protests and knows immediately the game that Caiaphas is playing. For whatever reason, this man has fallen from favor or has been otherwise deemed as a threat to their status quo. Whatever the case, Pilate knows that the priests are lying and trying to manipulate him into carrying out their dirty work. He also realizes that Yeshua has masterfully tossed the ball into his court by saying, *"Is it YOU who says I am"* in answer to the question of kingship. After some brief mulling, a brilliant thought comes to his mind.

He says with all authority, "You say that this man is a Galilean. Therefore, he is under the jurisdiction of Herod Antipas. Take him and let Herod decide his fate. As for me, I find no fault in this man."

Pilate immediately rises and leaves the room, leaving no doubt that this conversation is over. Despite their continuing protests, the priests are left with no choice but to proceed to the palace of Herod to plead their case. High Priest Caiaphas is fuming especially, knowing fully that Pilate and, therefore, Yeshua have won this round. He realizes now that Pilate is not only a worthy adversary but a major obstacle to the achievement of his agenda.

Simon and his group are waiting outside as the priests and their beloved Yeshua emerge. Simon is both shocked and angered by the sight of the obvious physical abuse that Yeshua has received at the hands of the Sanhedrin and their thugs. He wants to do something, but what? He snaps back to the moment at hand when one of the followers announces that Yeshua is being taken to the Royal Palace of King Herod for judgment. As much as Simon would like to believe that Herod might show some leniency, being that Yeshua is a Jew, he knows too that there is no loyalty when it comes to this level of politics. These are lessons that he has learned well during his days of dealing with the politicians of Cyrene. Simon's group follows the crowd to the next stop on this sordid journey and takes their place to await the next outcome.

Herod greets his visitors with great zeal. He has long been wanting to meet Yeshua, mainly with the hope of witnessing one of his legendary miracles.

"Well, well, well, at least I get to behold you, Yeshua of Nazareth. Your name is on the lips of everyone in the land! I must say, the stories of your supposed miracles are especially most intriguing. Will you indulge us with a small display of your powers?"

Herod's court has been assembled to witness this meeting and is quite vocal regarding Herod's request. Reveling in their drunken state, they all begin to shout out their sarcastic requests.

"Turn these rocks into bread, or better yet, GOLD!" says one.

"How about turning this water into fine wine!" jeers another.

"Perhaps we could bring him a corpse to raise!" comes another jest from Herod, garnering much laughter.

Yeshua stands silently, giving no reaction to the scene whatsoever. His quiet stand is aggravating Herod.

"Wait!" shouts Herod, bringing the room to silence. "I almost forgot! You are the King of the Jews, aren't you? I could not tell without your robes. Guards, bring me a purple robe of State!"

A guard quickly produces one and places it on Yeshua's shoulders. In a moment of inspiration, the guard says, laughing, "Is it true that if I strike you, you will turn the other cheek?"

The guard looks at Herod, who gives him a nod of approval. The guard cocks his arm and strikes Yeshua's face with a resounding slap, much to the delight of the mocking audience. Then, to the chagrin of the witnesses, Yeshua straightens himself and raises his head as if ready to be struck again. The treatment continues for a

The Cyrenian

few more moments until Herod, now starting to become uncomfortable on the inside, stops the onslaught. Perhaps he has visions of his past encounter with John the Baptist.

Whatever the motivation, he declares, "This Yeshua is no Messiah and is not a king. Send him back to Pilate!"

The priests suffer yet another defeat, making them even more desperate to accomplish their goal. Caiaphas knows that he must figure out a way to turn up the heat on Pilate, and soon. As things stand, he is losing this contest, and all that he is and holds dear is on the line.

Simon gets word that Yeshua is being sent back to Pilate. While he has been waiting, he has been listening intently to the people surrounding him and their thoughts about the rabbi. There are many who have been healed or were witnesses to healings. The story of Bartimaeus, a well-known resident of Jerusalem and the first blind man that Yeshua healed, is heard over and over. Others speak of having demons cast out of them, diseases cured, and debilitating depression as well as mental illness removed. The hungry fed. The dead raised. All their lives are forever changed, regardless of race, color, gender, or creed. All because of the unconditional love of one man. And now some want to kill him for it. The whole thing is so irrational.

Then there are the others. Some are unbelievers who are convinced that Yeshua is a fraud who is in league with evil spirits. Others are trembling with the fear that Rome is going to punish them all for his transgressions. This thought brings Simon to a monumental epiphany. He comes to realize that the opposite is true. *Yeshua is being punished for the transgressions of all men!* Most amazingly, he is doing it of his own free will. He could no doubt eliminate his enemies with little or no effort, yet he is taking their abuse. Why would someone with his power subject himself to this? What does he stand to gain? Why sacrifice oneself this way?

At this moment, Simon hears the words of Yeshua in his memory, saying, "It is for this purpose that I came into the world. Not to condemn it but to save it. It is not my will or my Father's that even one soul be lost. I am the Good Shepherd who would leave the ninety-nine sheep in his flock alone to go and seek the one lost sheep, to save it, and bring it home because I value him the most."

It is as if he is hearing these words again for the first time. The questions they breed are coming fast and furious. Can it be that Yeshua is simply trying to save as many lost sheep as he can, even the ones who would seek to destroy him? If so, what kind of love is this? Is there any so unconditional? At what cost does this redemption come?

The priests and a now more beaten and weakened Yeshua make their way back to the Praetorium and Pontius Pilate once again. It is obvious that the priests have not succeeded in their mission. Simon's fears are reaching a pinnacle, as he knows that seeing Pilate a second time cannot be a good sign.

This time, the meeting is held outdoors in the open, where all might witness the encounter. Pilate is seated as they bring a staggering Yeshua back before him.

"So, what is Herod's verdict?" he says gruffly.

The Chief Priest Annas replies, "Herod would not condemn him. He says that it is for Rome to do."

Turning to Yeshua, Pilate again questions him, "Your own nation and priests have brought you to me. What have you done? Are you the King of the Jews? Am I a Jew, your subject?"

This time, Yeshua speaks.

"You are right to call me a king. It is for this cause that I have come into the world that I should bear witness to the truth. Those who are about the truth hear my voice."

Pilate stands to his feet and asks, "What is truth?"

The pressure is mounting, but Pilate once again comes up with a clever plan to again diffuse the situation. Turning back to the priests,

The Cyrenian

he says once more, "I find no fault in this man at all. However, you Jews do have a custom at Passover, where you will have me release to the people a prisoner of their choosing. Shall I release to you this King of the Jews?"

Caiaphas realizes immediately the shrewdness of Pilate's move. If the people say yes, then the matter is done and at their own behest. The cries from the crowd on Yeshua's behalf begin. Caiaphas comes up with an equally shrewd counter, "Release to us Barabbas!"

Pilate is shocked that they would ask for this bloodthirsty killer and robber over Yeshua. He did not see that coming.

"Barabbas is a condemned murderer and a thief. Why would you want him over a man who is only guilty of being somewhat delusional?"

Caiaphas and the other priests now incite the crowd to begin chanting, "Release Barabbas! Release Barabbas!" at an ever-increasing volume. Pilate realizes that he is being fast backed into a corner. He decides on a compromise.

"I will not crucify an innocent man. However, as a warning and a lesson to him against starting trouble, I shall have him scourged."

Scourging is a most violent and painful punishment, entailing the use of whips and devices specially designed to inflict the highest levels of pain possible. The *flagella* whips are the most prevalent tools utilized. They are made of leather and have multiple "tails" so that a single blow is the equivalent of being lashed several times at once. To escalate the suffering, the tails are usually embedded with lead balls and/or sharpened glass or bone on the ends to tear the flesh as the victim is beaten. The soldiers usually chosen to administer the punishment are those of powerful, muscular stature and often have the meanest of spirits. They also often wet down the whip and the victim to increase the pain. In fact, it is quite common for a prisoner to die either during or soon after a scourging.

Simon is shaken to his core to learn what Yeshua is about to endure. He sees his beloved rabbi being dragged away for the order to be carried out amid the crazed shouting of the mob, who is incensed at the lack of the pronouncement of a death sentence. While the outsiders cannot see the victim as he is flogged, there is no mistaking the sound, from which there is no escape. With each lash, Simon cries out, all the while cringing in anticipation of the next strike, convulsing almost in unison. His mind is racing like never before in his lifetime. One part of him wishes that there was a way to rescue him and vanquish Yeshua's captors once and for all. But it is the other part of him that takes control.

He starts to cry out to God. "My God! Is there not a way to save him from this? I believe that he is Your Son, as he told us. Why would you suffer him to endure this? He does not deserve this! He has done nothing to deserve this!"

Just then, it is as if Simon has been transported to another place. The sounds of the mob and the scourging disappear, and he is standing in a place of great light, coupled with a strong sense of peace. A voice, gentle yet powerful, says to him,

"Simon, there is so much more involved here than you can ever see or comprehend. But let me share this much with you. What you see is not defeat. It is the greatest victory that man will ever know. What you see and hear is not an ending but a beginning to a life without end for all mankind. My Beloved Son is the Lamb… unblemished and perfect, that will take away the sins of the world, past, present, and future. Only he can do this. He is the sacrifice that will restore man and all the earth to its original glory, as it was from the beginning, as it was meant to be. Because of what he does now, man will live with us forever in paradise. He alone can make this possible because he is pure, without sin, and loves as I do, for he has chosen of his own free will to take all the sins of mankind upon himself. While the price of sin is death, he has chosen to pay it for everyone, regardless of who they are. His sinlessness will atone for *all* sin. No matter what one does or has ever done, if he believes in my Son and in Me, he will inherit all that I have given my Son.

The Cyrenian

You are all children of the King, with every right and privilege that comes with it, including eternal life. From the day you come, just as you are, and say yes to the gift that is free to all, nothing can separate us ever again. Nothing you can ever do can come between us. This is true for anyone who will just believe. You can't earn this or buy this. It is a gift. All you need do is accept it. That's all there is to know. Ask, and it shall be yours. Here. Now. Don't worry about what you will see, hear, or even feel sometimes. There are some things that everyone on earth has to experience, but I will see you through. All of you. I know that you will have many questions, and in time, you will get every answer, I promise you. For now, just trust Me. I know that can be harder than it sounds, but don't worry. I won't let you down, and I will never leave you. Do you understand?

Simon feels a warmth and a love come over him as he answers, "Yes, Father, oh yes!"

Once again, God speaks to him. "Now, I have a job for you. You will help to share with the world all that I have told you. You will also help my Son complete his task."

"How can I help him with a task so great?" Simon asks.

"When the time comes, you will know, My son. Thank you for all that you are about to do. Go now in peace, and remember, I am with you."

The volume of the crowd increases to where it was prior to his heavenly encounter. Simon looks up just as Pilate pronounces the sentence of death by crucifixion over Yeshua. The priests have won the day by threatening Pilate with reporting to Caesar his failure to keep the peace and allowing a Jew to proclaim himself King of the Jews, even above the will of Caesar. This is a threat that Pilate cannot afford to ignore. After an unsuccessful final plea to Yeshua to say anything that he can use to free him, Pilate reluctantly passes the final judgment. He symbolically washes his hands, signifying that the case is closed and that he bears no responsibility for the blood that is about to be spilled.

Simon dries his eyes as Pilate dries his hands and says aloud, "Thank you, Lord, for all that You are about to do."

CHAPTER 32. THE FINISH LINE CROSSED

The mob is now in a full-blown and blood-thirsty frenzy as Yeshua is led away, beaten, and bleeding profusely. He is still wearing the purple robe, and in adding insult to injury, the Roman soldiers have fashioned a crown out of large thorns, which they have cruelly mashed down into his head. Even now, they are still striking him while he struggles to walk despite being obviously very weak from his ordeal.

Simon and the others follow the crowd that will be making the death procession to a place on a hill outside of the city walls. It is called Golgotha in Hebrew, also known as Calvary. The name means: "The Place of the Skull." The name comes from the appearance of the hill itself, which resembles a human skull, right down to the two caves which form the eye sockets and rugged crannies forming the nose and mouth. It is a most fitting name, too, because it is a place of death, a traditional place of crucifixion. Simon walks silently, deeply lost in his thoughts. His divine encounter with God has cleared up many questions in his mind. He recalls many things that Yeshua has said and shared with him, which now have taken on new meaning. He is remembering Yeshua's words when Menachem died. "Greater love has no man than he who lays down his life for a friend." Simon now realizes that Yeshua was also referring to himself. Only this time, his friend is the entire human race.

The Cyrenian

Things that Yeshua shared that were at the time ambiguous prophesies of his impending death now have full clarity in his mind. Yeshua knew. He always knew. It's why he came. Every event of his life was leading him up to this moment. His mission is almost complete. However, at the same time, Simon wonders what God meant when He said that he would help Yeshua complete his task. He is all but dead now. What can there be left to do?

The procession stops in front of the Antonia Fortress, where the full complement of soldiers joined those escorting Yeshua to provide crowd control. Joining the soldiers is Drusus, whose men are among the ones assigned to do this duty. Added to the procession are two condemned thieves who will also be crucified alongside Yeshua. They all will be led down the Via Dolorosa Street, the traditional processional route to Calvary, roughly a half mile away. The public will gather along the route to witness the passing of the condemned and to either mourn or mock them as they pass. Just before the entourage begins the trek, each prisoner is given the crossbeam of their cross to carry to the site of their execution. While a full cross could weigh well above 300 pounds, the crossbeam would weigh around a hundred pounds on average. Even still, it represents a cumbersome burden, especially for an exhausted and injured man. However, in the case of Yeshua, Rome is going to great extra lengths to increase the discomfort.

After watching the soldiers join, Simon decides to proceed to find a place closer to the end of the march to minimize his contact with the Romans. Yeshua is already quivering beneath the beam and needs the help of two soldiers on either side of him to stand him up. At the front of the procession are soldiers blowing horns and beating out the cadence on drums so that all within earshot can know that they are coming. Others are carrying flags and the Roman standards. This procession is more than just a pronouncement of executions. It is a statement of Roman power, strength, and authority. It is also the message to all who would seek to oppose the will of Caesar in any way, shape, or form, "Beware and obey! Rome will destroy you. Make no mistake!"

As Simon tries to make his way through the crowd, which is becoming an increasingly difficult thing to do, he glances over his shoulder to see what is going on behind him. He looks with angst at the fallen figure of Yeshua, the rugged beam on top of him. Simon stops his advance, wanting instinctively to run back and help. However, he knows that it is impossible to cut back through the crowd, and he dares not walk out in the street. He decides to wait where he is until the parade gets to him and try to follow from there.

Even though Simon knows now just what is underlying all of this, his emotions are hard to keep in check. How can they continue to beat a man who obviously cannot continue? And you also command him to carry such a heavy beam besides knowing that he can't? Concern and sympathy fast become anger and spitefulness. At that moment, however, the calming voice of God comes through. "You will help Him complete His task. You will know the time." Simon stands down. He knows that Yeshua *must* complete this journey. Mankind depends on it. Then it strikes him. If he somehow does not make it to the end, will man be lost forever? Is that possible? After all, at this moment, he is only human. How much more can he possibly endure? Besides, the forces of evil are surely doing all that they can to sabotage God's plan. Then he wonders if maybe this is the moment where he calls down the heavenly host and lays waste all his enemies, as promised in the prophesies. But would that be fair? If the salvation of man depends on the blood sacrifice of the only perfect human, the Lamb of God, then it stands to reason that God cannot interfere. This is the final showdown between good and evil, and everything for all eternity is on the line. Whatever it takes, Yeshua must make it to Calvary.

Not far from him, Simon sees Yeshua fall again. He must get up. He must get up! Simon feels himself moving ever slowly in Yeshua's direction. He is close enough to clearly see the agony and pain in the normally gentle, smiling, and loving face of his rabbi. He realizes now that Yeshua is carrying much more than his cross. He has the weight of every sin in this world upon his shoulders. Sins past, sins present, and sins yet to come are all upon him. Yeshua staggers forward until he is directly in front of Simon. For an instant, their eyes meet, full on. Then Yeshua falls again, this time in such a way that it is clear he will not be able to go on. The timber comes to rest across him once more, thudding loudly as it falls. There, lying on the heavily cobbled stone street, gasping for air, is the trembling, battered, and bleeding out Son of Man, looking more victim than conqueror. Simon cannot bear it any longer. He starts to move into the street.

Simon's heart is beating out of his chest when, once again, he falls into another dream state. However, this time, it is not the voice of God he hears but the intense sound of the mob growing louder than ever before. And instead of the bright and lovely light of his last encounter, there is the harsh glare of a burning, merciless noonday sun. The love that was so easily felt in his talk with God is replaced by an intense feeling of hatred and evil that defies description. While the circumstances are unique, the experience is all too familiar. The cold sweat running down his cocoa-brown forehead is the sign that his frequent nightmare has returned, only this time, he is awake, or so he thinks. He starts to move forward when he hears that booming, fierce voice, just as he has time and time again during his nightmare. Then come the eyes. Those same fiery eyes that have haunted him night after night for so long, but this time, the face behind them is beginning to take form.

"YOU!" Simon hears as he simultaneously feels the point of a sword resting on his chest. Just then, the face before him takes full form. It is Drusus who had told him in no uncertain terms to never let their paths cross again. Now, there is nowhere to run and no place to hide.

"YOU! *Cyrenian!* Pick up this man's cross and carry it!" Drusus shouts.

The very words *"Pick up this man's cross and carry* it" set in motion flashes of the very conversations on the subject that Simon and the others have had with the rabbi. Now, he understands their full meaning.

"I said, YOU, Cyrenian! Pick up and carry his cross NOW before I get one for YOU!"

Simon pushes down the sword gently away from his chest in willing compliance. As he begins to bend down, he hears the most unexpected words from Drusus that he could ever imagine hearing.

Drusus moves his lips closer to Simon's ear and says softly, "Help him. Help him as you have helped me."

Drusus immediately pulls away and steps back to his ranks in the most no-nonsense fashion, watching as Simon carries out the command.

Simon hoists the beam up onto his shoulder while, at the same time, he puts his free arm around Yeshua, attempting to hold him up. He can feel just how weak he is at this point. In fact, Simon utters a prayer for them both to receive divine strength for the journey. Slowly, they begin to put one foot in front of the other.

Simon says to Yeshua, "Out of love, you have taken up my cross. Today, I take up yours, and I will carry it for as long as I live."

Again, no other words pass, but a momentary meeting of the eyes says all that needs to be said.

Simon quickly gets a new perspective of the journey from this vantage point. He is being spat on by the people trying to defile Yeshua. Some are throwing rotten food and even animal dung as they pass. The jeering is incessant. "Save yourself, you who claimed that you can save nations!" "Hail King of the Jews!" "Liar!" "Blasphemer!" On and on, they continue, every step of the way, to Mount Calvary. Simon says to Yeshua, "I thank you, Lord. You have saved us all. Even them." Yeshua raises his head for a moment. He says

The Cyrenian

not a word, but the look in his eyes speaks a volume of words. Amid all of the evil spectators, there are the others. Many are on their knees. Most are weeping and wailing aloud. Many have torn their garments and put dirt in their hair in the Jewish tradition of mourning the death of a loved one. The contrast is most gripping, to say the least, as one display of emotions happens directly next to the other. Yet, even at this darkest hour of his life, Yeshua still finds a way to put others before himself.

Passing a group of weeping and lamenting women, Yeshua turns to them and says, "Daughters of Jerusalem, weep not for me, but for yourselves and your children."

After what seems to have been forever, Simon, Yeshua, the thieves, the Romans, and the multitude who have followed them arrive at their final destination. Shoving Simon violently to the ground, the Romans waste no time in getting down to the business of crucifixion with brutal efficiency.

It is widely accepted that crucifixion is, without a doubt, the cruelest, most gruesome, and most painful way to kill someone. While the Romans did not invent crucifixion, they most certainly perfected it. The facts of the overall procedure leave little, if any, room for doubt. It was conceived from the very start with suffering in mind to dissuade those who witness it from perpetrating the types of crimes that would warrant this form of capital punishment. Sometimes, the victims are even left hanging and on display after death as a warning. It is designed to be a slow, painful death, thus coining the word "excruciating" or literally "out of crucifying." It is also meant to be public and humiliating, with the victims stripped naked before the punishment is administered. Long iron nails are then hammered through the hands of the outstretched arms and feet to attach the victim to the cross itself. Engineered in true Roman fashion to inflict the maximum constant pain possible on its victim, death can take hours or even days, depending upon the methods used by the executioner and the health of the victim. Death can come in many forms or combinations, including cardiac rupture or failure, acidosis, hypovolemic shock, asphyxia, arrhythmia, dehydration, and exposure, or sepsis from the wounds or scourging. Even animal predation is the cause of death in some cases. All in all, there is not a worse way to die known to man.

After enduring the nailing of his flesh to the timber, Yeshua is raised up on his cross for all to see, flanked on both sides by the two condemned thieves.

Simon is riveted to his spot as he gazes at what is left of the man he has come to know and love so much. He still is having a hard time picturing the Son of God this way. Deep inside, there is still a small part of him that hopes that he is wrong and Yeshua will vanquish his enemies right here and now. But then, he snaps back to reality after remembering what the grand plan is. He looks around and sees a multitude of mourners looking upon the face of the man who changed their lives forever. Simon recognizes some of the faces of people that were healed and restored. Walking towards him, Simon recognizes Yeshua's mother, Mary, and her sister, also named Mary. With them also is Yeshua's beloved disciple, John, and Mary Magdalene. John is the only of the twelve who is present. All the others are hiding at the safehouse. Simon greets them, and he shares in this moment of welcome reunion and support. Not many words pass as they stare transfixed at Yeshua's face. Before long, Simon feels a most tender touch on his aching shoulder. He whips around and sees the face of his beloved and unexpected Chana. He grabs her, and the two embrace each other as if there is no tomorrow. Alexander and Rufus join them, along with Gideon. Johanna, Susanna, and all the women who have traveled with Yeshua over the past three years are present, along with many of the new followers who have joined them along the way. Simon suddenly changes his focus and asks his dear wife, "Why are you here? You all should be in Bethany! There is danger here!"

Chana only whispers softly, "We had to be here."

The Cyrenian

Simon instantly understands. How could he not understand their need?

The group listens in disgust to the raucous mocking from the mob.

"You!" one yells. "If you are the Messiah, the Christ, then save yourself!"

The religious leaders join in the chorus. "You say that you will destroy the Temple and restore it in three days! You say that you are the Chosen of God, yet while you claim to be able to save others, you yourself you cannot save!"

One priest jokes, "Maybe Elijah will save him!"

Yeshua, hearing all of this, looks to heaven and says aloud, "Father, forgive them. They don't know what they are doing."

Again, Yeshua seizes yet another opportunity to share his love and grace, even to those who put him here. All those who hear the words are struck with amazement.

The charge to save himself is repeated everywhere, including from the crosses beside him.

One of the thieves challenges him, "If you are the Christ, then save yourself and us with you!"

However, the words from the other thief are much different. Rebuking his comrade, he says, "Have you no fear of God even now? We are guilty of our crimes and are being justly punished, but this man has done nothing wrong!" Speaking to Yeshua, he says, "Lord, remember me when you come into your kingdom."

Yeshua answers, "I assure you today you will be with me in paradise."

Yeshua sees his mother and says, "Woman, behold your Son." Then, looking at John, he says, "Behold your mother." John realizes that Yeshua is signaling for him to take Mary to his home and care for her. He gathers her and does just that.

Yeshua now calls out from thirst. The soldiers mockingly offer him a mixture of sour wine vinegar, but Yeshua refuses it. A soldier then takes a ladder and posts a sign atop Yeshua's cross, written in Greek, Latin, and Hebrew, listing the death charges. It says, "YESHUA OF NAZARETH, THE KING OF THE JEWS," which absolutely incenses the religious elites.

During the sixth hour (noon), a sudden eerie darkness takes over the sky as far as the eye can see. This is no ordinary darkness. This is blackness. Blacker than night. Blackness that you can almost touch. A cold wind begins to grow stronger, and fear starts to grip those present. Yeshua cries out, "My God! My God! Why have you forsaken me?" What the mortal man cannot know is that all his sins are now being borne by the Savior in full force. He has literally become the sins of man. God the Father, being unable to look upon the face of sin without destroying it, has veiled His face from His Son. For the first time ever, the two are truly separated. Meanwhile, the Temple veil, which separates man from the divine and literal presence of God, made of thick pelts and skins, is torn from top to bottom without human hands, signifying that the ritual of sacrifices for the atonement for sins is no longer necessary. Yeshua is the ultimate sacrifice, and he has made the ultimate sacrifice on man's behalf. Yeshua has completed his mission. God is now with man, and man is now with God directly, through His Son, forever.

Upon the hill, Drusus exclaims, "This man was truly a righteous man!" He knows now that he is witnessing a supernatural event. Meanwhile, his men are joking and gambling with dice to win Yeshua's infamous seamless outer garment as a trophy. The fact is that this act is yet another fulfillment of the prophecies about the Messiah. It is written in the scriptures, "They divided My garments among them, and for My clothing, they cast lots."

It is now the ninth hour (three o'clock), and the whole multitude who were condemning and ridiculing are starting to run for cover as the weather has become fierce. The faithful are crying and beating their breasts in sorrow.

Suddenly, from high up on the cross, the voice of Yeshua rings out. "Father, into Your hands, I commend my spirit!" He looks up to heaven and proclaims in a loud voice, louder than anyone would ever expect, *"IT IS FINISHED!"*

With that, Yeshua's head falls for the last time. He is dead. The very earth proclaims his passing. At the very moment he utters his final words, an earthquake of great magnitude unleashes its force. The winds of a great gale whip up as if out of nowhere, and the heavens sound off with thunder and lightning. The clouds also burst forth with a cold rain. It is as if all of nature is proclaiming the death and triumph of the Lamb.

Once again, Drusus speaks out, dropping to one knee, saying, "Truly, this man was the Son of God." He is thankful for the rain that is hiding his tears as he weeps openly.

Simon and his family, along with Yeshua's family, huddle together at the foot of the cross. Now, it is close to sundown, and the Sabbath is approaching. It is against Jewish law to have dead bodies hanging on a cross during the Sabbath, and the priests approach Pilate for help in the matter. To hurry the deaths of the men, Pilate sends the order to have the legs of the men on the crosses broken so that they will die quickly from being unable to support themselves to breathe. The soldiers do so with the thieves, but when they get to Yeshua, they can see that he is already dead. Therefore, there is no need to break his legs. Just to be sure, however, a soldier pierces Yeshua through his side and into the chest cavity. Blood and water spew out, confirming his death. Again, prophecy is fulfilled, as it is written in the scriptures, "Not one of His bones shall be broken. They shall look on Him who they pierced."

Just then, a Chief Priest named Nicodemus, with whom Yeshua shared a most intriguing and intimate conversation one evening, and a man named Joseph of Arimathea, who is a secret disciple of Yeshua, approach the cross. They have gained permission from Pilate to take Yeshua's body to be laid in a brand-new garden tomb of Joseph's that is nearby, right there at Calvary. The group, including Simon, gently lower the body of their dearest Yeshua from the cross and bear it down to the tomb. Since it is too close to the Sabbath, there isn't enough time to properly anoint the body, but the women there quickly wrap him in linen strips and stow a hundred pounds of fragrant myrrh and spices to complete the anointing after the Sabbath, according to custom. They will come back the day after Sabbath and complete the burial procedure properly. After they have finished, they roll a large stone in front of the entrance of the tomb to secure it, and everyone hurries home to make preparation for the Sabbath.

It has been an unforgettable, exhausting, and sorrowful day for all involved. For Yeshua's emotionally spent people, this Sabbath day of rest will be one most desperately needed. For Yeshua, it will be the Sabbath day rest of Victory. For his enemies, it will be anything but restful.

CHAPTER 33. NO REST FOR THE WICKED

The morning comes and brings with it some semblance of normalcy. The Shabbot call to worship sounds as the multitude of Hebrew residents makes their way to the Temple. As to be expected, the events of the previous day are hot on everybody's lips. One can tell that there is a deep sense of urgency among the people to be in the Temple today. Nobody is taking a chance on whether they are right with God or not after yesterday. The sales of sacrificial animals are brisk today. Not many, if any, of the people know the story of the Temple veil, so they are most eager to be cleansed and forgiven.

At Pilate's residence, there is a much different scene. Pilate and his wife are still in bed, awake and trying to put yesterday's ordeal behind them. As one would guess, there has been no sleep in the house whatsoever. There will not be a break today, either. A servant comes to the bed chamber, bowing most nervously.

"Please forgive me, Prefect, but some of the Chief Priests are here, demanding that they see you immediately. I tried to get them to return later, but they are most insistent."

"Of course they are!" mutters Pilate, along with some other colorful figures of speech.

"Tell them to wait!" he growls as he looks for his tunic.

"Yes, my lord!" says the servant, who is most glad to flee the scene.

The Cyrenian

Pilate turns to his wife, Claudia Procula, and says, "When this is over, we will be spending a lot of holiday time on the Isle of Capri. That is if it will ever be over!"

She smiles at him and says, "It will pass, my lord!"

Pilate emerges and walks down the steps of the Praetorium towards the trembling priests.

"Why do you disturb me now?" Pilate asks in a most edgy tone. "Did I not deliver your victim to you as you asked? What is the matter now? Did he die too quickly for you?"

Chief Priest Annas speaks up, "No, Prefect, what you did was excellent; however, there is a new problem. A big problem."

Pilate sighs a heavy sigh and asks in disgust, "What is it now?"

Annas continues, "When that deceiver was alive, he said that in three days from his death, he will rise again."

Pilate explodes. "You SAW him crucified! Are you not convinced? You are supposed to be men of wisdom. Don't tell me that you seriously believe this nonsense, moreover that you expect ME to believe it!"

Annas backs off, realizing that he is in an undesirable position. "No, Prefect, it is just this. Many of the people believe it. If the disciples should somehow remove the body and spread the rumor that he has arisen as promised, this deception will be worse than the original. The problem could quickly multiply exponentially!"

Pilate paces for a moment, obviously understanding the plight. "What, then, do you want of me?" he asks.

Annas responds, "We are asking you to post guards at the tomb and seal it with a Roman seal until the three days have passed. Then, they cannot succeed in creating this false miracle, and the people will see that he was a liar. After that, the myth will finally die with him."

"Fine," Pilate answers. "You have your guard. I will seal the stone of the tomb and set the guards to watch without ceasing, under penalty of death, until your feared three days have passed.

But I warn you, your plan had better unfold as you have said. There is a limit to my patience, even with priests. Now go, and trouble me no more!"

"Thank you, Prefect. It shall be as you ask," Annas says as they depart.

"Just one more thing to keep me from sleeping!" Pilate says to himself as he makes his way back to his bed chamber.

In the house of Mary, Martha, and Lazarus, the mood is deeply somber. It is a far cry from the days of joy and wonder that normally fill the residence. Everyone is trying to process the events of the previous day, as well as trying to figure out what will happen next. Simon is in deep thought while those around him are voicing their concerns.

Lazarus says aloud, "I cannot believe that he is dead. He raised me from the tomb, yet he did not save himself from the same fate. And now, what happens to us? Are we to be fugitives, in hiding forever? I do not understand."

Mary Magdalene responds, "He has never done anything that didn't have a purpose attached to it. I cannot believe that his death would be any different."

Chana comments, "I agree. It won't end here."

Changing the subject slightly, Joanna says, "We must be careful now. Pilate may decide to come after Yeshua's followers. I think after we anoint his body, we should go home to Galilee."

"I think that is wise," says Simon. He stands up and shares his thoughts.

"Do not worry, Mary. There is so much to do from this day forward to spread his word. All his ministry and all the works he has done would be for nothing if it all ended here. There is still more to this story than we know. God has got a plan. And he has promised me that he will see us through in any situation, that he will never leave us or forsake us. Yeshua has always told us to have faith. That's how he works. This is the moment when we need to exercise it more than at any other time we've ever faced. There is an answer, I am sure of it! Remember all that I have shared with you about my divine encounter. I truly believe that God is speaking even now."

Martha looks up through her tears and says, "I pray that you are right, Simon."

Simon thinks to himself, *Yeshua has given us all the answer already somewhere in his cryptic conversations with us. In time, when God is ready, we'll know what it is.*

Over in the garden at Calvary, the Roman Guard has arrived, including Drusus and his men. After the arduous task of rolling the almost six-foot-tall, one-and-a-half-ton wheel of stone back enough to verify that Yeshua's body is as it should be, they waste no time in making sure that the tomb is secured once and for all. With the Roman officers as witnesses, the Roman seal is affixed. The process entails strapping thick and heavy cords across the breadth of the stone and affixing them to the outer stone walls of the tomb with clay. Before the clay hardens, it is stamped with a metal stamp that depicts the seal of the Roman Empire. If the seal stays intact, there can be no doubt that the tomb has remained undisturbed in any way.

After they are done, the squad serving on the first watch takes their posts while the rest of the soldiers, including Drusus, return to the fortress. Drusus has heard the reasons why all these precautions are being taken. Despite his newfound respect for Yeshua's power, he is convinced that no one will dare to attempt breaking into this tomb. As far as he is concerned, the legends will all end here.

CHAPTER 34. VICTORY COMPLETE

The crackling fire serves to stave off some of the chill of the night as the soldiers keeping watch commiserate about their assignment. The Sabbath is over, and it is well before sunrise.

"So, this is what our careers have come to. Guarding dead bodies in the cold of the night," says one.

"No, guarding dead Jewish bodies in the cold of the night," says another.

Still another soldier pipes up, "I'll bet the body in that tomb is warmer than I am right now!"

The squad leader takes this moment to both try and instill some discipline and stifle the complaining. "Whatever the case, be careful that you do not fall asleep on this watch, or you'll get the chance to find out for sure!"

Though it is seemingly being said in jest, there is a great deal of truth to the statement. They all know that to be caught sleeping on guard duty will mandate the sentence of death by crucifixion.

"Besides," he says sarcastically, "it's only a twelve-hour watch!"

After a silent pause, one says, "Well, at least it is almost morning. Thankfully, the sun will start to warm things up around here." Everyone agrees and goes back to trying to warm themselves.

A few minutes later, the flame of the roaring fire strangely begins to flicker and reduce without explanation and then eventually flames

The Cyrenian

out, leaving them in total darkness. At that instant, the unmistakable rumbling and tremors of an earthquake begin and grow in intensity. As they increase, the soldiers begin calling out to each other like frightened children. While trying to find to locate any source of support in the uncanny dark, their panicked voices quickly begin to reach the height of their crescendo. Out of nowhere, a dazzling light and a spectral being land beside the stone at the entrance of the tomb. The being seems to have human traits, though he is much larger than any man that they have ever seen. The being, an angel of the Lord, his garments flashing like lightning, glances at the men and, with nothing but a mere touch, rolls the stone away with such force that it skips out of its groove and across the garden many yards away. Despite wanting to flee, the men literally faint and fall to the ground.

After a time, they begin to come around. The light is gone. The being is gone. Strangely enough, though, the fire has been rekindled to its previous intensity. One soldier manages to make his way into the tomb. A small oil lamp is still burning inside, and as he peers in, to his horror, THE BODY IS GONE! He runs out, tripping and falling multiple times. "He's gone! He's gone!" he yells in a nervous shriek. "We have lost him, and now the Prefect will come for us!"

Everyone is now on their feet, each man suddenly as sober as a newly ordained priest. Panic is now setting in. Another expresses his fears.

"If we tell Pilate what really happened, he will never believe us. He will swear that we were all drunk or fell asleep on our watch. Whatever the case, we are all dead men!"

The squad leader speaks up, "Wait! Silence!" The soldiers immediately comply. "We will go to the High Priest and their Elders, who will give us sanctuary per their law. We will explain what happened, turn ourselves in to them, and they will help us. I am betting that this is not a story that they will want the people to hear! Not now!"

They quickly do exactly that. After hearing their story, Caiaphas sternly instructs the soldiers, "You will say that the disciples overpowered you and stole the body, do you understand? You will keep your tongues and never tell a soul what you say you witnessed! *No one* must *ever* hear what you have described to us! In the meantime, we will secure your positions with Pilate and compensate you handsomely for your silence, as you have value as 'witnesses.' However, if you cross us in any way, we will say to Pilate that you lied to us, and we will personally see to your deaths. Do we have an understanding?"

The soldiers are most willing to agree. And so, it is done. In fact, the fabricated story will be repeated for generations to come and be accepted as truth by many.

The first rays of the sun announce to the world that morning has arrived. Everyone has been awake for hours. Joanna, Susanna, and Mary, mother of James, accompany the other women to the tomb to complete the anointing of Yeshua's body. As they walk to the site, Joanna says to Susanna, "I am concerned about the stone. It is too large for us to move. I hope that we will be able to find men to help us."

"I know," Susanna says in agreement. "I pray that God will send us help."

The group arrives in the garden and stops dead in their tracks, thrust into a state of pure shock. They gasp almost in unison as they behold the sight before their eyes. The stone has been rolled away, exposing the entrance of the tomb. The women sprint to the tomb and enter, only to find the tomb empty except for the linens that they wrapped their precious Yeshua in, neatly folded upon the resting place. They exit in a flurry of nervous chatter, and they are perplexed beyond words. Was his body stolen? Moved? Who could or would do this? Why?

As the women exit, they are confronted by two men who appear as if out of thin air, dressed in garments that are shimmering in a blinding white light. The women fall and cover their faces in fear.

The men say to them in comforting voices, "Do not be afraid. Why do you seek the living among the dead? He is not here, for *he is risen!* His very words to you in Galilee bear witness to the fact. Do you remember when he said to you, 'The Son of Man must be delivered into the hands of sinful men, and be crucified, and on the third day, rise again?' Do you remember these words?" Their eyes fly wide open upon this jogging of their memories.

"Yes! Yes! I remember!" Joanna cries out.

The angels continue. "Go and tell the other disciples, especially Peter, that he will see them in Galilee as he said he would."

"Thank you, my lords!" Joanna exclaims as the group heads with speed to the safe house where the twelve are hiding. When they arrive and share the great news, they are met with the most unexpected response, one of total disbelief. It also seems that the women are not the first of the group to learn that Yeshua has risen. Someone else has already told her story.

Mary Magdalene shared how she had gone to the tomb early and discovered it empty, except for two angels sitting at the head and foot of the resting place. She said that they asked her, "Why are you weeping?" She says she answered, "For they have taken away my Lord, and I don't know where they have laid him!" She told them how in her panicked grief, she bolted from the tomb and approached the first person she saw. It was a man that she assumed was a gardener. She described how she begged him to tell her where her beloved Yeshua had been taken so that she could take his body with her. She broke out in tears of joy when she described the moment when she heard the gentleman say to her, "Magdala," his special name for her and something nobody else could or would ever know. She then said that Yeshua asked her not to embrace him, for he was going to ascend to his Father, our Father, his God and our God.

However, they did not believe her, convinced that if his resurrection were true, he would have appeared to them first.

Each disciple takes his turn discounting the stories and writing them off to mass-hysterical, delirious female ravings fueled by overwhelming grief. Each disciple, that is, except for Peter. He takes off, running to the tomb as fast as his feet can carry him. Breathless, he enters to find the tomb and the linens, just as the women described. He is dumbfounded at the wonder of this moment. He paces aimlessly, just trying to comprehend the magnitude of what he has just witnessed. Slowly at first, then in a moment of unbridled joy, he realizes that his failure of Yeshua was not a failure at all but a footnote of the greatest story that will ever be told. "He is risen! It is true! *HE IS RISEN!*" he yells over and over as he runs back to tell the others. All through that blessed third day, there are sightings of Yeshua in multiple places, including two disciples who Yeshua eventually reveals himself on the road to the village of Emmaus. The news is spreading with blinding speed.

The women disciples return to the house of Mary, Martha, and Lazarus and share their glorious news. Simon is especially amazed and enraptured by what he hears. This is the confirmation that he has been hoping and waiting for. He knows in his heart that every bit of the story is true. Everything has come full circle. The victory is complete! Mankind has been saved for all time! Yeshua has completed his mission! Now, if only man can grasp the magnitude of this story! Death has been conquered and is no longer the end of life! What good news this is! The story must be told. Told everywhere. Over and over. Suddenly, so much of what Yeshua taught is making sense and falling into place for Simon. He can barely contain himself.

It is now time to go to the Temple for the daily services. Simon wonders if anyone there will have heard what he has. He cannot wait to find out.

CHAPTER 35. THE POWER AND THE GLORY

It is late in the afternoon, and the daily Temple services are over. Simon and the men are on the road back to Bethany and the house of Mary, Martha, and Lazarus. There was much commotion in the Temple today, as naturally, the events of the crucifixion are the topic of every conversation. Surprisingly, the news of the risen Yeshua has not quite hit the Temple yet. But even more than the crucifixion, there is a deeper, more baffling, and most mysterious occurrence topping the headlines of discussion this day.

There are people, literally walking to and within the city, *who were previously deceased!* Many were considered "saints" at the time of their deaths, but today, they are as alive as anyone else walking around! The power unleashed upon Yeshua's death has raised them. These once-departed souls are not ghosts or roaming spirits at all. They are fully restored, radiant, and in perfect health. In fact, they look much younger than they did when they died! Not even their clothing has aged. From what is being said, these people have all their mental faculties and claim to have just awakened from a good night's sleep. They also seem to be completely unaware of the fact that they were dead and are, therefore, partakers in the greatest miracle of all time!

As to be expected, those who are believers are rejoicing to the fullest of their abilities. The unbelievers are cursing Yeshua and his followers to the highest, convinced that he and they are in league with demons. Then there are those who are simply paralyzed with fear, not knowing what to believe or what side to take, if any.

Simon and others listen to stories of wonder being told and wonders to himself, *Is it possible that Menachem could be among their number? After all, should not the greatest act of love, according to Yeshua, receive the greatest reward?* How very much Simon wants this to be true. However, his mind is reeling from all he has witnessed and experienced, and frankly, these new thoughts are too much for him to process. If only he could know the mind of God, he thinks.

Gideon hears the stories, too, and runs up to Simon to ask his opinion.

"Do you think that my father can be alive as well?" he asks, trembling with anticipation and hope for a positive answer. But Simon is unwilling to give the youth a possible false hope. He is reluctant to give him that answer, even though in his heart now, he knows that nothing with God is impossible.

"I don't know, Gideon. I just don't know," Simon responds, believing that he has chosen the right response for the moment. The fact is, it's the truth. Gideon's eyes fall, and he walks away. After a few steps, he stops and turns back toward Simon.

He says with all the conviction he can muster, "Yeshua has promised me that I will see my father alive again. He has promised me, and I believe Him. I believed Him then, and I will not stop believing Him." Gideon turns and starts to walk faster to catch up with Alexander and Rufus.

Simon whispers, "So great is the faith of a child. Your faith may be just enough, my son; at least I will pray to that end."

As they near the last bend in the road before their destination, Gideon notices what he thinks is a familiar form walking ahead of them. He squints his eyes to try and bring a face into focus but cannot, as the person is walking away from them and, therefore, not showing his face. He decides to try and catch up to the person and get a good look. "Could it be? Can it be?" Gideon whispers to himself as he quickens his pace. Whoever it is, he walks like Menachem and has the same imposing physique. Gideon is now jogging and gaining on the man. His heart starts pounding as he notices the similarity between the man's clothing and his father's. He decides to take the chance and call out to him. After all, what has he got to lose? In the worst case, it would be merely a case of mistaken identity and, therefore, nothing to be embarrassed about.

"Father!" he yells out. The man turns around. "It *is* you!" Gideon shrieks, now starting to cry. The man wheels around and opens his arms to catch the boy, who leaps into them as if on cue.

"My son! My son, I've searched all over the city for you! I was going back to where we were camped at the Mount of Olives to see if you were there along with everyone else! I am so glad to find you! Where were you? I woke up from a nap and found myself alone. Why was everyone gone? Where is Simon?" Menachem asks each question in rapid succession.

"Oh, Father, there is so much to tell you. You will not believe what I will be telling you!"

By that time, they are nearing the house. The women are cooking the evening meal. As they arrive, Susanna looks up and cannot believe her eyes. She drops the fish she is carrying in her stunned state, which is only for a moment. Given the recent day's events, she instinctively guesses what has happened. Now, it is her turn to run to Menachem. She throws her arms around him and begins to cover his face with kisses.

"God has brought you back to me, my love! May he be forever praised!"

Menachem is puzzled by all this attention but is enjoying it all at the same time. He looks at his son and says, "You're right; there is a lot for you to tell me!"

The Cyrenian

Susanna cradles Menachem's face in her hands and says, "You will never leave me again. I won't let you!"

Menachem, now smiling, says to her, "I have no desire to ever be without you. But I must say, if this is what a nap can do for one, I may have to take them more often!" He laughs and then sees Simon looking at him and smiling. He can also see the welling of tears in his eyes.

"My brother," Simon says while grabbing his shoulder, "welcome home."

The twelve are locked up in the upper room of the safehouse, steeped in deep discussion about the news they have heard from Mary Magdalene and the other women. The men are quite anxious. They don't know if they are being hunted by the Jews, and moreover, the resurrection stories have them on edge.

Andrew speaks up, "I don't know what to believe. I find it strange that the women would know anything before us."

"Moreover, we are being given instructions by them that are supposedly directly from him. It can't be true," says James.

His brother John adds, "After all, aren't *we* his chosen? Is it not up to us to continue his work? Why then would he not at least appear to us and give us his instructions directly?"

Peter takes a stand, "He will come to us! He does nothing without a reason. Perhaps we are being tested."

Just then, Yeshua appears, standing in their midst. "Peace be with you," he says to his startled and frightened disciples.

"How do we know that it is truly you, Lord, and not some aberration?"

Yeshua smiles and raises his hands, showing him the nail wounds. Then he showed them the spear wound in his side. "Why are you troubled?" he asks. "Why do you doubt? Ghosts do not have flesh and bones as I do. And they don't *eat* either. As for me, I am hungry!" he says, laughing. "Do you have any food here?"

They share with him what they have to eat. They know now that this was not a ghost, and they are very glad to see him.

"LORD!" they cry. "You are truly risen!"

He eats with them and then says, "Peace be upon you. As my Father has sent me, so I send you. Now receive the Holy Spirit."

He breathes upon them, and a wind is felt throughout the room. "By the Spirit, you will forgive sins, and they will be forgiven."

After he says this, he is gone, right before their eyes.

Soon after, Thomas, the twelfth disciple, returns to the room with supplies. He was not present when Yeshua appeared. The excited disciples are trying to share their joy with him when Thomas stops them in their tracks.

"I do not believe what you are saying! In fact, I will not believe until such time that I see his nail wounds and put my fingers in his side!"

"Thomas, why would you doubt him, or us, for that matter?" asks Peter, trying his best not to lose his temper. And so, the argument rages on for another week, when on the same day of the following week, Yeshua appears again in the same upper room. "Peace to you!" comes the familiar strain of Yeshua's voice. Thomas spins around and meets the smiling gaze of his precious rabbi.

"Thomas, come to me. Put your hands here in my wounds. Put your hand in my side. Do not unbelieve, but believe," he says while guiding Thomas' hands.

Thomas does so and cries out, "My Lord and my God!"

Yeshua says to him gently, "Thomas, you have believed me because you have seen me. Even more blessed are those who believe me and have never seen me." Thomas immediately understands this message of *faith*. In his heart, he is also thankful that his Lord does not hold it against Him for asking questions or needing proof. *What love*, he thinks to himself.

Over the next days, Yeshua goes with his disciples into the city and surrounding villages, performing many signs and wonders in

The Cyrenian

their presence, leaving no doubt whatsoever that he is the Christ, the Son of God, and that by believing, all may have life eternal, in his name.

CHAPTER 36.
COMMISSIONED

It has been many days now since the miracle of the resurrection, but its impact is far from diminished. On the contrary, there has never been a time that a single event has brought about such change. Those who have had a direct encounter with Yeshua are now speaking out unabashedly. More and more people are wanting to become followers of Yeshua's teachings. They are desperately seeking those who would be their new rabbis. Of course, this is creating more than its share of problems for the Pharisees and Sadducees in Jerusalem. There is a new wave of exodus from the Temple, as many of the congregants seek out new teachers and traditions. This is especially true of the poor and the downtrodden, who have found new hope and empowerment in Yeshua's words and ways.

Rome is also unsure of this new doctrine. While there is plenty of controversy, there is so far no form of rebellion, so for now, there is no trouble. However, anything that unites the people in such a way bears watching. And watched is what they will be.

Simon and his family are sharing some quiet time back in Galilee and Joanna's home. As they often do nowadays, they share their feelings about their future. Whatever it be, they know that their lives will truly never be the same.

Chana asks her husband, "Where do you see us now? So much has changed. Do we stay here, or do we go back to Jerusalem?"

The Cyrenian

Simon responds, "I'm not sure, dear wife. I think that things in Jerusalem are going to get tougher with time for Yeshua's followers."

Chana nods and says, "I agree with you, but is this not where the greatest need will be in terms of ministry? I only know that serving matters more to me now than it ever has before."

Rufus chimes in, "Father, I would like to stay and study to become a rabbi and teach others."

"Alexander, what say you?" Simon asks.

"I wish to take what we have learned back to Cyrene. I wonder if anyone there has heard anything about what has happened here."

Simon strokes his beard. "You make a good point. Cyrene is what we know, and there are many who I believe would love to learn what we know. There is just so much that we don't know. How do we even begin to share the story?"

"Just that way. Just share the story," Chana says with peaceful conviction.

"That is a profound thought, Chana," says Simon. "We just need to pray constantly for God's guidance here."

Off in the distance, the figures of the twelve are walking towards them from the hills. As they draw near, everyone can see that they have experienced something. There is an undoubted look of awe and, at the same time, a glow of joy on their faces.

Joanna asks Peter, "What is going on? Where is Yeshua?"

Peter responds, "He is gone. He has ascended into heaven to sit at the right hand of God, his Father, our Father.

Simon stands up and asks, "Just like that? Did he leave any word or instructions for us?"

"Oh yes. He has commissioned us. All of us!"

Peter and the other disciples sit down in the grass. Everyone there does the same, focused and silent, waiting with keen anticipation for Yeshua's final words.

He begins. "He has instructed us all to go into all the world and preach the Gospel, the Good News, to everyone. He has told us all to make disciples of all the nations and to baptize them in the name of the Father, the Son, and the Holy Spirit. We are to teach them all the things as he has taught us and commanded us. We are above all to love God with all we are and love one another and everyone we encounter, as he loved us."

Simon soberly says to him, "This is a task that is so much larger than we are. I know that I don't think that I know enough yet to do this most crucial task properly."

"I felt the same way when he spoke to us on the subject," Peter continues. "I am nobody by comparison, and I expressed this to him. He told us that he has given us all authority in heaven and on earth. He has sent the Holy Spirit to us as a Helper. He has opened our eyes so that we can better understand and, therefore, teach his word. He will do the same for you when your time is come. Most blessed of all, he has promised us that he will return and take us home with him to be with him in paradise for all eternity. Us, and all who will believe in him. For now, however, he has commissioned us all to 'feed his sheep,' in other words, those who we will be ministering to. By his spirit and in his name, we will heal the sick, feed the hungry, cast out demons, and even raise the dead as he did. He will reveal the Gospel and his teachings to each of us so that we can each go where he sends us and speak with his authority and knowledge to save souls for his kingdom. Best of all, He has promised that in all things, he will never leave us or forsake us. He will be with us always, even to the end of time. These are his own words."

Simon and the others sit in silence as they come to terms with all that they have just learned. He turns to his loving wife, and referencing their previous conversation, he says, "Isn't this just like him? Before we can ask him the question, He gives us the answer!"

Andrew pipes up, "Just like him, indeed!"

Chana answers, "May that *never* end!"

"AMEN!" shouts one of the disciples, igniting a continuous chorus of praise from everyone else.

The Cyrenian

During the singing and praising of God, Peter whispers to Simon, "We all know what you did for our Lord. Thank you for answering his call. Your act has brought some of his most important words to life for all of us. Now, we must dedicate our lives to helping each other carry our crosses as we carry his cross throughout the world."

Over time, each of the twelve will go their separate ways to begin their part in Yeshua's continuing ministry, as do many of the other disciples. There will be many stories to tell. Simon is looking forward to him and his family adding their own to the list.

The sea spray feels good on the faces of Simon and his family as they walk the ship's deck on their way back to Cyrene. This is a much different ship journey for him than the last one, there can be no doubt. He thinks to himself, *We came as fugitives, our lives hanging in the balances. Now, we are going home with the weight of the world no longer on our shoulders and with no prices on our heads. Word has it that High Priest Caiaphas has fallen from grace as well as Pontius Pilate and that they both will likely be removed from office very soon. We are the eternally saved. We are the eternally redeemed. We are the eternally pardoned. We are the prisoners, eternally set free.*

"All praise be to God," Simon utters out loud.

"Amen! Blessed is His name!" says his family all together.

Alexander asks, "Father, what shall we do when we get home?"

Simon answers, "I have unfinished business. Much unfinished business and many things to put right. Only now, the purpose is different. Starting today, we begin yet another new chapter. Perhaps even a new book altogether. I only know that there is much to do, and it will take *all* of us to make it work. Some of it, no doubt, will be very difficult, but God has promised His help. So, are you all up for the challenge?" Of course, Simon already knows the unanimous answer.

Without hesitation, Alexander responds with an exuberant "Yes!"

"Me too, Father!" beams Rufus. Gideon looks at his father, who gives him a wink.

Simon looks at his best friend and asks, "What about you, Menachem?"

He chuckles and says, "I'll have to ask my wife!"

Susanna answers, smiling at her new, adoring husband, "We'll see!"

Chana squeezes her husband and whispers, "That's a *yes*."

The two of them grin from ear to ear.

Once more, Simon raises his eyes to heaven. He lifts his voice aloud in prayer, saying, "Lord, may our new lives be as you will them. We are each ready to serve You and to daily take up our cross…your cross."

Simon feels as if all of God's creation is answering for him with joyous approval and peace. The sea is calm, the day is beautiful, and the wind is perfect. If this keeps up, they will be home, *truly* home, in record time.

Printed in the USA
CPSIA information can be obtained
at www.ICGtesting.com
LVHW061945110324
774145LV00001B/125